Diasporic Media beyond the Diaspora ··············

Diasporic Media beyond the Diaspora

Korean Media in Vancouver and Los Angeles

•••••• Sherry S. Yu

UBCPress · Vancouver · Toronto

27 26 25 24 23 22 21 20 19 18   5 4 3 2 1

Printed in Canada on FSC-certified ancient-forest-free paper
(100% post-consumer recycled) that is processed chlorine- and acid-free.

Library and Archives Canada Cataloguing in Publication

Yu, Sherry S., author
    Diasporic media beyond the diaspora : Korean media in Vancouver and Los Angeles / Sherry S. Yu.

Includes bibliographical references and index.
Issued in print and electronic formats.
ISBN 978-0-7748-3578-7 (hardcover). – ISBN 978-0-7748-3579-4 (paperback)
ISBN 978-0-7748-3580-0 (PDF). – ISBN 978-0-7748-3581-7 (EPUB)
ISBN 978-0-7748-3582-4 (Kindle)

    1. Ethnic mass media – British Columbia – Vancouver – Case studies 2. Ethnic mass media – California – Los Angeles – Case studies 3. Koreans – British Columbia – Vancouver – Case studies 4. Koreans – California – Los Angeles – Case studies. I. Title.

P94.5.M552C365 2018   302.23089'957   C2017-906476-2
                                                     C2017-906477-0

Canadä

UBC Press gratefully acknowledges the financial support for our publishing program of the Government of Canada (through the Canada Book Fund), the Canada Council for the Arts, and the British Columbia Arts Council.

Printed and bound in Canada by Friesens
Set in Scala and Minion by Artegraphica Design Co. Ltd.
Copy editor: Joyce Hildebrand
Proofreader: Kristy Hankewicz
Indexer: Cheryl Lemmens
Cover designer: Will Brown

UBC Press
The University of British Columbia
2029 West Mall
Vancouver, BC V6T 1Z2
www.ubcpress.ca

To my parents

Contents

..... Tables and Figures

TABLES

FIGURES

Preface

Some say diasporic media will disappear with the growth of younger generations of immigrants, while others say these media will continue. The history of journalism in North America supports the latter prediction, since diasporic media date back to the 1700s when international migration to North America began (Hayes, 2003). Although it is more of a history of indifference than of recognition, the argument is that if these media were to disappear, it would have already happened. Recent statistics place even more weight on this argument. International migration continues to grow, especially in Canada and the United States. Annual migration has been steady in the past decade, at around 250,000 for Canada and a million for the United States (OECD, n.d.). Added to this number are the Syrian refugees each country has welcomed since 2015. Between November 2015 and January 2017, over 40,000 and 17,000 refugees arrived in Canada and the United States, respectively (Citizenship and Immigration Canada, 2017; US Department of State, 2017). Given this flow of migration, the expansion of existing diasporic communication infrastructures, along with the development of new communicative space, is a more likely scenario than their disappearance. For migrants, diasporic media are an indispensable part of their lives; these media are historians of and everyday companions in the process of settlement and integration. For established diaspora, diasporic media are a community in and out of themselves. *La Opinión,* a newspaper that is almost a century old, is a living example. For young diasporas, on the other hand, diasporic media are a window to a broader society. A high dependency on the mother tongue and limited sociocultural and linguistic capacity often makes diasporic media a critical source of information during settlement and integration.

Canada and the United States already boast a strong diasporic media sector. There are approximately 1,300 and 3,000 diasporic media outlets in these countries, respectively, although these are conservative figures registered with the Canadian Ethnic Media Association (n.d.) and New America Media (n.d.). What is new in this sector is the recent transformation brought about by new media technologies and generational shifts. In parallel to so-called first-generation media, new communicative spaces initiated by young hyphenated descendants of immigrants and cross-cultural and -linguistic groups have emerged to offer new alternative voices. News/magazine blogs and websites such as "Angry Asian Man" and "Alhambra Source" are good examples. What is more, major news networks have introduced services such as Fox News Latino, NBC News Latino, and HuffPost Latinovoices.

In this time of interesting continuities and changes, this book explores some important questions: Do diasporic media serve their respective communities exclusively, or are they also *available* and *accessible* to members of greater society at large to serve as *media for all*? To what extent has the discourse produced by these media been made available and accessible, and what are the factors that promote and hinder broadening availability and accessibility? These are new questions in diasporic media studies. To date, studies have focused primarily on the autonomous roles of diasporic media within respective communities without due consideration for their role within the broader society. Certainly, there is more to learn about these autonomous roles: new projects constantly add new value to diasporic media.

Nonetheless, the exploration of *availability* and *accessibility* of diasporic media for the broader society is equally important and timely. In particular, how multicultural cities, diasporic communities, and diasporic media operate in an increasingly multicultural, multiethnic, and multilingual society and its media system is an important area of inquiry, especially when the growing gap in public discourse among increasingly fragmented audience segments is considered. Amidst the continuing under- and misrepresentation of minorities in mainstream media content and employment (Gandy, 2000), the increasing dependency on social media news aggregates for quick newsfeeds in the digital era further limits the opportunities for members of a multicultural society to attend to alternative voices and acquire "cultural literacy" (Wood and Landry, 2008, p. 250). According to a Pew Research Center study, over 60% of adult Americans use Facebook and 50% of those users (who account for 30% of the general population) obtain news from Facebook (Holcomb, Gottfried, and Mitchell, 2013). The question is whether the Facebook news aggregator includes news produced by diasporic media, and if not, where does that 30% of the population obtain news about the rest of society? Indeed, an information void amidst abundance is a reality. This trend continues in parallel with growing public distrust among ethno-cultural groups. Over 50% of adult Americans believe that conflict between immigrants and people who were born in the United States is the most ser-ious social conflict in that country – more serious than the conflict between rich and poor, or blacks and whites (Pew Research Center, 2009).

This book proposes a notion of an *intercultural media system* in which mainstream and diasporic media are not only *available* but also *accessible* for all members of society so that voices from diverse communities are ad-equately created, circulated, contested, and cultivated in everyday discourse and that all members of society experience a full sense of belonging and have sufficient cultural literacy to make informed democratic choices. This system allows members of society to engage in a two-way conversation – to speak and to listen – by providing a proper access point to diverse voices.

Perhaps this concept sounds too ideal, but the actual need of it is rather real and urgent. The purpose of this book is thus to envision such a media system and begin a conversation on collective efforts to enable it. This book is, after all, an exploration of my long-time query throughout years of dias-poric media research that has observed the theoretical and administrative reinforcement of diasporic media as *media for the Other* rather than *media for all*. The history of cultural and linguistic hierarchy influences how cul-ture, race, ethnicity, language, and citizenship, among other aspects of iden-tity, are *theorized, organized, managed,* and *practiced* in a multicultural society. The consequence is the perceptual or substantial marginalization of alternative voices that hinders opportunities for proper intercultural dia-logue. The questions that remain are these: Are we fine with continuing this arrangement? What would be the consequence of missing opportunities for listening to diasporic voices and acquiring cultural literacy in a society that is only becoming more multicultural, multiethnic, and multilingual?

Building an intercultural media system requires a collective effort from government, media sectors, industry associations, and academic institu-tions. The chapters in this book carefully examine the past, present, and future outlook of diasporic media through a study of Korean media in Van-couver and Los Angeles and their challenges and possible contributions to building an intercultural media system. The focus is on the still-dominant form of diasporic media of young diasporas, which produce content in their respective ethnic languages. Understanding their challenges and contribu-tions in terms of broadening availability and accessibility for a broader audience helps us to properly address the areas in need of attention as we move forward.

I hope that this book opens up a conversation, an opportunity to speak about and listen to the ways in which individuals in a multicultural society can be more culturally literate and have culturally literate conversations in the years to come. Diasporic media are certainly one of the ways, if made properly accessible.

Abbreviations

AAJA	Asian American Journalists Association
ACHP	Advisory Council on Historic Preservation
ASEN	American Society of Newspaper Editors
AURN	American Urban Radio Networks
BET	Black Entertainment Television
CAB	Canadian Association of Broadcasters
CBC	Canadian Broadcasting Corporation
CCTV	China Central Television
CEMA	Canadian Ethnic Media Association
CRTC	Canadian Radio-Television and Telecommunications Commission
CSO	civil society organization
CTF	Canadian Television Fund
FCC	Federal Communications Commission
IMF	International Monetary Fund
ISS	Immigrant Services Society
KABA	Korean American Bar Association
KAC	Korean American Coalition
KACF	Korean American Community Foundation
KADC	Korean American Democratic Committee
KADNO	Korean American Democratic National Organization
KAVC	Korean American Voters' Council
KBS	Korean Broadcasting System
KCC	Korea Communications Commission

KCCD	Korean Churches for Community Development
KCCLA	Korean Cultural Center of Los Angeles
KCWN	Korean Community Workers Network
KHEIR	Korean Health, Education, Information, and Referral Center
KIWA	Koreatown Immigrant Workers Alliance
KRC	Korean Resource Center
KYCC	Koreatown Youth and Community Center
MBC	Munhwa Broadcasting Corporation
NAKASEC	National Korean American Service and Education Consortium
NAM	New America Media
NBC	National Broadcasting Company
NEPMCC	National Ethnic Press and Media Council of Canada
OCA	Organization of Chinese Americans
SBS	Seoul Broadcasting System
SMC	Shaw Multicultural Channel
SKDTV	Seoul Korea Digital TV
SMC	Shaw Multicultural Channel
SUCCESS	United Chinese Community Enrichment Services Society

Diasporic Media beyond the Diaspora

Introduction: Understanding Media in Multicultural Cities

Canada and the United States were among the top 10 destinations for more than 200 million international migrants in 2010 (United Nations, 2015). The presence of foreign-born immigrants, significant in both countries, is continually growing and, as of 2010/2011, accounted for 20% (equivalent to seven million) and 13% (equivalent to 40 million) of the population in Canada and the United States, respectively (Statistics Canada, 2011a; U.S. Census Bureau, 2010a).[1] Especially in cities like Vancouver and Los Angeles (L.A.), a large proportion of the population speaks languages other than the official language(s): 40% and 60%, respectively (Statistics Canada, 2011b; U.S. Census Bureau, 2010a).[2] In addition to this constant flow of immigration, the resettlement of refugees further intensifies ethnocultural and linguistic diversity. Between November 2015 and January 2017, over 40,000 Syrian refugees arrived in Canada and 17,000 arrived in the United States (Citizenship and Immigration Canada, 2017; U.S. Department of State, 2017).

Such ever-growing diversity, coupled with the advancement of new media technologies and the influence of transnational economics and politics, has been reflected in the growth of the diasporic media sector across North America in recent decades. As evidence of this, there are roughly 1,300 and 3,000 broadcast, print, and online diasporic media (or more broadly known as "ethnic media") organizations in Canada and the United States respectively (Canadian Ethnic Media Association, n.d.; New America Media, n.d.). The actual number could be higher, since these listings tend to be based on voluntary membership. In fact, Murray, Yu, and Ahadi (2007) found nearly 150 diasporic media outlets in 22 languages in Metro Vancouver alone. Similarly, in Los Angeles County alone, there are more than 100 such outlets, and this figure represents newspapers only (see County of Los Angeles, 2011).

What are the implications of this growth for diasporic communities and the broader society? Literature on diasporic media has focused on the former. I have discussed elsewhere (Yu, 2017) that among other topics, studies have explored diasporic media as a communicative venue (Couldry and Dreher, 2007; Georgiou, 2005); as a public sphere and political agency (Downing, 1992; Downing and Husband, 2005); as a facilitator of national identity and shared understanding (Bailey, 2007; Georgiou, 2002, 2005; Kosnick, 2007; Sinclair, Yue, Hawkins, Pookong, and Fox, 2001; Sreberny, 2000, 2005; Sun, 2006); as a provider of a sense of belonging (Ball-Rokeach, Kim, and Matei, 2001; H.L. Cheng, 2005; Karim, 2002; Lin and Song, 2006; Murray et al., 2007; Ojo, 2006); and as a distributor of business information to help enable new business start-ups (Zhou, Chen, and Cai, 2006). The role of diasporic media in the process of immigrants' settlement in and integration to the broader society is indeed significant.

Certainly, more studies on these autonomous roles of diasporic media within their respective communities are needed, especially as factors such as the advancement of new media technologies and the demographic shifts across generations constantly transform the nature of diasporic media and offer new opportunities and possibilities. Specifically, new media technologies have enabled diasporic communities to go online. So-called digital diasporas formed online by and for media organizations and ordinary migrants help these user communities connect to one another locally in new countries and globally across diasporas and with home countries (Brinkerhoff, 2009; Chan, 2006; Hiller and Franz, 2004). Added to this dynamic is the expansion of homebound transnational media that reach out to a global diasporic audience, especially to transnational, cosmopolitan migrants (Sun, 2006; Punathambekar, 2014).

Demographic shifts across generations also facilitate the expansion of diasporic media beyond the domain of first-generation immigrants and open up opportunities for their discourse to reach a broader audience. Culturally and/or racially hybrid second- and third-generation descendants of early immigrants create "communicative spaces" (Couldry and Dreher, 2007, p. 80) of their own. Online news and magazine blogs such as "Schema Magazine" and "Angry Asian Man" have emerged to represent the voices of the younger generations. These new spaces suggest that just as the diasporic experience is unique for each group within and across communities, so too is the utility of diasporic media. The growth in population of the younger generation, particularly in the United States, explains this trend. Between 1998 and 2013, the second-generation population – defined as "U.S. native (born in the United States or territories) with at least one foreign-born parent" – grew by 23% from 30 million to 36 million (Trevelyan et. al, 2016, p. 1). What is more, cross-cultural, -ethnic, and -linguistic communicative spaces emerge to test possibilities for new communicative platforms for intercultural dialogue. Grassroots initiatives such as "Alhambra Source" (a multilingual news site in the city of Alhambra) and LA Beez (a former hyperlocal news site in L.A.) have been tried as innovative ways to facilitate dialogue across cultural and linguistic groups on a local level (Yu, 2017). In the private sector, new media ventures such as Saavn.com and DramaFever.com invite producers and audiences from the broader society to be involved in production and consumption of ethnocultural content (Yu, 2015). Indeed, DramaFever.com, an online streaming service of international television programs, was established by Korean Americans but is watched primarily by non-Koreans (Nawaz, 2015).

These continuities and changes within the diasporic media sector confirm the "inevitably dialectic nature" of diasporic media, which constantly pushes diasporic media beyond their former boundaries, despite the general understanding that diasporic media are *only by, for, and about ethnic communities*" (Yu, 2015, p. 133). Diasporic media are indeed both *here* and *there*, both *universal* and *particular*, and both *in-between* and *intercultural* (see Chapter 1). This dialectic nature of diasporic media, especially its increasingly intercultural nature, provides the reason for the need for new research focusing on the broader implication of diasporic media within a multicultural society – along with continued research on the autonomous roles of diasporic media within their respective communities. The question is: Do diasporic media serve their respective communities exclusively, or are they also available and accessible to members of greater society at large to serve as *media for all*? This book focuses specifically on the extent to which diasporic media are *available* and *accessible*, not only for diasporic communities but also for the broader society, as a means to improve cultural literacy, intercultural dialogue, and civic engagement in a multicultural society.[3] In doing so, this book explores the *structural* (policy) and *institutional* (media organization) conditions that promote or hinder broadening the availability and accessibility of diasporic media, as well as how these conditions fare in constituencies where multiculturalism is implemented differently – in the case of this study, Canada and the United States.

These are indeed new questions in diasporic media studies. Theories, policies, and practices related to media and cultural diversity in general and diasporic media in particular have focused primarily on diasporic media within their respective diasporic communities, without due consideration for their role within the broader society. Such a tendency is certainly related to how culture, race, ethnicity, language, and citizenship, among others are *theorized, organized, managed,* and *practised* in a multicultural society. Diasporic media have long been confined as *media for the Other* rather than *media for all.* This is manifested in public perception, policy articulation, industry practices, and academic research, which collectively have overlooked the significance of availability and accessibility of diasporic media for the broader society. The consequence is detrimental: the continued marginalization of minority voices and limited access to those voices for the rest of society hinders opportunities to listen and be listened to. In the words of Charles Husband (1996, 1998), both "the right to communicate" and "the right to be understood" for all members of a multicultural society are at risk (see Chapter 1 for a full discussion). How are these missed opportunities manifested in a society that is only becoming more multicultural, multiethnic, and multilingual?

The growing gap in public discourse among ever-fragmented audience segments warns us of possible repercussions. Illustrating this reality is a recent finding by the Pew Research Center (2009): over 50% of adult Americans believe that the conflict between immigrants and people who were born in the United States is the most serious social conflict in the country – more serious than the conflict between rich and poor or blacks and whites. Perhaps this should not be a surprise, given continuing under- and misrepresentation of ethnocultural minorities in media content and media employment (Gandy, 2000). The changing news media habits in the digital era further sets up a double whammy and widens the gap in public discourse. In the United States, over 60% of adults now use Facebook, and 50% of those users (who account for 30% of the U.S. population) obtain news from Facebook (Holcomb, Gottfried, and Mitchell, 2013). The question is whether the Facebook news aggregator includes news produced by diasporic media and, if not, where that 30% of the population obtains news about the rest of society.

What all these findings suggest is that without having a set of mechanisms in the media system that helps individuals in a multicultural society *access* diverse voices, "living together" in mutual respect amidst increasing differences is hard to achieve (Fleras, 2011, p. 249). Thus, a new model that helps to critically reassess theories, policies, and practices concerning media and cultural diversity in general, and diasporic media in particular, is indeed necessary. As its starting point, this book introduces the notion of an *intercultural media system* in which mainstream and diasporic media are not only *available* to but also *accessible* for all members of society. This system would mean that voices from diverse communities are adequately created, circulated, contested, and cultivated in everyday discourse and that all members of society experience a full sense of belonging and have sufficient cultural literacy to make informed democratic choices. This system would allow members of society to engage in a two-way conversation – to speak and to listen – by providing a proper access point to diverse voices (see Chapter 1 for a full discussion).

The need to envision an intercultural media system emerges from immediate necessity rather than utopian idealism. Certainly, this media system requires the examination of both mainstream media and diasporic media. In particular, understanding the extent to which mainstream media are available to, and accessible for, new members of society as well as existing ethnocultural minorities is as important as diasporic media being available to and accessible for members of broader society. This book focuses on diasporic media and attempts to initiate a conversation on how government, media sectors, industry associations, and academic institutions can work together to build a more interculturally available and accessible media system and help individuals in a multicultural society to become more culturally literate, have meaningful conversations across communities, and actively engage in civic matters that are common to *all*.

The focus is on the still-dominant form of diasporic media that produces content in the respective languages of its audience. A case study of Korean media in two multicultural cities, Vancouver and Los Angeles, helps us understand the challenges and possible contributions of diasporic media as a community, a civil society, and a market, which are governed by locality and/or ethnicity.

Why Korean Media and why Vancouver and Los Angeles?

This is the first comprehensive international comparative study of Korean diasporic media in the two most multicultural cities in North America. Korean media in Vancouver and Los Angeles were selected primarily for two reasons: the uniqueness of the Korean media, on the one hand, and of the cities, on the other. With respect to the uniqueness of Korean media, first, the Korean media sector provides rich case-study material in terms of availability of services in these two cities. During the time of study, more than 20 Korean media outlets operate in Vancouver, and 50 to 100 operate in L.A., depending on the source (see Chapters 3 and 4). The rate of growth of Korean media stands out within the diasporic media sector. Especially in Vancouver, Korean diasporic media are the fastest-growing media segment among 22 language groups tracked (Murray et al., 2007). Korean media are also available on all media platforms – in broadcasting (over-the-air, cable, satellite) and print (newspapers, magazines) as well as in online and offline formats (e.g., websites, e-papers, online community bulletins, online streaming services). They are also available across all major cities in North America. *The Korea Times* and *The Korea Daily*, the two leading transnational media organizations, for example, operate branches in L.A.; Seattle; Atlanta; Washington, DC; Chicago; Texas; New York; Vancouver; and Toronto.

The second reason for selecting Korean media is the adequacy for an in-depth international comparative analysis. In terms of development paths, for example, the comparison is between young and mature infrastructures. The first Korean media outlet in Vancouver was founded in the 1980s, when L.A.'s Korean media sector had already formed all genres of media outlets. Beginning with the launch of *The Korea Times* in 1969, L.A.'s Korean media now boast nearly 50 years of history. In terms of ownership, the comparison is between the sector of solely immigrant media and the sector of immigrant and transnational media combined. Korean media in Vancouver are owned entirely by local immigrants, with the leading outlets being independent franchises of either L.A.'s branches or headquarters in Korea. L.A.'s media, on the other hand, consists of immigrant media and branches of transnational media that operate under the auspices of their headquarters in Korea (see Chapter 4).

Korean media in these cities can also be compared in terms of micro and macro market structure – not only the sheer number of media outlets, as mentioned above, but also the size of the average monthly advertising market – in 2011, $500,000 for Vancouver compared to $5,000,000 for L.A. (see Chapters 3 and 4). The stronger presence in L.A. of local branches of Korean transnational corporations such as Samsung, Korean Air, and Hyundai Motors is one of the contributors to the expansion of the local advertising market. Exploring how these different conditions influence local Korean storytelling in each city can provide significant insights.

With respect to the uniqueness of the cities, first, Vancouver and L.A. are under the governance of Canada and the United States, which take different approaches to multiculturalism. Chapter 2 details how these understandings of multiculturalism – as a political philosophy (in Canada) and as an ideology (in the United States) – influence the policies for media practices, especially that of diasporic communities. This structural difference provides a rationale for a more thorough examination of diasporic media practices across cities.

Second, these cities are two of the most popular destinations for Korean migration to Canada and the United States, which provides a rationale for the Korean communities to develop a strong enclave economy and communication infrastructure. Not only have Canada and the United States been the primary destinations for Koreans migration in the past two decades – accounting, respectively, for over 30% and 50%, on average, of the total global Korean migration (see Table I.1) – but also the province of British Columbia and the state of California, where the research sites are located, host over 30% of the Korean migrants in each country (see Table I.2; Republic of Korea, Ministry of Foreign Affairs and Trade, 2009, 2010). Specifically, Vancouver is home to the second-largest Korean diaspora in Canada, after Toronto, and the city was also chosen as the top destination for Korean entrepreneur immigrants in 2001 (British Columbia. B.C. Stats, 2001). L.A.'s Korean community is by far the largest Korean diaspora in North America in terms of the size not only of the Korean population but also of the enclave economy. As mentioned, most branches of major Korean transnational media, as well as Korean corporations, are located in this city (see Chapter 4).

Third, the Korean communities in these cities are one of the largest monolingual, first-generation–dominant diasporas in Canada and the United States. First-generation Koreans account for 83% and 74% of the total Korean populations, respectively, in Canada and the United States (Statistics Canada, 2011c; U.S. Census Bureau, 2011). Dependency on the mother tongue is therefore common. In the United States, 79% of Koreans speak Korean at home and 45% "speak English less than 'very well'"; these figures increase when narrowed down to Koreans in L.A., where 87% of Koreans speak Korean at home and 59% "speak English less than 'very well'" (U.S. Census Bureau, 2011). This explains the dependency of Korean immigrants on Korean diasporic media (E.T. Chang, 1988; A.Y. Chung, 2007; I. Kim, 1981; Min, 2006b) and provides a rationale for the rapid growth of Korean-language media.

TABLE I.1

Global Korean migration, 1990–2009

Year	Total	Canada	U.S.	Australia	New Zealand	Latin America	Europe	Asia and other
1990	23,314	1,611	19,922	1,162	119	456	14	30
1991	17,433	2,651	12,754	1,113	308	550	3	54
1992	17,927	3,407	11,473	1,093	1,320	594	11	29
1993	14,477	2,735	8,133	538	2,569	467	14	21
1994	14,604	2,356	7,975	542	3,462	257	4	8
1995	15,917	3,289	8,535	417	3,612	49	2	13
1996	12,949	3,073	7,277	519	2,045	24	–	11
1997	12,484	3,918	8,205	216	117	3	–	25
1998	13,974	4,774	8,734	322	96	–	–	48
1999	12,655	6,783	5,360	302	174	8	–	28
2000	15,307	9,295	5,244	392	348	–	1	27
2001	11,584	5,696	4,565	476	817	1	–	29
2002	11,178	5,923	4,167	330	755	3	–	–
2003	9,509	4,613	4,200	256	435	5	–	–
2004	9,759	4,522	4,756	350	127	4	–	–
2005	8,277	2,799	5,083	327	67	1	–	–
2006	5,177	1,605	3,152	357	49	14	–	–
2007	4,127	1,517	2,227	347	15	21	–	–
2008	2,293	820	1,034	405	6	4	2	22
2009	1,153	383	599	158	7	–	2	4

NOTE: The numbers represent Korean migrants who declared their destination to be either the United States or Canada on departing Korea. Those who changed their status in their respective countries are excluded here.
SOURCE: Republic of Korea, Ministry of Foreign Affairs and Trade (2010).

Finally, the Korean communities in the two cities have different local experiences, which means that diasporic media fulfill different roles in the two cities. In a comparison of factors such as immigration history, demographic profiles, and interracial relations, Vancouver's Korean community was found to be much younger, less settled (with more of a floating population; see Table I.2), and more peaceful. L.A.'s Korean community is older and more settled (with a greater naturalized citizen population; see Table I.2) and has experienced intense interracial relations such as during the 1992 L.A. riots (see Chapter 4).

Thus, this study uses the city as a conceptual reference from three perspectives for a comparative analysis. First, the city as a legal reference is subject to the constitutional and legal frameworks of multiculturalism, immigration,

TABLE I.2

Koreans in Canada and the United States, 2009

	Canada		B.C.		U.S.		California	
	N	%	N	%	N	%	N	%
Korean total	223,322		76,712		2,102,283		622,100	
Canadian/U.S. citizens	98,860	44	23,228	30	1,003,429	48	359,200	58
Korean citizens	124,462	56	53,484	70	1,098,854	52	262,900	42
• Permanent resident	80,705		35,133		524,084		105,900	
• Visa student	22,249		7,599		105,242		20,800	
• Other	21,508		10,752		469,528		136,200	

NOTE: Extracted for Canada and the United States only.
SOURCE: Republic of Korea, Ministry of Foreign Affairs and Trade (2009)

citizenship, and media. Second, the city as a socio-urban reference is subject to the structure in which immigrant settlement and media undertakings actually take place. Finally, the city as a geographic reference is subject to the area in which local stories are told. The two cities examined in this book refer to Metro Vancouver, on the one hand, and L.A. County (and the adjacent Orange County, as needed, as these two are the major markets of Korean diasporic media), on the other.

In addition to these city-specific references, political and sociocultural changes in (or initiated by) Korea and the rest of the world make this study timely, including Korea's 2009 election law, which extended voting rights to overseas Koreans, and the widespread popularity of the Korean Wave around the world (see Chapter 6).[4] These push factors originating from Korea create new dynamics in the relationships among Korea, the Korean diaspora, and Canada and the United States, dynamics that occur on sociocultural, economic, and political levels and are worth exploring in the study of Korean media.

Data Collection and Interpretation

COLLECTION OF DATA

Peter Dahlgren's (1995) fourfold typology of the public sphere provides a useful guide for exploring structural and institutional factors across cities

(Vancouver and L.A.) and ethnicity (Korean). Dahlgren's "four dimensions" are "social structures" (e.g., "historical conditions"), "media institutions" ("organization, financing, and legal frameworks"), "media representation" (e.g., news topics, "modes of discourse," "character of debates and discussion"), and "interaction" (e.g., "people's encounters and discussions with each other") (Dahlgren, 1995, pp. 11, 17, 11, 12, 15, 18). The first dimension helps explore structural conditions – as in policy frameworks for immigration, citizenship, and media – while the remaining three dimensions help explore institutional conditions pertaining specifically to Korean media organizations. Because each dimension requires a different approach, a multimethod approach was chosen, as detailed below, using in-depth interviews, content analysis, and observation. The fieldwork was conducted in Vancouver and Los Angeles, between May 2009 and April 2011.

In-depth Interviews

Using in-depth interviews to examine the first two of Dahlgren's dimensions, social structures and media institutions, this book explored the history of the community; the demographic profile of media practitioners and community organization leaders; and the organization's history, day-to-day operation and production, financing, and regulation. For the regulation, in particular, the level of awareness of relevant multicultural and media policies among media practitioners was explored. Fifty semi-structured, in-depth interviews were completed with individuals from two groups: (1) media practitioners (e.g., owners, editors, reporters, staff writers) involved with diasporic (or multicultural/multilingual) media – whether printed, broadcasted, or published online or offline – that are directed to immigrants in Canada and the United States; and (2) nonprofit, nonpartisan CSO (civil society organization) representatives who serve immigrants in Canada and the United States. The semi-structured interviews involved a self-administered importance-satisfaction rating survey on news production and on institutional collaboration both between media and CSOs and among media institutions. These attributes were developed based on findings from earlier studies (Murray et al., 2007; Yu and Murray, 2007).

Content Analysis

A content analysis of news items and surrounding ads was conducted to explore the third dimension – media representation, described by Dahlgren

(1995, p. 15) as "what the media portray, how topics are presented, the modes of discourse at work, and the character of debates and discussion." The analysis helps us understand not only Korean discourse in general but also both the potential influence of media policies (Chapter 2) and institutional conditions (Chapters 3 and 4) on editorial directions and the level of availability and accessibility of diasporic discourse in broader society. The analysis was based on answers to the following questions: What news items are covered most frequently? What news of *here* (country of settlement) and *there* (country of origin) are covered? Is this coverage consistent with what media practitioners claim to cover? How do these media situate their community in the national and local discourse? How civic and engaging are these media in terms of covering *here* and working towards improving cultural literacy? Thus, the focus is more on what is covered than on how it is covered, the latter usually being the focus of cultural studies through semiotic or narrative analyses.

A content analysis of the ads surrounding news items was also conducted to increase understanding of not only the types of businesses that constitute the Korean enclave economy but also the level of economic embeddedness and social belonging of Korean immigrants in the local economy, as an indicator of mutually constitutive socioeconomic activities. A content analysis is more useful than a semiotic analysis for this study, since the majority of ads provided brief business and/or contact information in spaces smaller than a business card rather than using the artistically designed images usually associated with full-fledged commercial ads.

Data were collected from a full range of media platforms (television, radio, and newspapers) and ownership types (local immigrant, transnational, and multicultural media). A three-week sample (Monday to Saturday) of more than 1,800 news items and more than 2,800 surrounding ads was collected in total in March (newspapers and TV) and April (radio) 2010. From the total of 18 days, 6 days were selected to form a "constructed week" that assumes "cyclic variation of content for different days of the week and requires that all the different days of the week be represented" (Riffe, Aust, and Lacy, 1993, p. 54). The coding was done entirely by the author followed by the intercoder reliability testing on a "reliability subsample" (10% of the total 1,839 items) by a second coder to ensure that "the obtained ratings are not the idiosyncratic results of one rater's subjective judgment" (Tinsley and Weiss, 1975, p. 359). A variety of measurements was used to check the level of agreement and covariance, and the result was satisfactory on all measurements.[5]

Additionally, along with the news items and surrounding ads, more than 300 online community bulletin board threads were analyzed. The threads were retrieved from the so-called community section of the websites of all dailies during the time of study. This analysis was designed to address Dahlgren's fourth dimension – interaction. Although the online threads represent virtual encounters, readers share events or announcements (e.g., congratulatory messages, social programs, job postings, cultural events, new business promotions or updates), raise concerns or questions (e.g., regarding immigration, health, the job market, studying abroad), buy and sell items, or promote locally originated blogs. This rich community section provides useful information for understanding reader-initiated conversations on the topics that matter to them, in addition to the topics selected by publishers. The threads posted in the first three weeks of March 2010 (Monday to Sunday) were collected six months after the initial posting in order to provide enough lead time for readers to respond to the posts and for the analysis to measure hit frequency.

Unobtrusive Observation

Finally, the purpose of observation was to have a closer look at media announcements of the events that actually took place during the fieldwork period. The advantages of observation are "subjective understanding," "being there: seeing the unseen," "immediacy," "grounded research," and "richness and colour" (Deacon, Pickering, Golding, and Murdock, 2007, pp. 255–260). For this study, observing events through a series of questions helped develop an understanding of what was considered worthy of an announcement in the media on the part of media practitioners and how people (who may or may not have been the consumers of diasporic media) in the local community responded to and utilized the information in their everyday lives. Some of the questions asked were the following: What is the event about (what)? Who is hosting the event (who)? When does it take place (when)? Where does it take place (where)? How is the event structured (how)? Who are the participants? What are the demographic specificities, and how do those vary with type of event? What are their main issues and concerns? What is the purpose of the event? For those events that media practitioners attended and reported on, this type of observation facilitated the understanding of media's actual roles as well as their interactions with the audience. The audience members' comments also revealed how they made sense of communication infrastructure. Thus, the observation in this study achieved a dual purpose in that it not only "put flesh on the bones of quantitative methods" but also added to and enriched the findings (Deacon et al., 2007, p. 259).

INTERPRETATION OF DATA

In discussing the politics of interpretation, Ang (2006, p. 184) argues that "the 'empirical', captured in either quantitative or qualitative form, does not yield self-evident meanings; it is only through the interpretive framework constructed by the researcher that understandings of the 'empirical' come about." This conception of the "interpretive framework" is heavily indebted to the ethical injunction for researchers to aspire to "reflexivity," since "the ethnographer and his or her language are inevitably a part of the phenomenon that is being investigated" (Spencer, 2001, p. 450). According to Alasuutari (2004, p. 26), the researcher's standpoint is a reflection of who she or he is in totality:

> Standpoint researchers draw a radical conclusion by emphasizing that what you observe and how you conceive of reality depends on your perspective, and that different perspectives are mutually incommensurate. Consequently, as part of a research report the researcher must give an account of his or her characteristics and standpoint so that readers can assess its effect on the results.

In this study, the author depended on the author's own hyphenated identity as the "interpretive framework" when interpreting the data. The lived experience of a "cultural negotiator" between the two cultures, Canada/United States and Korea, offers a view of the in-between, which is the very nature of diasporic media as well.

The pros and cons of this double in-between standpoint are discussed in a body of literature. Bissoondath (1994) illustrates the dilemma that people with hyphenated identities face, both inside and outside of the subscribed ethnocultural boundaries. From inside, the second generation is often labelled "banana," which implies "yellow on the outside, white on the inside," and is considered less authentic, mostly because of low proficiency in its own ethnic language (Bissoondath, 1994, pp. 105–106). From outside, the foreign appearance constantly evokes questions from the dominant culture such as "What nationality are you really?" (Bissoondath, 1994, p. 111). This dual foreignness is also raised by Ang (2002) in her autobiographic work *On Not Speaking Chinese: Living between Asia and the West*. Her self-claimed identity as a multiple migrant ("an ethnic Chinese, Indonesian-born and European-educated academic who now lives and works in Australia") contributes to the idea that "there can never be a perfect fit between fixed identity label and hybrid personal experience" (pp. 11, 34).

The author's own hyphenated (or culturally hybrid) identity may lack the authentic in-group representation; however, cutting across two different cultures may offer new possibilities in accessing and understanding the practices of cultural negotiation. Therefore, the interpretation that this study presents is neither the in-group narration speaking on behalf of the Korean community nor the out-group narration looking in at the Korean community from the third-person perspective. Instead, it is the narration of a cultural negotiator who attempts to offer the contact point between the two cultures. Such a standpoint (or the reflexivity that the author assumes) has two implications. First, it is reflective of not only the author's own identity but also the overall objective of this study – to see possibilities for connecting multicultural "sphericules" (Gitlin, 1998, p. 173) – to work towards building an intercultural media system. Second, the author's standpoint is not only a deliberate and natural choice of self-positioning as a narrator but also an almost automatically prescribed and expected role imposed by the study participants; they expected the author to serve the community as a spokesperson or a negotiator between the Korean community and the broader society (or the broader media system) by delivering to the broader society the community's messages, such as calls for advertising support or policy recommendations.

Structure of the Book

This book is structured to guide readers through a comprehensive overview of the multicultural mediascape in North America, followed by a specific case study. Chapter 1, "Conceptualizing Media in a Multicultural Society," examines theoretical debates on media and cultural diversity in general and diasporic media in particular and conceptualizes an intercultural media system as a conceptual tool for reassessing existing theories, policies, and practices of diasporic media. The chapter also conceptualizes diasporic media by problematizing existing terminologies that are used to refer to media of this nature and introduces the three dimensions of diasporic media explored by this book – diasporic media as a community, a civil society, and a market. Chapter 2, "Multicultural or Intercultural? Policies and Media Practices in a Multicultural Society," attempts to understand the relationship between policies and actual practice: how cultural diversity is organized and managed in policy influences the actual practice, such as the availability and accessibility of diasporic media for *all*. The chapter begins with an examination of the relationships among policies concerning multiculturalism, immigration, citizenship, and languages, and the historical trajectory of diasporic media as an outcome of that relationship. This chapter further explores the relationship between the media policies and the multicultural mediascapes of Canada and the United States by providing an overview of multicultural media options on various platforms, and discusses the structural issues pertaining to the availability and accessibility of diasporic media for *all*.

Chapter 3, "Korean Diasporic Media in Vancouver," and Chapter 4, "Korean Diasporic Media in Los Angeles," discuss the findings of case studies on Korean media. Both chapters examine three dimensions of Korean diasporic media: as a community, a civil society, and a market. Each dimension specifically illustrates the level of availability and accessibility of Korean discourse for members of diasporic communities as well as of the broader society and identifies areas of strength and weakness. Challenges and prospects for broadening availability and accessibility are revealed through the analysis of data gathered via three research methods: interviews with media practitioners and civil society organization leaders; a content analysis of selected news items, advertising, and online bulletin board threads from Korean diasporic television, radio, and newspapers; and observation of community events.

Chapters 5 and 6 return to the notion of an intercultural media system and discuss the importance of collective efforts by government, media sectors, industry associations, and academic institutions in building an intercultural media system. Chapter 5, "Locality, Ethnicity, and Emerging Trends," identifies city-specific and ethnicity-specific factors and discusses the similarities and differences in how structural and institutional characteristics across cities fare in developing functioning communication infrastructure. This chapter revisits the findings discussed in Chapters 3 and 4 and explores potential contributions of and expectations for diasporic media; it includes a brief discussion relating to mainstream media institutions. In addition, the chapter examines the emerging new factors – other than structural and institutional characteristics – originating in Korea. Special attention is given to the rise of the Korean Wave.

Chapter 6, "The Intercultural Media System and Related Policy Areas," focuses on policy areas that are in need of attention if an intercultural media system is to be built. This final chapter revisits Chapter 2 and projects the comments from media practitioners onto the existing policies in order to provide policy recommendations for government, media sectors, industry associations, and academic institutions to consider for building an inter-cultural media system.

1

Conceptualizing Media in a Multicultural Society

The media in a multicultural society is a complex one. Beyond the distinction between "mainstream" and "minority" media, a variety of terms are used to describe minority media practices. Cultural and technological transformations of the mediascape that bring about innovations and new possibilities further challenge the existing distinctions and definitions. Where does this conceptualization of media originate and where is it headed? A critical examination of the existing theoretical approaches is necessary in order to properly understand the media in a multicultural society. This chapter conceptualizes a media system and the diasporic media that operate within that system.

Conceptualizing an Intercultural Media System

Theoretical debates and policy initiatives for the media system in a multicultural society tend to start from a binary distinction between mainstream media and diasporic media. As I have argued elsewhere, there is a persistent academic and public perception that diasporic media are "media *only* by, for, and about ethnic communities" (Yu, 2015, p. 133) whereas mainstream media are media by and for the "mainstream of society" – the mainstream in the United States (and similarly in Canada) being "individuals with European heritage" – with reservation that demographic changes in the past decades challenge the notion of mainstream (Matsaganis, Katz and Ball-Rokeach, 2011, p. 10). In this binary framework, diasporic media are *media for the Other* and are considered ancillary rather than complementary to the broader media system.

Such a distinction is no surprise and in fact corresponds to the ethnocultural hierarchy that is manifest in many policy practices. Especially in Canada, the distinction reflects the ideals of Canada's 1971 multiculturalism policy:

For although there are *two official languages*, there is *no official culture* [emphasis added], nor does any ethnic group take precedence over any other. No citizen or group of citizens is other than Canadian, and all should be treated fairly ...

... National unity, if it is to mean anything in the deeply personal sense, must be founded on confidence in one's own individual identity ... A vigorous policy of multiculturalism will help create this initial confidence. (House of Commons Debate, October 8, 1971 in Cameron, 2004)

The irony of multiculturalism within a bilingual framework is that language is not considered as part of culture. Although this approach can be considered an advancement from the Royal Commission on Bilingualism and Biculturalism (B and B Commission), which hierarchized *both* language and culture, the hierarchy of language continues, as defined in "other ethnic groups." Language was used to determine the level of "us" and "them":

Canadians who are of neither British nor French origin are covered by our inquiry in two ways: 1) to the extent that they are integrated into *English- or French-speaking society*, all that is said of Anglophones or Francophones applies to them; and b) to the extent that *they* remain attached to their original language and culture, *they* belong to other ethnic groups, whose existence is definitely beneficial to the country. (Royal Commission on Bilingualism and Biculturalism, *Book I*, 1967, p. xxv, emphasis added)

Biculturalism also resurfaces whenever it is necessary. The Canadian Radio-Television and Telecommunications Commission (CRTC) defines an "ethnic program" as "one, in any language, that is specifically directed to any culturally or racially distinct group *other than* [emphasis added] one that is Aboriginal Canadian or from France or the British Isles" (CRTC, 1999b). In this case, the emphasis is less on language but more on culture, placing diasporic media as *media for the Other*. Any media that are not for English, French, and Aboriginal Canadians are *ethnic*.

Liberal multiculturalism theories envision a public sphere in a multicultural society from a similar perspective, in that multicultural sphericules (diasporic media) are added to *the* public sphere rather than creating a public sphere (media system) that is interculturally engaged. Kymlicka suggests "institutional integration" (2001, p. 167) by having a "societal culture" (1995, p. 76) for multicultural citizens created within common mainstream institutions (e.g., education, government, legislature, workplace, police, health) for proper exercise of "multicultural citizenship" grounded in "group-differentiated rights."[1] This idea of not "re-creating a separate societal culture" aims to "contributing new options and perspectives to the larger anglophone culture, making it richer and more diverse" (Kymlicka, 1995, pp. 78–79).

For ethnocultural minorities, institutional integration is an advancement as it accommodates ethnocultural options as part of "fair terms of integration": that is, "the common institutions into which immigrants are pressured to integrate provide the same degrees of respect and accommodation of the identities of ethnocultural minorities that have traditionally been accorded to the majority group's identity" (Kymlicka, 2001, p. 162). This accommodation is important in order for not only immigrants but also members of society in general to be able to participate in the public sphere:

> The need to engage in public discourse arises from the fact that the decisions of government in a democracy should be made publicly, through free and open discussion. But the virtue of public discourse is not just the willingness to participate in politics, or to make one's views known. It also involves the willingness to engage in a conversation: to listen as well as to speak, to seek to understand what others say, and to respond respectfully to the views of others, so as to continue the *conversation*. (Kymlicka, 2002, p. 289, emphasis added)

Ultimately, if this informed conversation is possible, it is, in essence, "shared citizenship" that we can expect to pursue universal projects of broader society. Shared citizenship,

> goes beyond the sharing of citizenship in the formal legal sense (that is, a common passport) to include such things as: feelings of solidarity with co-citizens, and hence a willingness to listen to their claims, to respect their rights and to make sacrifices for them; feelings of trust in public institutions, and hence a willingness to comply with them (pay taxes, cooperate with police); feelings of

democratic responsibility, and hence a willingness to monitor the behavior of the political elites who act in our name and hold them accountable; and feelings of belonging to a community of fate (that is, of sharing a political community). (Kymlicka, 2007, p. 33)

While this book focuses on these notions of "conversation" and "shared citizenship" as a way of having healthy intercultural dialogue, it is also important to note the consistent pattern in the conceptualization of multiculture: that is, multiculture is what the dominant culture (anglophone culture) is *not* rather than the culture *itself*. Consistent with the above definition of "ethnic program," ethnocultural options are options for *the Other* and not for *all*. Nonetheless, these options are expected to be added to the "anglophone culture" to make it "richer and more diverse." The assumption here is that ethnocultural options are culturally and linguistically flexible and that they can be easily added to the dominant culture, when in reality this may or may not be the case, especially those options that are created for first-generation immigrants. From this perspective, the absence of discussion on accessibility of ethnocultural options for members of broader society is a natural consequence: these options are *assumed* to be accessible. Thus the focus so far has been only on creating ethnocultural options and making these options *available* within the dominant institutions, not on making these options *accessible* for all members of society. The irony is that availability alone without broader accessibility cannot make the dominant "anglophone culture" "richer and more diverse."

A further consequence is the "parallel societies" (Hafez, 2007, p. 130) or "communicative ghettos in which relatively homogenous audiences consume a narrow diet of information, entertainment and values" (Husband, 1998, p. 143). Charles Husband (1996, 1998, p. 144) has long proposed "the right to communicate" and "the right to be understood" as human rights. In other words, the right to speak entails the obligation to listen. Thus, if creating spaces in which ethnocultural voices can speak is the first step, creating an "interactive media infrastructure" that allows these voices to be heard is the next step:

In essence the facilitation of a multi-ethnic public sphere requires the state to fulfil its first generation human rights obligations by creating the space for the expression of individual, and collective, communicative freedoms. And informed by group-differentiated rights principles the state should also fulfil its second generation human rights functions in enabling the emergence of a diverse and interactive media infrastructure appropriate to the ethnic diversity present within the society. And finally, consistent with third generation human rights thinking, the state should promote "the right to be understood" as a principle informing the legitimacy and implementation of the two prior functions. (Husband, 1998, p. 144)

This book thus focuses on both *availability* and *accessibility* of diasporic media in the broader media system. Unlike previous studies, the book goes beyond the creation of communicative spaces for sociocultural expression for members of diasporic communities and explores the possibility of having these spaces as options for members of the broader society, so that the infrastructure for intercultural dialogue can be established. In effect, an *intercultural media system* is being conceptualized. This is a media system in which mainstream media and diasporic media are not only available but also accessible for all members of society, so that voices from diverse communities are adequately created, circulated, contested, and cultivated in everyday discourse and that all members of society experience a full sense of belonging and have sufficient cultural literacy to make informed democratic choices. Wood and Landry (2008, p. 250) define "cultural literacy" as "the ability to read, understand and find the significance of diverse cultures and, as a consequence, to be able to evaluate, compare and decode the varied cultures that are interwoven in a place." Accordingly, a city where cultural literacy is developed so that "people can understand and empathize with another's view of the world" is an "intercultural city" (p. 250). In this framework, diasporic media are thus not *media for the Other* but part of *media for all.*

In multicultural cities, access to diasporic media and the discourse these media produce is increasingly important for both the general public and media businesses when considered in relation to changing dynamics in both the public sphere and the market. For the general public, a media system that enables a functioning democracy, allowing for the ability to properly exercise citizenship based on informed decision-making, is particularly important for cities like Vancouver and Los Angeles, where 40% and 60% of the population, respectively, speak languages other than the official languages, as mentioned earlier. In reality, mainstream media in those cities ultimately serve only half of the population, while the rest of the people (especially members of young diasporas whose English is limited, as is the case for the Korean diaspora) resort to their own mother-tongue language diasporic media. The consequence is that mainstream media users remain largely uninformed about diasporic communities.

As evidence, a study found that local mainstream newspapers in Vancouver dedicated only 5% of their front-page news to ethnocultural minorities during the 2008 Canadian federal election, thus inadequately informing the broader society about the concerns of those minority communities (Yu and Ahadi, 2010). Yet it is also important to note that limited access to diasporic discourse may be a concern only for the general public and not for political interest groups. I discussed this elsewhere (Yu, 2016b) in reference to the case of Citizenship and Immigration Canada, which had silently monitored ethnic news media between 2009 and 2012 at taxpayers' expense, but the findings of this monitoring were only available to interest groups (Cheadle and Levitz, 2012). Certainly, "the right to communicate" and "the right to be understood" (Husband, 1998, p. 144) are at risk for *all*.

Likewise, for media businesses, accessibility to diasporic media is increasingly important, since business relationships between diasporic and mainstream media are changing as a result of the growing vibrancy of the diasporic media sector. Indeed, according to Juana Ponce de Leon, director of the Independent Press Association of New York, "ethnic media is the only print media sector that is growing in the United States" (Pew Research Center, 2006). Cross-ethnic ownership has also become more visible, as I discussed elsewhere in reference to the following cases in Canada and the United States (Yu, 2017a). Canada's Star Media Group, which publishes *The Toronto Star*, also publishes *Sing Tao Daily*, a leading Chinese-language daily in major cities in North America, as well as *Canadian Immigrant*, a monthly English-language magazine targeting a broad audience (Jin and Kim, 2011). These types of partnerships are no surprise to media industry stakeholders, who have seen ongoing efforts by Canadian mainstream media to tap into the ethnocultural market. Initiatives by the Canadian Broadcasting Corporation (CBC) and *The Vancouver Sun* to offer multilingual translation services to growing ethnocultural populations are good examples. After much trial and error, which led to a realization of the technical impossibility of automated translation, *The Vancouver Sun* launched a Chinese-language website, "Taiyangbao.ca," in early 2012 – which is now the English-language "Asia-Pacific" (Vancouversun.com/tag/asia-pacific) as of 2017.

In the United States, more aggressive cross-ethnic partnerships are evident. For example, in 2002, Telemundo, a Spanish language television service with an average prime-time audience of fewer than a million, was acquired by the National Broadcasting Company (NBC) for $2 billion, with the approval of the Federal Communications Commission (FCC; Rutenberg, 2002). Black Entertainment Television (BET) was acquired by Viacom in 2001, and TV One, which also targets African American viewers, was launched by Comcast in 2004 (Matsaganis et al., 2011; Comcast, 2011). All of these channels have attracted significant audiences, with BET and TV One reaching, respectively, more than 77 million households in the United States, Canada, and the Caribbean (in 2007) and 28 million households in the United States (in 2006; Matsaganis et al., 2011). These cases suggest a growing recognition of the business potential in cross-ethnic collaboration and competition in the dwindling media industry in the past couple of decades.

Does owning these by these companies change the portrayal of ethnic groups?

Thus, availability and accessibility of diasporic media is increasingly important for *all* as members of a multicultural community, civil society, and market. The level of availability and accessibility is, however, governed by multiple factors: immigration and media policies, demographics, the history of immigration, the development of communication infrastructures of diasporic communities, the language in which the content is produced (ethnic languages vs. English), the level of public awareness and promotion of diasporic media, and access costs, among other factors. Thus this book explores *structural* and *institutional factors*. Structural conditions inherent in a particular locality include immigration and media policies that are specific to each country (Chapter 2), while institutional conditions include media logics driven by diasporic media outlets themselves in the production and distribution of diasporic discourse (Chapters 3 and 4). Amidst these conditions, the city-specific factors that are bound to locality and the ethnicity-specific factors that are common to ethnic groups can be discerned and provide further insights.

Particularly in relation to the structural factors, it has been argued that government intervention is critical – whether to initiate a two-way "conversation" or to build an "interactive infrastructure" (Kymlicka, 2002, p. 289; Downing and Husband, 2005; Husband, 1998, p. 144). Through measures such as "the regulation of commercial media," "the policies of public service broadcasters," and "programs of education and training" (Downing and Husband, 2005, p. 209), the state is expected to fulfill the civil and political rights of multicultural citizens. Dreher's "listening" project further reminds us of the importance of government intervention with respect to accessibility in the discussion of the politics of voice and listening:

> If the politics of voice emphasizes the (re)distribution of means and opportunities for speaking, a politics of listening would seem to align more closely with struggles around recognition. The challenges are not merely individual but also institutional – where are dominant media institutions and hierarchies of value open to challenge and change? How is the challenge of difference contained? – perhaps through a reluctance to engage with community, alternative or multicultural media. (Dreher, 2009, p. 454)

The chapters that follow examine existing policy measures (Chapter 2) and present the voices of media practitioners concerning these measures (Chapters 3, 4, and more thoroughly in Chapter 6). In terms of institutional conditions, this book specifically explores the various dimensions of diasporic media – as a community, civil society, and market. While these dimensions have been studied in different projects, they have been considered only within their respective communities rather than in relation to the broader society. This book explores availability and accessibility of diasporic media as a community, civil society, and market for members of diasporic communities as well as those of the broader society and identifies the areas of relative strength and weakness in working towards building an intercultural media system. The following sections discuss these three dimensions in detail.

Conceptualizing Diasporic Media

Why "diasporic media"?

Before proceeding with the discussion of the three dimensions, it is important to explain why, among all the possible terms, this book uses "diasporic media." I discussed elsewhere the terminological issue in the research community that various terms are used inconsistently to refer to minority media practices (Yu, 2017a). While the most commonly used blanket term is "ethnic media," other terms include "ethnic community media," "ethnic minority media," "minority media," "minority language media," and "multicultural media" (Yu, 2017a, p. 160). This variety of terms is certainly a natural consequence of these media being pursued and experienced differently across communities. Thus, many of these terms are inadequate as a generic term since each one reflects only one of many projects pursued by these media.

This book uses the term "diasporic media," derived from Vertovec's definition of "diaspora" (1997, p. 277): "practically any population which is considered 'deterritorialised' or 'transnational' – that is, which has originated in a land other than that in which it currently resides, and whose social, economic, and political networks cross the borders of nation-states or, indeed, span the globe." Vertovec's three meanings of diaspora and the "combined working" of these meanings are useful for the purpose of this study: diaspora as (1) a "social form" that constitutes "social relationship[s]," "political orientations," and "economic strategies"; (2) a "type of consciousness" as in the "awareness of multilocality" of being "both 'here' and 'there'"; and (3) a "mode of cultural production" as in "the *production and reproduction of transnational social and cultural phenomena*" (emphasis in the original document, pp. 278–279, 281–282, 289). The Korean communities in Vancouver and L.A., and especially Korean media in everyday production, manifest all of these multifaceted dimensions of diaspora in their local-transnational continuity.

From this perspective of multilocality and transnationality of diaspora, I build on my earlier discussion on terminologies (Yu, 2017a) and argue that the term "diasporic media" is useful for three main reasons. First, as compared to "community media" or "ethnic community media," "diasporic media" reflects the increasingly transnational nature of these media, with the advancement of new media technologies and the expansion of transnational media from the country of origin. The focus is on availability or the origin of production (Yu, 2017a). Georgiou (2005) argues that diasporic media are available at all geographic levels, from local to national and international, and that they create an interesting "universalism-particularism" tension within diasporic lives (see below for further discussion). Indeed, De Leeuw and Rydin's (2007) study on media practices of immigrant children and their families confirms that the consumption of diasporic, national, and global media works to help them negotiate their identities.

Karim (2009) and Naficy (2003), on the other hand, focus on the origin of production, although the term "diasporic media" is not used in the same context. Karim (2009) differentiates "ethnic" and "diasporic" media, with the former originating in the host country and the latter in the country of origin. To Naficy (2003, pp. 51–52), referring to Middle Eastern television programs aired in L.A., "diasporic" media are media for exiles whereas "transnational" media are equivalent to Karim's diasporic media. Such different uses of the same term reflect the complexity and diversity of media offerings within diasporic communities.

The increasingly transnational nature of diasporic media is enabled by new media technologies that connect not only local diasporic media with the local community but also transnational media corporations with globally dispersed diasporic communities. In the Korean diaspora, for example, MBC America, a branch of the Munhwa Broadcasting Corporation (MBC) in Korea, provides MBC program content through local over-the-air, cable, and satellite services, not only to the Korean community in L.A. but also to that of Vancouver. Another example is Saavn.com, which I discussed elsewhere (Yu, 2015), referring to Punathambekar's (2014) work on South Asian diasporic media. The case confirms that the boundary of diasporic media expands geographically by connecting Bollywood with cable companies in the United States in order to tap into the growing South Asian American market. In this sense, geographically bound terms such as "community media" or "ethnic community media" are self-limiting. Whether local or transnational, homebound or host-bound, one form of media does not replace the other. Rather, these media coexist to serve the diasporic communities and beyond. Recognition of this coexistence broadens the horizon of understanding and helps conceptualize media for diasporic communities despite the variety of projects pursued by them.

Second, the term "diasporic media" is useful because it captures the collective diasporic experiences that are unique and authentic in their own "in-betweenness" (Siapera, 2010, p. 96). Hybridity results from mixing and mingling with other cultures. Korean Canadian/American culture, for example, may contain some Korean cultural forms maintained over generations, but it is largely Canadianized/Americanized Korean culture and thus is different from the Korean culture experienced among Koreans in Korea. Siapera (2010, p. 96) argues that diasporic media emphasize "elements of continuous development, of being in between places, of similarity of experience, but not necessarily of nostalgia for a homeland." The term "ethnic media," in this sense, is self-limiting: it implies culture in its authentic form from the country of origin rather than as a new hybrid culture that is locally developed by immigrants and people of multiple identities. The term thereby overemphasizes ethnicity and underemphasizes the fluid, transforming, and hybrid nature of diasporic identity.

The term "ethnic media" is also self-limiting by implying only visible minorities, when nonvisible European ethnicities, for which media are developed, are also ethnic categories. Indeed, Murray et al.'s (2007) B.C. ethnic media directory lists not only media of visible minorities (e.g., *Ming Pao, The Indo-Canadian Voice*) but also media of European origin (e.g., *Germany Today, L'Eco d'Italia [Il Marco Polo]*). Therefore, the term "ethnic" undermines the diasporic experience of European groups. Furthermore, given that new media ventures, like the aforementioned DramaFever.com, appeal to a broader audience rather than just to the audience from their respective communities, the boundary between ethnic and mainstream media becomes blurry.

To this end, the question raised is whether "ethnicity" as a sociocultural character or identity is becoming less relevant. Post-ethnic scholars like Hollinger (1995, p. 116) have long proposed the conception of post-ethnic identity, which "prefers voluntary to prescribed affiliations, appreciates multiple identities, pushes for communities of wide scope, recognizes the constructed character of ethnoracial groups, and accepts the formation of new groups as a part of the normal life of a democratic society." Similarly, Brubaker (2004, p. 11) also proposes the conception of "beyond groupism," which respects the fluid nature of ethnicity, race, and nation, and treats these "not in terms of substantial groups or entities, but in terms of practical categories, situated actions, cultural idioms, cognitive schemas, discursive frames, organizational routines, institutional forms, political projects, and contingent events." Debates on these pan-ethnic perspectives continue since ethnicity is still an important variable in policy administration.

Third, the term "diasporic media" is useful because as transnational and in-between diasporic experience demonstrates, it conveys the breadth of the diasporic or intercultural projects pursued by these media. As I discussed elsewhere (Yu, 2017a), some are subaltern, such as *Hua Xia Wen Zhai* – digital diaspora for the Chinese community – while others are purely for entertainment purposes, such as media that relay telenovelas for the Hispanic community. Still others bridge the gap between immigrant communities and the broader society, such as Britain's London Greek Radio (Georgiou, 2005) and Germany's Radio MultiKulti, for the Turkish community (Kosnick, 2007). Thus, the term "minority media," positioned in contrast to the majority or dominant media as a location of power struggle or a counter-public, can be an overstatement. Again, as one of many projects pursued by diasporic media, it is pursued by only select media organizations. Diasporic media can simply function in a variety of ways – as a channel to deliver home content to various diasporas with minimal editorial revision, as a political vehicle to pursue a local political agenda, or as an innovative and creative project that the younger generation might bring to the sector.

THE DIALECTIC NATURE OF DIASPORIC MEDIA

If diasporic media are approached more conceptually, the fundamental nature of these media can be discerned. The interplay of international politics and economics is evident in international migration to North America, and so is the development and practice of diasporic media. In particular, considering neoliberal immigration trends in which "global citizens" or "multiple passport holders" emphasize a transnational sense of belonging and a multiple or hybrid identity (Ong, 1999), diasporic media facilitate discourse that is both "'here' and 'there'" (or "multilocality"), both universal and particular (or "universalism-particularism continuum"), and both in-between (or "in-betweenness") and "intercultural" (Vertovec, 1997, p. 282; Georgiou, 2005, p. 483; Siapera, 2010, p. 96; Wood and Landry, 2008, p. 250). In other words, diasporic media are venues where both the country of settlement ("here") and the country of origin ("there"), both the broader society ("universalism") and the diasporic community ("particularism"), and both hybridity ("in-betweenness") and diversity (interculture) coexist and communicate. The transnational and universal projects indeed challenge the conventional notion of diasporic media as media *only* by and for members of diasporic communities.

Vertovec's concept of "multilocality" is empirically confirmed by H.L. Cheng's (2005) analysis of *Ming Pao*, a Cantonese newspaper in Vancouver. Cheng discusses how "transnational, multilocal sense of belong" to both Vancouver (*here*) and Hong Kong (*there*) constructed by local ethnic newspapers challenge the traditional dichotomy of either here or there (p. 146). Cheng suggests that it is not *either* but rather *both* localities that immigrants comfortably identify themselves with. Lindgren's (2011) analysis of Chinese newspapers in Toronto, and Murray et al.'s (2007) analysis of Chinese, Korean, and Punjabi media in Vancouver, further confirm Cheng's notion of transnational, multilocal sense of belonging. Although the media examined in both studies emphasize news about country of origin, the coverage of *both* here and there reinforces attachments to both. To note, I raised elsewhere (Yu, 2017a) this home-country orientation hypothesis, which diasporic media are often subjected to, needs further exploration in terms of whether it demonstrates a genuine interest in the country of origin or is the result of the political economy of the media industries in general. As will become clear in this book, it is more often the latter than the former.

Looking specifically at the concept of "here," Georgiou's "universalism-particularism continuum" is useful for explaining diasporic media's dialectic nature – being both the broader society (*universal*) and the diasporic community (*particular*). Georgiou (2005, p. 482) points to "the continuities and interdependencies between diasporic, national and local cultures, minority and majority media, and projects of local, and national and transnational participation." In other words, the practices of diasporic media support both universal projects of the broader society and particular projects of the diasporic community. Such a conceptualization is consistent with Fleras's (2009, p. 726) typology, in that multicultural media have "both reactive and proactive, as well as outward and inward" natures. Specifically, these media are *reactive* in that they show "a minority reaction to media mistreatment," but they are simultaneously *proactive* in that they "celebrate minority successes, accomplishments, and aspirations" (p. 726). These media are also simultaneously *outward*, "by supplying information of relevance and immediacy to the intended demographic, including how to navigate the labyrinth of a strange new society," and *inward*, "by reporting news of relevance to the community through a perspective and tone that resonates more meaningfully with its audience" (p. 726).

This "inevitably dialectic nature" (Yu, 2015) of diasporic media operates on multiple levels and further intensifies their hybrid (*in-between*) and diverse (*intercultural*) characteristics. Whether it be about broader societal issues – a federal election, for example, or newly enacted laws – or diasporic community issues such as cultural events and immigrant services, diasporic discourse communicates multiple senses of belonging as well as the tension created by this dialectic nature.

On one level, the geographic focus of *here* and *there* can be discussed not only as country of settlement versus country of origin but also as *local (here)* versus *North America (there)*. Although the current situation for the Korean diaspora suggests that Korean discourse is largely hyperlocal, the online communities developed in Korean media suggest a potential for wider diasporic communication among the geographically dispersed Korean diasporas across North America.

On another level, *universal* and *particular* can be discussed in the tension between the diasporic storytelling pursued by immigrant media and that of transnational media branches: the former pursues aspiration for *integration* (*universal*) and the latter pushes for *home connection* (*particular*). This storytelling is never uniformly either universal or particular; rather, both qualities are manifest to varying degrees across diasporic media organizations. The diversity within the diasporic media sector and the different editorial goals lead to variations in the focus of news content.

In this sense, diasporic media production and consumption coexists in terms of geography and culture and is continuously transformed in the interaction between *here* and *there* and the *universal* and the *particular*. In short, it is the *in-between* and *intercultural* discourse about issues that matters to all.

This increasingly complex and dialectic nature of diasporic media raises a critical question: *Are diasporic media only for members of diasporic communities, or are they also for members of the broader society?* That is, are diasporic *media for the Other* or *media for all*? This book attempts to answer these questions by exploring diasporic media within three functional dimensions: as a community on the local level, as a civil society that bridges diasporic communities and the broader society, and as a market in the media industry. Within what dimensions are diasporic media more or less *our media* rather than *Other's media*? These dimensions help identify area-specific strengths and weaknesses of diasporic media in their availability and accessibility.

THREE DIMENSIONS OF DIASPORIC MEDIA

In discussing availability and accessibility of diasporic media, three dimensions – diasporic media as community, civil society, and market – help us to unpack the notion of diasporic media and to understand the level of availability and accessibility more clearly.

Community

Diasporic media serve as a community on two levels. First, these media are a community that holds geographically dispersed members of a diasporic community together as a culturally and/or linguistically friendly haven. Second, they are a bridge to the broader community that facilitates cross-community engagement. Ball-Rokeach's communication infrastructure theory (CIT) addresses the function of diasporic media on these levels.

The communication infrastructure consists of two elements (Y.C. Kim and Ball-Rokeach, 2006, p. 413):

(a) *a neighborhood storytelling network* of everyday conversations and neighborhood stories that people, media, and grassroots organizations create and disseminate, and (b) the *communication action context* encompassing the tangible and intangible resources of residential areas that promote communication between residents (e.g., residential stability, ethnic heterogeneity, institutional resources, neighborhood milieu, collective memories, etc.).

This storytelling system operates on three levels: macro storytelling of the city, the nation, and the world; meso storytelling of more geographically focused areas; and micro storytelling by neighbours. The function of meso storytelling is critical, since it links macro and micro storytelling, and thus, if successful, it serves as a civil society by offering a storytelling system that is "broad (from world to neighborhood referents), deep (many stories about all referents), and integrated (strong linkages between macro, meso, and micro storytelling production systems)" (Ball-Rokeach et al., 2001, pp. 397–398). It is at the meso level where diasporic media can contribute to increasing community bonding, within and across communities, by providing "geo-ethnic storytelling" – that is, stories that are "ethnically or culturally relevant to a particular ethnic group" and that are "geographically bound and concern primarily the happenings in the community" (Lin and Song, 2006, pp. 367–368).

In exploring the level of intercultural efforts on a community level, this book pays attention to the sociocultural capacity of the diasporic community as a meso storyteller. The underlying logic of the CIT is that if diasporic media are effectively connected with local diasporic community members and organizations, as well as with their mainstream counterparts on varying geographic levels, diasporic media can serve as highly effective intercultural agents, allowing diasporic storytelling to reach the broader community in everyday communicative action contexts. However, the question that remains is whether all diasporic media are socioculturally capable of playing such a role.

Language is an important criterion in this communication context, and if the English language has been assumed as the language of communication, only those media organizations that produce content in English or bilingually are likely to participate. Does the CIT then consider only those established, older immigrant communities – those whose members are more likely second- or third-generation immigrants? Examples of established, older communities would be early European immigrant communities such as the Hungarians, Czechs, and Slovaks, who are a majority now through integration and assimilation (Glazer, 2005) and whose cultural identities have been "symbolically erased" within the Euro-American bloc in the national census (Hollinger, 1995). Or does the CIT envision a communication infrastructure that is multilingual? This book attempts to explore these questions with a case study on Korean-language media, which help identify challenges and prospects for diasporic media to serve as an intercultural agent in the process of two-way integration of third-language communities and the rest of society.

Civil Society

Meso storytelling essentially envisions a civil society in which diasporic communities are connected with the broader society on different geographic levels. The case studies on Korean media in Chapters 3 and 4 show how diasporic discourse pushes for political representation of minorities and how diasporic media are considered by political interest groups as intermediaries through which to connect with diasporic communities. This function is critical, since ethnocultural minorities have historically been undervalued and underrepresented, not only in media content but also in media employment (Gandy, 2000). Without their own media to represent themselves, ethnocultural minorities continue to be unseen and unheard.

Indeed, diasporic media are an important part of the "societal culture" that enables the exercise of "multicultural citizenship" and the "group-differentiated rights" (Kymlicka,1995), as discussed earlier. Kymlicka argues that "recognizing minority rights would actually strengthen solidarity and promote political stability by removing the barriers and exclusions that prevent minorities from wholeheartedly embracing political institutions" (Kymlicka, 2001, p. 171). Similarly, media scholars discuss "the right to communicate" and "the right to be understood" and expect a stronger role for public broadcasting (Curran, 2000; Downing and Husband, 2005; Husband, 1998, p. 144). Curran's working model for contemporary television, for example, illustrates a binary composition of centre and periphery media, led by public service television and followed by four individual sectors – private enterprise, civic, professional, and social market. Among these spheres, ethnic services are positioned within public services.

Public broadcasters are, however, often known to be financially incapable of meeting public mandates. As evidence, the Canadian Broadcasting Corporation (CBC) and the Public Broadcasting Service (PBS) of the United States are at the lowest funding levels of public media among 15 leading democracies: U.S.$30.42 and U.S.$3.75 per capita, respectively (Benson and Powers, 2011, p. 61). It is no surprise that ethnic-language services are unseen in this sector and instead are offered by periphery media in the private sector. (See Chapter 2 for further details.) Such a reality adds weight to the role of diasporic media as a civil society, and it is critical that their sociocultural capacity to play this role within and across communities be explored.

Market

How available and accessible are diasporic media as a market? They are part of the local economy – the local marketplace in general and the media industries in particular. One of the common immigrant settlement patterns is a high concentration of small businesses, and diasporic media are promoters of these businesses and are themselves among these businesses. Examining the businesses promoted through these media is a good way to understand the level of economic integration of immigrants. The growth of diasporic media as businesses, however, is related to the neoliberal immigration policies such as Canada's Business Immigration Program of 1986. The subsequent influx of entrepreneur/business-class immigrants who favoured media as a business to start in a new country contributed to this growth (see Chapter 2). The growth is not only in the actual number of media outlets but also in revenue. The Chinese print media in Canada, for example, boasts a $50 million advertising market (Szonyi, cited in Zhou et al. 2006, p. 51).

What is more, among the three dimensions of diasporic media, the market is where intercultural initiatives are most actively pursued by both diasporic and mainstream media, as a response to the challenges in the media industries in the past couple of decades. The continual mergers and acquisitions of leading media conglomerates during the economic downturn in the 2000s, the transition to digitalization and adaption of new media technologies, and the resulting new political economy of the media industries characterize the media market (Havens and Lotz, 2012; Winseck, 2012). Demographic changes in multicultural cities like Vancouver and Los Angeles further challenge the division between mainstream and diasporic media. Audiences use both or either type of media for everyday news consumption, and that makes cross-cultural expansion an important marketing strategy. One consequence of this is the aforementioned cross-ethnic media partnerships such as Canada's Star Media Group and *Sing Tao Daily* and the American NBC and Telemundo. Chapters 3 and 4 discuss these intercultural efforts within the market and the factors that promote and hinder diasporic-mainstream partnerships.

Conclusion

An increasingly multicultural, multiethnic, and multilingual reality is both cause and consequence of an equally multicultural, multiethnic, and multilingual mediascape. The cultural and technological transformation across generations and the new media technologies enable production and consumption of new voices from diverse communities, which challenge – or require us to challenge – the conventional understanding of diasporic media as media *only* by and for members of diasporic communities. This challenge is healthy for a functioning democracy in which members of a multicultural society are fully informed of diverse voices and make informed choices. But how available and accessible are these diverse voices for members of both diasporic communities and the broader society?

This question requires a new theoretical approach to provide a critical understanding of the media system in a multicultural society. This chapter conceptualized an intercultural media system. This system takes a holistic approach by asking how available and accessible mainstream media are for new members of a multicultural society, and conversely, how available and accessible diasporic media are for a broader audience. In this book, the focus is on the latter to critically explore the limitations of existing theories that discuss only the availability of diasporic media for diasporic communities. This book brings accessibility into the debate in order to initiate a discussion on ways for members of a multicultural society to access diverse voices and have a conversation based on sufficient cultural literacy about diasporic communities to which they do not belong. Both speaking without having anybody listening and being expected to listen without having adequate means to commit to listening present barriers in intercultural dialogue among members of a multicultural society.

The question of mutual availability and accessibility also requires a new conceptualization of diasporic media. Having available a variety of terms to describe the same media is healthy, since these varied terms reflect the variety of projects that these media pursue. Nonetheless, it is important to examine the strengths and weaknesses of each term and to challenge the common assumption underlying all existing terms – that these media are *only* by and for members of diasporic communities, with no consideration of members of the broader society as an audience. This is not to say that the term "diasporic media," which this book uses, is perfect. Nonetheless, it delivers a sense of the inevitably dialectic nature of diasporic media as being both *here* and *there*, both *universal* and *particular*, and both *in-between* and *intercultural.* Considering the continuing transformation of the nature of diasporic media, even this conceptualization is likely to be transitional. Nonetheless, it is important to have a point of reference. The conceptualization of an intercultural media system and of diasporic media is only the beginning of new conversation about a media system that is much needed for a multicultural society.

2

Multicultural or Intercultural?
Policies and Media Practices in
a Multicultural Society

An intercultural media system as a model for communication in multi-cultural societies requires a systematic understanding of multiculturalism – as a political philosophy, as policy, and as everyday practice, as demonstrated by Kymlicka (1995). Kymlicka emphasizes that it is important for scholars not to lump these separate units of analysis together under the name of multiculturalism or assess the effectiveness of multiculturalism without reference to the specific units, since this makes it difficult to judge and systematically respond to problems, should they arise. This type of conceptual distinction is equally important for the analysis of media, since how multiculturalism is understood and articulated in policies influences the direction of media policies and practices with respect to cultural diversity. How do policies influence media practices? In particular, how do they influence *availability* and *accessibility* of diasporic media for *all* in the media system? Are diasporic media multicultural – that is, available and accessible only for members of the respective cultural communities – or intercultural – that is, available and accessible for *all*? Building on the theoretical discussion in Chapter 1, this chapter reviews the relationship between policies and media practices, first by looking at the relationship between the policies concerning multiculturalism, immigration, citizenship, and foreign relations and the development of diasporic media in different phases of immigration, and then by examining the relationship between media policies and the development of media with respect to cultural diversity in general and diasporic media in particular.

Multiculturalism Policies and Diasporic Media Practices
A brief look at the history of transnational migration to Canada and the United States helps us understand how the multicultural mediascape as it exists today came to be. As I discussed elsewhere (Yu, 2017a), the history

of immigration policies confirms the influence of these policies on the development of diasporic media in the country of settlement. Both countries have a dark history of immigration policies in the early years. Discriminatory approaches to the migration of ethnocultural groups were common until the 1950s. Canada's Chinese Immigration Act (1885–1923) and a series of Gentlemen's Agreements in the early 1900s are good examples, as are the Chinese Exclusion Act of 1882 and the Gentlemen's Agreement of 1907–1908 in the United States, followed by the Immigration Act of 1917 (Abu-Laban and Gabriel, 2002; Burnet and Palmer, 1988; James, 2000; Mall, 1997). Looking specifically at policies with respect to political rights, Chinese, East Indians, and Japanese were excluded from voting in political elections in Canada until the 1940s (Abu-Laban and Gabriel, 2002). Similarly, in the United States, Asians were categorized as aliens ineligible for citizenship until the McCarran-Walter Act of 1952, which relaxed regulations that limited Asian immigration (Min, 2006a). The history of Korean immigration to the United States began as early as the 1800s, with the conclusion of the Treaty of Peace, Amity, Commerce, and Navigation between the Kingdom of Chosun (Korea) and the United States on May 22, 1882 (Republic of Korea, Ministry of Foreign Affairs and Trade, 2007).

In these early years, most visible diasporic newspapers in Canada were created by European-origin immigrants and were allied with political parties (Burnet and Palmer, 1988). The Icelandic-Canadian newspapers backed by the Conservatives and Liberals are good examples: *Heimskringla* by the Conservatives, and *Lögberg* by the Liberals (Burnet and Palmer, 1988). (Note that these two newspapers were merged in 1959 to become *Lögberg-Heimskringla* [see Lögberg-Heimskringla's "What is Lögberg-Heimskringla?"]). In the United States, while African American and European media were dominant – such as *Philadelphische Zeitung* (est. 1732), *Freedom's Journal* (est. 1827), *L'Eco d'Italia* (est. 1849), and *Echo z Polski* (est. 1863) – Asian and Hispanic newspapers were also present, such as *El Misisipi* (est. 1808), *The Golden Hills News* (Chinese, est. 1854), *Nippon Shuho* (est. 1892), and *Shinhan Minbo* (est. 1905; Hayes, 2003). World War I was a difficult time for foreign-language newspapers, especially the German press, since Germany was the major opponent of the Allied forces, including the United States (Folkerts, Teeter, and Caudill, 2009). American legislation such as the Espionage Act and the Trading with the Enemy Act, both enacted in 1917, censored communication from and to foreign countries and restricted foreign-language newspapers' activities by, for example, imposing unfavourable mailing rates and requiring translation to be filed with the government (Folkerts et al., 2009). This eventually led to the "decline and death" of diasporic press during this time (p. 303).

Shifts in immigration policy emerged in the 1940s, when the United States began to ease immigration and naturalization for its World War II allies. In appreciation of China's role as an ally of the Americans against Japan in the Pacific War, the United States enacted the Magnuson Act of 1943 to loosen the immigration restriction on the Chinese by repealing the anti-Chinese measures, and Canada followed suit in 1947 (Min, 2006a; Li, 2007; Lo, 2006). The Chinese Confession Program of 1956 further encouraged undocumented Chinese people from the exclusion era to confess and obtain legal status (Li, 2007). For other Asians, the United States passed the Luce-Celler Act of 1946, which granted the right of naturalization to Filipinos, and the Immigration and Nationality Act of 1952 (also known as the McCarran-Walter Act), granting the same right to Koreans and Japanese (Võ, 2004, pp. 20–21). The close military, political, and economic ties established between the United States and Korea during the 1950 Korean War helped ease the immigration of Koreans to the United States. Similarly, in Canada, the military connection with Korea through Canada's participation in the Korean War also helped ease immigration to Canada (Wang and Wang, 2011). For Japanese Americans, peace came after much struggle during World War II. Japan's attack on Pearl Harbor in 1941 led to the internment of more than 110,000 Japanese Americans (Folkerts et al., 2009; Conrat, Conrat, Lange, and California Historical Society, 1972). This meant a temporary cessation of Japanese American media, although some publications were founded by detainees (Soga, cited in Matsaganis et al., 2011).

In addition to foreign relations, the global economy is a factor that influenced immigration directives. The liberalization of immigration policies began in the 1960s in both countries as they joined the "global race for highly skilled migrants" (Kobayashi, Li, and Teixeira, 2011, pp. xxi–xxii). Canada's introduction of the points system in 1967 and the U.S. Immigration and Nationality Act of 1965 (also known as the Hart-Celler Act) meant the elimination of a racial or country-of-origin quota, which resulted in an unprecedented increase of immigrants in general and Asian immigrants in particular (Joppke, 2005; Li, 2007; Li and Skop, 2007; Lo, 2006; Ong, 2003).[1] More importantly for Canada, this was also the era in which the multiculturalism policy was officially announced (in 1971), making Canada an inclusive society – officially.

Korean immigration started to see changes in this period as well although with some distinctive differences between Vancouver and Los Angeles owing to local situations, as I have discussed elsewhere (Yu, 2016a). The impact of the points system on Korean immigration to Canada was not immediate, since it was not until 1963 that diplomatic relations between Canada and Korea were established, and in 1965, the Korean Embassy was instituted (M. Kwak, 2004). The Immigration and Nationality Act of 1965 made a significant impact on Korean migration to the United States (A.Y. Chung, 2007; K. Lee, 2000; Min, 2006b; Martin, 2005). Indeed, between 1965 and 1980, approximately 300,000 Koreans immigrated to the United States, and Korean migration continued to grow in the 1970s and the 1980s (Republic of Korea, Ministry of Foreign Affairs and Trade, 2010). The growth factor was mainly economic as L.A. offered a competitive job market, especially in the garment industry (Light and Bonacich, 1988). Forever 21, a multinational fashion retailer, is a prime example. Established in L.A. by a Korean American couple in the 1980s (H.K. Lee, 2011), it is one of the most popular "American Dream" success stories among Koreans in L.A. and a source of much pride. This was also the time when major transnational Korean media launched branch offices in Los Angeles, including *The Korea Times* (or *Hankook Ilbo*) (1969), *The Korea Daily* (or *JoongAng Ilbo*) (1974), and Korean Television Enterprise (now KBS America, 1983). This later peak of Korean immigration – despite the earlier immigration dating back to the 1800s – makes the Korean diaspora relatively very young.

In more recent decades, neoliberal initiatives have characterized immigration and citizenship policies. The cutbacks to government funding programs that started in the 1980s (e.g., Canada Council for the Arts, CBC, the Medical Care Act, the Canada Pension Plan) drew attention to the "model immigrant/citizen" (Abu-Laban and Gabriel, 2002, p. 66; Brodie, 2002). The government endorsed not only the self-sufficiency of immigrants "who will not make demands on the social programs of the welfare state" but also economic contributions of entrepreneur/investor immigrants who would bring outside capital into Canada (Abu-Laban and Gabriel, 2002, p. 65). As an example, the Business Immigration Program, launched in 1986 under the Mulroney government, targeted "urban, middle-class applicants with a particular trade or professional skills" and required a minimum personal net worth of $500,000 (Mitchell, 2001, pp. 169–170). The U.S. equivalent would be the Immigration and Nationality Act of 1990, which created a new investor visa category (EB-5) to attract "highly-skilled or affluent Chinese immigrants from Hong Kong, Taiwan, mainland China, Malaysia, and Indonesia" and the H-1B nonimmigration visa to attract temporary workers (Li, 2007, p. 218; Li and Skop, 2007).

During the 1990s and 2000s, Korean migration to Canada peaked, largely because of the introduction of the Business Immigration Program of 1986 and the subsequent Korea-Canada visa waiver (1994) and simplified medical examination (1997; M. Kwak, 2004). Other than these policy changes, a relatively easier immigration process compared to other countries and Vancouver's natural environment and geographical proximity to Korea also contributed to the growth of Korean migration (Oh, cited in Wang and Wang, 2011; M. Kwak, 2004, p. 17). Interestingly, economic factors are less critical to immigration trends in Vancouver compared to those in L.A.; in fact, Vancouver is generally not considered among Koreans to be a competitive market for business (M. Kwak, 2004). As in the United States, the peak in immigration to Canada meant a significant growth of diasporic media in general and Korean media in particular, suggesting a relationship between immigration policies (in this case, the Business Immigration Program of 1986 and the rise of business- and entrepreneur-class immigrants) and diasporic media as business ventures. New immigrants favour diasporic media as a new business venture (Zhou, Chen, and Cai 2006), and the case of Korean media supports this hypothesis. In addition, the drive to recruit highly educated and skilled labour in the 2000s further intensified this tendency. The 2002 Canadian Immigration and Refugee Protection Act – which strengthened the requirement of language ability, education, and work experience (Kobayashi et al., 2011) – and the Canadian Experience Class – which was also designed to attract Canadian-educated international students – may have contributed to increasing the flow of educated manpower to the diasporic media industry.[2]

If foreign relations and the global economy were pull factors that facilitated international migration to North America, there were also push factors from the countries of origin that motivated people to leave their country. Especially for Asian immigrants, lack of economic opportunities, social and political insecurity, and high competition in children's education in their country of origin were the main factors (Min, 2006a). Indeed, Korean immigration to the United States increased dramatically immediately after the 1965 Immigration Act and then decreased in the early 1990s "due mainly to significant improvements in economic, social, and political conditions in South Korea" (Min, 2006a, p. 22). Immigration bounced back again in the late 1990s, when Korea was undergoing a severe economic crisis, which led to a bailout by the International Monetary Fund (p. 22).

Multiculturalism and immigration policies, combined with push and pull factors in North America and the countries of origin, have continually created ebbs and flows of international migration to North America. The media for these migrant populations have gone through similar ups and downs, as seen in the decline or death of certain media outlets during World Wars I and II and the growth of others, including Korean ones, in the 1990s and 2000s. Following this discussion on multiculturalism policies and diasporic media, the section below explores media policies and diasporic media practices, specifically as related to availability and accessibility of diasporic media for all.

Media Policies and Diasporic Media Practices

As discussed in Chapter 1, policy support is critical in broadening the availability and accessibility of diasporic media for all. This section focuses on understanding the policy initiatives in this regard within a broader scheme of media policy-making concerning diversity. Conceptually, Riggins's (1992) five media policy models concerning the state's structural support for minority media are useful for understanding policy direction: (1) "the integrationist model," which supports minority media with the intention of assisting integration; (2) "the economic model" (also referred to as "*the new assimilationism*"), which supports minority media with the intention of assisting assimilation into the dominant culture; (3) "the divisive model," which encourages ethnic rivalry as a mechanism for "social control"; (4) "the preemptive model," which encourages the state to establish its own minority media in order to prevent minorities from establishing their own; and (5) "the proselytism model," which mobilizes minority media to promote state values (Riggins, 1992, pp. 8–10).

In *Understanding Ethnic Media,* Matsaganis et al. (2011, p. 193) categorize both Canada and the United States in the economic model in that "the state is not committed to multiculturalism per se, but rather to the economic advantages that a type of shallow multiculturalism can generate." In the case of Canada, the reference was Aboriginal media. Contrary to this argument, I have discussed elsewhere (Yu, 2017a) that Canada is close to the integrationist model as there are media policies in place to ensure diversity. This section advances this claim by carefully comparing policy directives of Canada and the United States concerning diasporic media practices and identifies the areas in need of more attention.

Canada

Complexities of Canadian Broadcasting

From the implementation of the Broadcasting Act in 1932 to the creation of the CBC in 1936 and the CRTC in 1968, the two primary mandates of Canadian media were enhancing "national identity" in linguistic duality and securing "cultural sovereignty" so as to minimize American cultural influence (Armstrong, 2010; Siegel, 1996; Vipond, 2000). These mandates are stated in section 3(1)(b) of the Broadcasting Act of 1991: "the Canadian broadcasting system, operated primarily in the English and French languages and comprising public, private and community elements, makes use of radio frequencies that are public property and provides, through its programming, a public service essential to the maintenance and enhancement of *national identity* and *cultural sovereignty*" [emphasis added].

Various measures have been adopted in Canada since the early 1920s to ensure market sovereignty and independence from the United States, including tariff protection, which serves as "the umbrella under which Canadian industrialists expanded and prospered," and a British Broadcasting Corporation (BBC) model of government-owned broadcasting, which led to the birth of the CBC in 1936 (Vipond, 2000, p. 26). More protective measures followed, including restrictions on foreign ownership and Canadian content rules. According to "Direction to the CRTC (Ineligibility of Non-Canadians)," "no broadcasting licence may be issued, and no amendments or renewals thereof may be granted, to an applicant that is a non-Canadian" (Canada, Ministry of Justice, 1997, p. 5). In the case of corporations that are "incorporated or continued under the law of Canada or a province," a strict 80% rule is applied in terms of overall Canadian ownership (p. 3):

(a) the chief executive officer or, where the corporation has no chief executive officer, the person performing functions that are similar to the functions performed by a chief executive officer, and not less than 80 per cent of the directors are Canadians;

(b) in the case of a corporation having share capital, Canadians beneficially own and control, directly or indirectly, in the aggregate and otherwise than by way of security only, not less than 80 per cent of all the issued and outstanding voting shares of the corporation and not less than 80 per cent of the votes.

Canadian ownership is favoured based on the assumption that Canadian owners are more likely to encourage "local creative expression" and profits are likely to be reinvested in the work of "local creators" (Grant and Wood, 2004, pp. 240–241). This rationale corresponds to the principles of Canadian content rules for Canadian television stations, which aim to limit American programs and encourage Canadian production, especially in private broadcasting (Vipond, 2000; Grant and Wood, 2004).[3]

Although there is constant debate among Canadian media scholars on the practicality, technicality, and ambiguity of the Canadian content rules – including discussion on whether they violate the Canadian Charter of Rights and Freedoms and on the skewed focus on quantity rather than quality of "Canadianness" (see, e.g., Grant and Wood, 2004; Vipond, 2000; Zolf, 1988) – the government intervention in content per se is indeed a notable difference that sets Canadian media policies apart from those of the United States.

Diasporic media are governed under the same rules. In particular, the benefit of the restriction on foreign ownership safeguards the locally grown immigrant media from the surge of transnational media corporations from the country of origin and the likely competition that would arise. However, stronger protection does not necessarily mean more minority ownership. In reality, minority ownership is absent in free over-the-air conventional television and is heavily concentrated in ethnic specialty services or brokerages for which users need to pay additional fees for services (CRTC, 1985; Roth, 1998).[4]

A short overview of ethnocultural options in the broadcasting sector will help to clarify the ownership status as a policy outcome. Ethnocultural options are available on various media platforms – such as radio, "over-the-air ethnic television stations," and "ethnic pay & specialty services" ("analogue ethnic specialty services" and "Category 2 digital ethnic pay & specialty services") and "non-Canadian third-language programming services" eligible for distribution in Canada (CRTC, 2007, pp. 89–90).[5] To be more specific, as of 2010, there were more than 30 third-language radio services in Canada, including five in Vancouver, and six over-the-air multicultural television stations, including one in Vancouver (CRTC, 2008a, 2011). Rogers's OMNI, Vancouver's multicultural television station, serves ethnocultural communities in more than 20 languages with a variety of programs and provides a venue for ethnocultural producers to offer programs to the community through brokerage.

The ethnic pay and specialty service sector is where ethnocultural minority ownership is most notable and ethnocultural options are most available. As of 2011, these options include five analogue ethnic specialty services – Fairchild Television (Cantonese), Telelatino (Italian and Hispanic/Spanish), Talentvision (Mandarin), Asian Television Network (South Asian), and Odyssey (Greek) – and 31 Category 2 digital services (CRTC, 2007, 2011).[6] Unlike over-the-air television, these services are carried by cable companies such as Shaw and Telus; thus, the users must be cable subscribers and are required to pay additional fees to access the channels. Cable companies also offer their own free multicultural channels. In Vancouver, Shaw operates Shaw Multicultural Channel (SMC), offering more than 20 third-language services to its subscribers and providing another venue for ethnocultural producers to offer programs through brokerage. In the case of Korean media, three out of four television services (TV Korea, KC TV, and Cakocom) offered programs through this arrangement during the time of study. In addition, 89 non-Canadian, third-language satellite services are authorized for distribution in Canada (CRTC, 2011).

With respect to policies related to cultural diversity, the change to the Broadcasting Act of 1991 was expected to provide more diversity in the broadcasting sector. After six years of "a unique process of public consultation and lobbying" of civil society groups and individuals between 1985 and 1991, the act incorporated cultural and racial diversity as "a fundamental characteristic of Canadian heritage and identity" (section 3[1][b] of the Canadian Multiculturalism Act of 1988 [Government of Canada, 1988]) through the insertion of section 3(1)(d)(iii) (Raboy, 2010, pp. 104), which declared:

> The Canadian broadcasting system should ... through its programming and the employment opportunities arising out of its operations, serve the needs and interests, and reflect the circumstances and aspirations, of Canadian men, women and children, including equal rights, the linguistic duality and *multicultural and multiracial nature of Canadian society* [emphasis added] and the special place of aboriginal peoples within that society.

Within this framework, the CBC, in section 3(1)(m)(viii), is also directed to "reflect the multicultural and multiracial nature of Canada," although this clause by no means changes the CBC's bilingual commitment (Raboy, 2010, pp. 111–112). All these changes, however, made possible the expectation that the "multicultural and multiracial nature of Canadian society" be represented in various media undertakings, including "programming" and "employment" (Raboy, 2010, p. 105). Reflecting these new mandates of the Broadcasting Act, the two main policy frameworks for ethnic broadcasting are "Building on Success: A Policy Framework for Canadian Television" and the "Ethnic Broadcasting Policy." Both, however, address only availability, and not accessibility, of diasporic media for a broader audience.

Policy Framework for Canadian Television
"Building on Success: A Policy Framework for Canadian Television" (CRTC, 1999a) sets out conditions for all conventional television licensees in order to ensure that "the on-screen portrayal of all minority groups is accurate, fair and non-stereotypical" and to create a system in which "producers, writers, technicians and artists from different cultural and social perspectives have the opportunity to create a variety of programming and to develop their skills." With regard to the portrayal of minorities, the CRTC required individual broadcasters and the Canadian Association of Broadcasters (CAB) to develop action plans in response to the CAB's earlier report, "Reflecting Canadian: Best Practices for Cultural Diversity in Private Television" (2004), which found an underrepresentation of Aboriginal peoples, Asian Canadians, and visible minorities on the air (Canadian Association of Broadcasters, 2004). As a result, the "Equitable Portrayal Code" was developed and approved by the CRTC in 2008 to replace the existing "Sex-Role Portrayal Code" (CRTC, 2008b). This new code broadened the coverage from the previous code "to overcome unduly negative portrayal and stereotyping in broadcast programming, including commercial messages, based on matters of race, national or ethnic origin, colour, religion, age, gender, sexual orientation, marital status or physical or mental disability" (CRTC, 2008b). The effectiveness of this measure is, however, questionable, since studies continue to find cases of the misrepresentation of ethnocultural minorities. Both the analyses of news content (Raboy, 2010) and interviews with journalists (reported in Chapters 3 and 4) confirm this tendency.

The quality of representation is one thing and the quantity of representation is another. It is the private rather than the public sector that provides quantity third-language options, as illustrated above. In the public sector, the CBC offers multicultural programs only in the two official languages targeting a broad audience, unlike private broadcasting, which offers third-language services targeting specifically ethnocultural audiences. This difference is a direct outcome of multiculturalism within a bilingual framework. Section 3(1)(m)(iv) of the Broadcasting Act of 1991 states that the programming provided by the CBC should be in English and in French (Raboy, 2010, pp. 111–112). Consequently, some examples of multicultural programming are the CBC's English-language sitcom, *Little Mosque on the Prairie* (2007–12), a story about Muslims and Christians living in the small town of Mercy, and recently launched *Kim's Convenience* (2016–), a story about a Korean Canadian family running a convenience store in Toronto's Regent Park neighbourhood.

Third-language programs are not completely absent from the CBC, however. According to the *Annual Report on the Operation of the Canadian Multiculturalism Act 2010–2011,* presented to Parliament (CBC/Radio-Canada, 2011), during that year, CBC's multicultural programs included an Indigenous news site (cbc.ca/indigenous), a Chinese news site, and *Hockey Night in Canada Punjabi Edition* (then in its third season). Although the Chinese website was available only until 2012, *Hockey Night in Canada Punjabi Edition* continues as of 2017, and it is, in fact, one of the most highly rated programs offered by CBC. Nonetheless, an overall lack of multicultural services in public broadcasting concerns many. Canadian media scholars attribute this lack to funding issues, among other reasons, in that it is a challenge for the CBC even to meet its bilingual mandate in the face of continual budget cuts (Raboy, 2010; Vipond, 2000). Vipond (2000, p. 138) argues that "the Broadcasting Act gives the CBC great responsibilities, and virtually every observer has pointed out that no government has given the CBC the resources with which to accomplish this task."

The representation of minorities, on the other hand, is marginal in both public and private media production. As discussed above, the emphasis on Canadian ownership embraces ethnocultural minority ownership only marginally. The CRTC, in fact, rejected the request for identity-based licensing by the Canadian Diversity Producers Association on the grounds that "the current regulatory structure has continued to support these sectors in a variety of ways, such as providing various opportunities for entry into the system, streamlined licensing processes for easier access by new entrants, as well as regulatory supports for existing services" (CRTC, 2008a). One of the "variety of ways" referred to in this statement may be the "Category 2 digital ethnic pay & specialty services," which was created to respond to the needs of diverse communities (CRTC, 2002). Obviously, this is the sector in which third-language services are concentrated.

In terms of employment, the CRTC follows the Employment Equity Policy by requiring all licensees with 25 to 99 employees to report on "the on-air presence of members of the four designated groups (women, aboriginal persons, disabled persons and members of visible minorities)" (CRTC, 1997). However, the effectiveness of this measure is also questionable, since minority employment in the media industry is marginal. The executive summary of 2014 CBC/Radio-Canada's *Employment Equity Annual Report* (CBC/Radio-Canada, 2014) reported that visible minorities and Indigenous people represented only 8% and 1.5%, respectively, of its "permanent positions" in 2014. The private sector is doing only slightly better. Bell Media Inc.'s Corporate Cultural Diversity Report 2012 to the CRTC reported that two of the four CTV Morning hosts are visible minorities (Bell Media Inc., 2013, p. 5).

Ethnic Broadcasting Policy
The second policy that is directly relevant to ethnic broadcasting is the CRTC's "Ethnic Broadcasting Policy," enacted in 1985 and updated in 1999 (CRTC, 1999b). This policy is indeed unique to Canada, reflecting the "multicultural and multiracial" mandate of Canadian broadcasting (Canadian Broadcasting Act, 1991). One of its most important aspects is the provision of an official definition of an "ethnic program": "An ethnic program is one, in any language, that is specifically directed to any culturally or racially distinct group other than one that is Aboriginal Canadian or from France or the British Isles." Again, as discussed in Chapter 1, ethnic programs are officially defined as programs for *the Other* (those who are not English, French, or Aboriginal); thus, accessibility to these programs for *all* is officially left out of the discussion.

Rather, the policy focuses on laying out licensing requirements for ethnic broadcasting – primarily its content. To summarize, ethnic radio and television stations are expected to devote at least 60% of their schedule to ethnic programming and 50% to third-language programming, outside of French, English, or Aboriginal languages. In order to protect multicultural or ethnic specialty stations from direct competition with nonethnic stations, the CRTC limits the amount of ethnic programming of nonethnic stations to a maximum of 15%. Furthermore, the same Canadian content rules are applied to ethnic stations as are required of nonethnic stations: 60% Canadian content overall and 50% during the evening broadcast period. The ethnic specialty service is also not exempt from Canadian content requirements: this service must have 15% Canadian content, compared to 35% for English and French specialty services (CRTC, 2000). Chapter 3 will discuss that the Canadian content requirement is both an incentive and a burden, depending on the sociocultural and financial mobility of media organizations.

United States

Deregulation, Liberalization, Internationalization, and the Diasporic Media

In contrast to the protective Canadian media policies, two significant characteristics of the U.S. media industry are the commitment to the First Amendment (although this is not to say that Canada is not committed to the Canadian Charter of Rights and Freedoms) and open competition through deregulation. Canada's proximity to the United States, as discussed earlier, has resulted in more conservative media policy directives. According to Katz (2005), American media policy has gone through three developmental stages. The first stage is identified with the "old structure of broadcasting," which focused primarily on public service and cultural aspects of broadcasting (p. 19). In particular, the commitment to the First Amendment guarantees freedom of content in that "no government – federal or local – has the authority to interfere with the right of the media to deliver whatever information they wish" (p. 23). This further limits the authority of the Federal Communications Commission (FCC) to regulating "technological and structural aspects" (p. 23).[7]

The second stage is characterized by deregulation. As early as the 1970s, the United States deregulated the cable industry and adopted an "open-skies policy" for cable and satellite, which permitted the importing of distant transmissions and allowed the cable industry to become "a fully commercial competitor to broadcast television" (Katz, 2005, p. 32). Later, in the 1990s, the Telecommunications Act of 1996 opened the market entirely by lifting the remaining restrictions on all communication services (p. 46). Finally, the third stage is characterized by the global media policy led by the United States, which has resulted in the reality that media policy and competition are no longer a local matter. Technological advancement allows transmissions to reach beyond national borders, thus calling for global governance. This has led to the "transfer of influence from the government sector to the free market" (p. 39).

In this context, availability and accessibility of diasporic media are largely governed by neoliberal market conditions. Foreign ownership and local content requirements are much more relaxed in the United States compared to those of Canada. In particular, concerning foreign ownership, the United States lays out no restrictions on the ownership of cable, satellite, print, or telecom services (Grant and Wood, 2004; McEwen, 2007). These sectors are not considered broadcasting. Such a relaxed environment allows for more availability of ethnocultural programs in these sectors and for significantly more channels compared to Canada. Indeed, the nation's leading satellite service providers, such as Dish Network and DirecTV, and cable service providers, such as Time Warner, offer international channels. During the time of study, Time Warner's "Espanol Tier" carried more than 60 channels, and the "Premium" channels carried more than 10 languages, including Korean, Japanese, Cantonese, Mandarin, and Farsi (Time Warner, n.d.).

In the broadcasting sector, however, a strict restriction is imposed, limiting foreign ownership to 25% of the voting stock of a licensee (McEwen, 2007). This is only slightly higher than Canada's 20%. Nonetheless, similar to Canada, more protection does not necessarily mean more minority ownership. No complete profile of ethnocultural services in the United States is available; however, the FCC report titled *Information Needs of Communities: The Changing Media Landscape in a Broadband Age* (Waldman, 2011) provides a snapshot. African American radio stations have included WERD in Atlanta (the first to be African American–owned) and the National Negro Network (NNN, a nationwide network of 40 stations). American Urban Radio Networks (AURN) is the largest such network in the U.S. today. Univision, one of the top five television networks in the United States, serves the Hispanic community, and KSCI-TV Channel 18 (or LA18, equivalent to the Asian version of Vancouver's OMNI), owned by Asian-Media Group, used to serve Asian communities (Waldman, 2011). (Note that LA18 cancelled its international programming format in July 2017, replacing it with English infomercials [Do, 2017; CBS Los Angeles, 2017]). Minority ownership in broadcasting is certainly higher than in Canada but is still extremely marginal by per capita population. African Americans (13% of the entire U.S. population) own only six television stations (equivalent to 0.33% of all full-power television stations) and 240 radio stations (or 1.6% of all full-power radio stations). Similarly, Latinos (14% of the population) own 1.11% of television stations and 2% of radio stations, and Asian Americans (4% of the U.S. population) own 0.44% of all broadcast television stations.

One of the reasons for this underrepresentation is weak financial status (Waldman, 2011).

The public sector similarly underserves the ethnocultural audience. Grant and Wood (2004, p. 212) assess the U.S. commercial media system to be "large, rich, productive and extremely competitive," while public broadcasting is "undernourished." Indeed, other than a few options on over-the-air, ethnocultural services are largely available in the unregulated cable and satellite sectors.

The FCC's "Diversity Objective"

Although the United States has aspirations to commit to "a unitary and new ethnic identity, that of American" (Glazer, 1983, p. 270), the increasingly multicultural and multiracial realities of its society, and the corresponding cultural demands, have required the U.S. media system to respond. There are no policies designed solely for ethnocultural minority broadcasting (such as the "Ethnic Broadcasting Policy" in Canada), however, that does not mean that diversity is a nonissue.

The FCC, in fact, addresses the issues concerning minorities in its broader commitment to "diversity objective": (1) "outlet diversity" ("the number of independently-owned media outlets"), (2) "source diversity" ("the availability of media content from a variety of content creators"), (3) "minority and female ownership diversity" ("the number of media outlets owned by minority race/ethnic groups and women"), (4) "program diversity" ("the variety of program formats and content provided by the media"), and (5) "viewpoint diversity" ("the availability of content reflecting a variety of perspectives") (Rennhoff and Wilbur, 2011, p. 3). Among these five objectives, minority and female ownership diversity and viewpoint diversity are particularly relevant to the discussion of diasporic media. Both, however, address only availability, and not accessibility, of diasporic media for a broader audience.

The FCC's diversity objective has two implications. First, there is an assumption that minority owners will produce minority-concerned content and thus that more minority owners would mean more diverse viewpoints available in the public discourse. Einstein (2004, p. 7) mentions that "structural diversity" is used to accommodate diversity, equating ownership diversity with viewpoint diversity. The justification of ownership diversity as a measure for content diversity is, however, ambiguous. Indeed, media scholars (e.g., Browne, 2005; Einstein, 2004) point out that there is no actual agreement on what diversity means among scholars and policy makers – whether it refers to an idea, product, producer (person), or production/ distribution outlet (entity). The social responsibility of minority owners is vaguely assumed but there is no empirical evidence to support it. Ambiguity of this nature makes it even more difficult to meet these objectives.

Second, the FCC's diversity objective consists of, after all, just objectives, rather than regulations, which would bear legal consequences if unmet. In fact, minority ownership is continually declining, especially during the recent economic downturn. Frank Montero, a Washington, D.C., communications attorney and an expert in broadcast finance and FCC regulatory matters, attributes the decline to the vulnerability of minority owners in the market: minority owners tend to be "under-collateralized and therefore vulnerable to economic downturns" (Waldman, 2011). More importantly, contrary to the FCC's objectives, a study of broadcasting policies and Spanish-language media found that the FCC's regulatory decisions since the deregulation in the 1980s increased the consolidation of ownership and the ownership by non-Latinos of Spanish-language broadcasting (Perlman and Amaya, 2013). This trend in the industry resulted in the weakening of Hispanic discourse and the endangering of Hispanic civic engagement in the public sphere. Notably, this dismissal of linguistic diversity is also related to the racial history in the United States in that regulatory responses in the post–civil rights movements were "crafted to address African American Civil Rights concerns and delimited how the policy-making community has conceived of minority media rights" (Perlman and Amaya, 2013, p. 144).

Measures for the "Diversity Objective"
In addition to the ambiguity of the objective, a broader question is whether there is a proper mechanism to meet that objective. A few measures do exist, but their effectiveness is debatable. With respect to minority ownership, between the 1960s and 1990s, the FCC introduced assistance programs that help facilitate minority ownership. However, these race-specific measures, quoted below, failed to obtain support from the Supreme Court and Congress (Waldman, 2011, p. 313):

(1) adopting a tax certificate program that allowed broadcast and cable companies to defer capital gains on the sale of media and cable properties to minority-owned businesses; and

(2) allowing for the "distress sale" of a broadcast station, thereby permitting broadcasters to sell properties to minority owners at reduced rates as an alternative to losing the broadcast assets due to non-renewal or revocation of their licenses.

With respect to minorities in media employment, the FCC, as part of the Equal Employment Opportunity rules and policies, requires broadcasting licensees with more than five employees to report annually on the minority composition of their workforce (Form 395-B) as well as on licence renewal (Form 396).[8] The aim of this requirement is to prohibit discrimination based on "race, gender, color, religion, or national origin" by broadcasters (Creech, 2007, p. 159; FCC, 2016). In the case of noncompliance, further actions such as forfeiture, short-term renewal, or nonrenewal can be taken (p. 159). In 2001, the FCC proposed an additional rule that required licensees to advertise job postings as widely as possible so that all qualified candidates have an equal chance to be informed and compete for jobs in the broadcasting industry (p. 160). The effectiveness of this measure, however, is debatable. A study has found that other factors such as the "diversity of the surrounding population, a station's desire to target minority audiences, minority ownership of the station, and the size of the market in which the station was located" were more influential in minority employment (Hollifield and Kimbro, 2010, p. 243).

Minority employment in print media is, in fact, declining. According to the American Society of Newspaper Editors (ASNE), there were approximately 5,300 minority workers in newspapers in 2010, down from 7,400 in 2007 (Waldman, 2011, p. 253). This figure is equivalent to 12.8% minority employees in newsrooms. Nonetheless, it is important that a precaution must be taken when considering ethnocultural representation in the media industry in terms of per capita population. One of the multiple factors that influence underrepresentation is the history of immigration and the level of sociocultural integration (and subsequent socioeconomic capital) of ethnocultural groups. For a young diaspora such as the Korean community, in which first-generation immigrants represent over 70% of the total Korean immigrant population in the United States, jobs in mainstream media institutions are less likely to be a career option. In other words, the absolute size of the population who would apply for mainstream media jobs is already small.

With respect to viewpoint diversity, the United States has no regulations comparable to the Canadian content rules. This is more of a concern for countries like Canada, in which imports of U.S. cultural products are significant. However, content requirements are not entirely absent. Grant and Wood (2004, p. 212) found that the FCC, as early as the 1930s, when it was established, set out various measures concerning local content in the name of "public-interest responsibilities" and encouraged licensees to respond to "local needs." These measures included the requirements for "the development and use of local talent," "program[s] for children," and "educational programs" in 1960, the Children's Television Act in 1990, and a three-hour quota for children's educational programming in 1996 (FCC, cited in Grant and Wood, 2004, pp. 212–214).

POLICY AREAS IN NEED OF ATTENTION
While these policy frameworks are in place to accommodate diversity, their focus is on *availability* through the representation of minorities in media content and media production, and on the management of available diasporic media practices in particular. There is no discussion about broadening *accessibility* to diasporic media for members of the broader society.

Availability and Accessibility
The two most important accessibility issues are language and cost. Multilingual services in various genres (e.g., news, current affairs, entertainment) are available within mainstream institutions; however, limited access to these options for a broader audience is an issue common to both countries.[9] First, English subtitles are provided for most over-the-air programs (except news programs), making these programs accessible for all audiences, but they are available only selectively for paid services. Multicultural television stations such as Vancouver's OMNI and L.A.'s LA18 used to provide local daily news in various languages, which could potentially serve as a window into diasporic discourse. However, no English or multilingual subtitles were provided, thus, they were not accessible to a broader audience. On that note, Canadian media scholars Beaty and Sullivan (2006, p. 144) support the idea that "Canada should cast wide its doors and welcome in as much third-language as possible, ideally with available French and English subtitles so that foreign-language programming can have the widest possible impact across Canada." Nonetheless, even this option still provides only one-way

access, which allows only majority-language viewers to have access to minority programs but not the other way around, leaving immigrants with limited linguistic capacity in the official languages in an information void. As mentioned in the previous chapter, this is the other side of an intercultural media system, a side that requires research attention. (See Chapter 6 for further discussion.)

The second accessibility issue relates to cost on the user's end. Except for the programs offered on over-the-air broadcasts, most multilingual services available on cable and satellite are paid services, available to subscribers only, as part of a regular subscription or at additional cost. In Canada, this is because the CRTC allows Category 2 specialty services to broadcast but imposes no obligations on cable companies to carry them, thereby requiring cable subscribers to pay an additional cost to receive third-language services (Beaty and Sullivan, 2006, p. 49). The CRTC's "Regulatory Frameworks for Broadcasting Distribution Undertakings and Discretionary Programming Services" (CRTC, 2008c) contains amended access rules for third-language services:

> All BDUs distributing any of the following ethnic services – Telelatino, Odyssey, Talentvision, Fairchild and Asian TV Network – as of the date of this public notice will be required to continue distributing them.
>
> Terrestrial BDUs will be required to distribute the appropriate above-noted ethnic service(s) when 10% of the population in the service area of the terrestrial BDU is of the ethnic origin targeted by the service(s).
>
> Non-Canadian third-language services can only be offered in a package with Canadian ethnic/third-language services in the same language(s) if one exists, in a ratio of one (1) Canadian service to up to three (3) non-Canadian services.

In addressing the language and cost issues, it is also important to pay attention to the growing nonprofit sector. Some grassroots initiatives contribute to broadening accessibility to the daily reporting of ethnocultural minorities. One example is New America Media, a network of more than 3,000 "ethnic media" outlets (see New America Media, n.d.). The organization "produces, aggregates and disseminates multimedia content and services for and from the youth and ethnic media sectors" such as *The Korea*

Times, The Korea Daily, India Currents, and Univision, among others (New America Media, n.d.). Another multiethnic online news platform that was tested in recent years is LA Beez, a former multiethnic collaboration of local ethnic media in Los Angeles. The site provided hyperlocal news feeds (again in English or translated into English) contributed by its local diasporic media members: "Alhambra Source," *Asian Journal, India Journal,* and *KoreAm Journal,* among others. If LA Beez was a professional collaboration, "Alhambra Source" is a multilingual community collaboration of local researchers, students, residents, organizations, and professional journalists; it offers stories in English, Chinese, and Spanish. All of these intercultural and multilingual online models respond to the language and cost issues one way or another, yet for them to grow in the digital era, policy support at various levels of government needs to occur to facilitate the growth. They also require more careful policy attention to themselves in order to grow in the digital era.

Funding

One of the sustaining conditions for broader availability and accessibility of diasporic media is funding. Although vigorous discussion of this issue has taken place in Canada, it has brought about no substantial outcomes. The CRTC acknowledged that there was a disconnect between some of the funding demands and the CTF (Canadian Television Fund; CRTC, 1999b).[10] As an alternative source of funding, the Panel on Access to Third-Language Public Television Services proposed "that third-language broadcasters ... be required to make a contribution to a third-language programming fund" of at least "10% of the funds they would receive from the Canadian distributors" (Lincoln, Tassé, and Cianciotta, 2004, p. 21). The logic is the same as that of the Canadian Television Fund, which subsidizes film and television production through public funds and contributions from cable and satellite distribution systems (Grant and Wood, 2004, p. 300). The rationale here is that cable and satellite companies make large profits by airing inexpensive foreign programs in place of local Canadian content (p. 305). The panel's proposal was, however, not new: their report noted that the fundamental idea had already been stated in the "Ethnic Broadcasting Policy" but had never been implemented (Lincoln et al., p. 21).[11]

The panel's recommendation received mixed responses – support from producers and related interest groups, and objections from major distributors (CRTC, 2004). The main argument of the latter was the ongoing contribution of non-Canadian services to the Canadian system "by providing greater programming choice and diversity and by virtue of the existing financial contribution to local expression, Canadian programming and community television required of all Canadian BDUs amounting to 5% of gross revenues derived from their broadcasting activities" (CRTC, 2004). Thus, additional financial requirements would discourage potential new services. Then, is self-funding within the third-language sector a possibility? The numbers in the CRTC's 2011 *Communications Monitoring Report* (CRTC, 2011) show that there is no guarantee. The revenue of third-language specialty services (analogue and digital combined) in 2010 was 3.7% ($78,044,000) of that of English-language specialty services ($2,109,877,000). The actual market share is small; however, the figure represents an approximately 16% increase from 2006 (or $67 million; CRTC, 2007).

Given this weak funding structure, it is a natural consequence that Canadian content requirements for diasporic media, equal to those for non-ethnic programs, is often considered a burden rather than an incentive, as the case study of Korean media reported in Chapter 3 reveals. While local production is much desired, limited production capacity makes third-language producers resort to imported programs from the country of origin, replicating Canadian mainstream broadcasters' dependency on U.S. programs. A potential new option is the Canada Media Fund's Diverse Languages Program, which "supports productions reflecting Canadian diversity by funding projects in languages other than English, French, or Aboriginal languages ... developed for distribution on at least two platforms, one of which must be television" (Canada Media Fund, n.d.). For-profit companies owned by Canadians and headquartered in Canada are eligible to apply (Canada Media Fund, 2016, p. 9).

The funding for print media is equally insufficient. One potential funding source for diasporic publishers is the Canadian Periodical Fund. Canadian-owned magazines or nondaily newspapers are eligible to apply if the publication contains at least 80% "Canadian editorial content" (or 50% for "ethnocultural periodicals") in a given financial year (Canada, Ministry of Public Works and Government Services, 2015, p. 8).[12] Some of the previous funds were made available to diasporic media outlets through collective efforts. According to the National Ethnic Press and Media Council of Canada (NEPMCC), its joint efforts with the Department of Heritage Canada (the former name of Canadian Heritage) resulted in the "inclusion of the members of the ethnic press in PAP (Heritage Canada Publications Assistance Program), in order to less the burden of postal expenditure, a privilege that has been enjoyed for so many years by the Canadian mainstream media" (NEPMCC, n.d.). The case of the PAP suggests that organizational efforts need to be mobilized in order to access additional sources of funding.

Conclusion

Overall, the current media system is multicultural rather than intercultural. Although ethnocultural options are available, they operate in isolation with limited access for a broader audience. The influence of the status of multiculturalism is apparent when the media policy framework in both countries is examined. In Canada, the official commitment to multiculturalism lays out more ethnicity-specific (group-differentiated) regulations. Policy measures for minority portrayal in media content and minority participation in production, such as the Canadian Association of Broadcasters "Equitable Portrayal Code" (CRTC, 2008b) and the "Employment Equity Policy" (CRTC, 1997), are also constantly studied and updated. Specifically, the Broadcasting Act not only embraces cultural diversity as an important mandate of Canadian media but also sets out policy directives for multicultural or ethnic broadcasting (e.g., the "Ethnic Broadcasting Policy"). Although some measures are still more conceptual than substantial and require further attention, they clearly show the impact of multiculturalism as part of the Canadian constitution. In the United States, however, ethnicity-specific initiatives are not supported, but nor are they absent. Minority participation through ownership and employment is encouraged and believed to be related to "viewpoint diversity." Multicultural and multiracial realities inevitably demand a certain level of policy support for minority media undertakings and have been answered in the name of "diversity objective." Overall, projecting onto Riggins's (1992) five media policy models, the Canadian policy framework is closer to the integrationist model than is the U.S.'s economist model.

Although Canada and the United States take different approaches, the outcome is similar: a mechanism that ensures accessibility to diasporic media for broad audiences is equally lacking in both countries. The policy focus is on availability of diasporic media or diasporic voices and the management of these practices rather than accessibility for a broader audience within a wider scheme of creating an intercultural media system. In the broadcasting sector, ethnocultural options have only limited availability on public over-the-air stations and are instead heavily concentrated in the private cable/satellite sectors, which require additional service fees to access. Even in Canada, the public broadcasting service offers only a few general multicultural programs for all audiences without any third-language programs specifically for ethnocultural audiences. What is more, all these existing measures concern only broadcasting, when it is the print media sector in which diasporic media are predominantly concentrated.

Access to third-language (or non-English, in the case of the United States) services requires policy attention that addresses the sociocultural and economic barriers (e.g., limited English subtitles or translation services, paid services) that prohibit access. The current system offers ethnocultural options only to those who know the language and are willing to pay extra fees to access these services. A hopeful sign is that online intercultural communicative spaces are emerging to fill this gap, although the effectiveness and impact of these spaces in bringing about an actual intercultural dialogue requires further monitoring. The next two chapters examine and compare Korean media in Vancouver and L.A. and explore how diasporic communication infrastructure, especially that operates in a third language, fares under these structural conditions.

3
Korean Diasporic Media
.... in Vancouver

The diasporic communication infrastructure – consisting of media, civil society organizations (CSOs), alumni networks, and religious institutions – is a central part of immigrants' lives. Earlier studies have found that religious institutions are particularly important for the Korean community; they provide a sense of belonging to Korean immigrants struggling in a new country and satisfy the "desire for communal ties" (Min, 2001, p. 186). Especially for those who suffer from "marginal man syndrome" – men who "feel loss of social status after having left Korea" – local Korean churches serve as venues to re-establish status (K. Lee, 2000, p. 83). This functionality is, however, not limited to churches. The findings discussed in this chapter confirm that local Korean media serve not only as a community but also as a civil society and a market. This chapter further expands the scope of discussion and explores the increasingly hybrid nature of diasporic communities and their relationship with the broader society in the community, the public sphere, and the media industry. Are Korean media available and accessible for the Korean community *as well as* for the broader society? What are the possible contributions of the Korean community and media to building an intercultural media system? What are the challenges in broadening accessibility for a broader audience? This chapter will explore these questions.

Availability and Accessibility of Korean Media: An Overview

NUMBER OF MEDIA OUTLETS

Korean diasporic media are an important part of the Korean diasporic communication infrastructure. A 2010 audience study by *The Korea Daily* (n = 136) found that 75% of Koreans depended on Korean diasporic media for news about Canada and Metro Vancouver whereas 16% use English-language media (J.O. Kim, 2010). Such a high dependency on mother-tongue media is indeed one of the reasons for the rapid growth and wide availability of Korean media for local Korean immigrants.[1] Murray et al.'s (2007) study identified 28 Korean-language media outlets in British Columbia in 2007: three television services, two radio services, three magazines, and 20 dailies and weeklies (see the B.C. ethnic media directory for further details at www.bcethnicmedia.ca). Korean is the largest single-language media sector (followed by Chinese- and Punjabi-language media, with 25 and 22 outlets, respectively) and has the highest per capita ratio of media outlets to population size.

Historical trajectory

The short history of Korean media compared to European and other Asian media makes its growth more significant.[2] The two oldest newspapers, *The Korean Canadian News* (or *Hanga Shinmoon*, 1983) and *The Vancouver Korean Press* (or *The Chosun Ilbo Vancouver Edition*), were launched in the 1980s. The following two decades, however, saw significant growth with the launch of television and radio services along with more than a dozen publications: *The Korea Times* (or *The Korea Times Vancouver* or *Hankook Ilbo*, 1992), KC TV (1995), *Kyocharo* TV Korea (1997), *The Korea Daily* (or *JoongAng Daily* or *JoongAng Ilbo*, 2001), Radio Seoul FM 96.1, Murray et al., 2007). This growth peaked in 2007. Six new specialty weeklies were launched in the first two quarters of that year including *The Vancouver Education Post* (or *Vancouver Kyoyook Shinmoon*), *The Korea Times Weekly* (or *Ilyo News*), *Canada Express*, and *The Bridge* (Murray et al., 2007).

This rate of growth, however, was not sustained. This study tracked the changes in the market since Murray et al.'s 2007 study and found that the continuing economic recession pushed at least five media outlets out of the market, including some of the weeklies that were launched in 2007: *The Bridge*, *The Donga Life Weekly*, and Radio Seoul. Interestingly, the market had its own dynamic. While a few outlets were discontinued, new players also entered the market regardless of the recession: All TV B.C. (2008), *Korean News* (2009), Enjoy &TV (2010), *Today's Money* (2010), and a few new back-to-back publications as part of existing weeklies (e.g., *Canada Express*'s *Vancouver Life Weekly*, *Kyocharo*'s *Golf & Cars*, and *Canada Edu News* [or *Miju Kyoyook Shinmoon*]). According to interviews with media practitioners, more were expected to emerge, including outlets that were preparing for a comeback after a few months of temporary closure (Media Practitioners 6 and 8).

Print media

In terms of media type, Vancouver's Korean media are available predominantly in the form of print. As mentioned earlier, the strong print media sector is a general characteristic of Vancouver's third-language media market, where 80% of media are print media (Murray et al., 2007). These are also predominantly specialty weeklies. Other than *The Vancouver Korean Press*, *The Korea Daily*, and *The Korea Times* (general newspapers that published three to five times a week during the time of study, and that are considered as "dailies" in this study), the majority of the weeklies specialize in one issue area and target a specific segment of the market: for example, real estate (*Korean Real Estate Weekly* [or *Boodongsan Vancouver*]), women (*Womanself News*) [or *Joogan Yuhsung Jashin*]), education (*The Vancouver Education Post*), and classifieds (*Kyocharo*). Relative ease of entry and regulatory structure compared to broadcasting media is the main contributing factor for this growth. As discussed in Chapter 2, the broadcasting sector is regulated by the CRTC, whereas the print media sector is out of the regulatory loop, with only voluntary membership in press councils or industry associations at the discretion of organizations. Another reason may be the absence of 24-hour Korean specialty TV until 2008, when All TV (CRTC, 2001a) was launched (Media Practitioner 8). Until then, print media had been the only media available for local Koreans since the 1980s.

In the digital era, most of these publications are also available online and are accessible for free. Their websites provide not only online news and e-papers but also various community services, such as reader-driven free posts of various topics, specialist Q and A, buy and sell, and community calendars. Indeed, online communities developed on or linked to these publications are a new form of communicative space in which various issues and concerns are discussed. (The section that follows shows the findings from a content analysis of online threads.) As I have discussed elsewhere (Yu, 2017b), online publications also provide additional revenue sources by creating extra advertising space. Thus, strategies to strengthen online business solely or in collaboration with regionally dispersed Korean media across Canada are well underway (Media Practitioner 1).

Broadcasting media

In the broadcasting sector, Korean radio has been discontinued, but TV continues and is available on cable and over-the-air. While print media operate largely in isolation, broadcasting media are relatively more integrated into and available in the broader media system, offering Korean options as part of multilingual programs. Korean programs have been, in fact, among the most common programs in the past couple of decades. According to Public Notice CRTC 2001–31 (CRTC, 2001b), Korean, at 19 hours per week, was indeed the most common language on the Shaw Multicultural Channel (a multicultural channel owned and operated by Shaw Cablesystems) in 2001 among more than 20 third-language programs; it was followed by Hindi (9.5 hours) and Italian (9 hours). By 2010, Korean had increased slightly (20.5 hours a week) but was a distant second after Mandarin (40 hours a week), according to the SMC spring 2010 schedule during the time of study.[3] Hindi was fourth with 10.5 hours after Punjabi with 14 hours, with some overlapping programs offered both in Hindi and Punjabi. Punjabi, Chinese (not specified, Cantonese, Mandarin), and Korean were, in fact, among the five most-spoken "immigrant languages" at home in British Columbia (Statistics Canada, 2011b, p. 9).

KC TV (est. 1995), Cakocom (est. unknown), and TV Korea (est. 1997) were three independent Korean producers/program providers that offered a variety of imported Korean programs (e.g., news, drama, entertainment) in the form of brokerage (see Chapter 2). During the time of study, the now-defunct TV Korea offered the most programming among the three providers (with 3.5 hours provided by KC TV and one hour by Cakocom), providing mainly imported news and entertainment programs from KBS (Korean Broadcasting System). In addition to its services through SMC, TV Korea provided local Korean-language news, *Korean News*, and *TV Korea Magazine* (a current affairs program), through OMNI, Vancouver's only over-the-air multicultural television channel. TV Korea stopped services in 2011, well before Rogers's decision to discontinue OMNI's multilingual daily news in 2015 (further details later in this chapter).

A 24-hour Korean specialty TV service is also available for cable subscribers at an additional fee. (Note that "ethnic pay & specialty services" is the sector in which ethnocultural minority ownership is concentrated.) All TV started a Korean service in British Columbia and Alberta in 2008 through Shaw and Telus TV, after its launch in Ontario in 2001 (All T.V., n.d.). The company provides programs from all three broadcasters in Korea: MBC (Munhwa Broadcasting Corporation), SBS (Seoul Broadcasting System), and KBS (Korean Broadcasting Corporation). This kind of program lineup is the exception rather than the rule, in contrast to L.A., where branches of Korea's three major broadcasters (KBS America, MBC America, and SBS International) compete with one another in the same market. In the absence of transnational branches in Vancouver, All TV enjoys a competitive advantage unseen in L.A. Another exception is that All TV offers programs almost in real time without subtitles: what was aired in Korea is aired the following day in Vancouver, whereas in L.A., there was a four-week hold-back period during the time of study owing to subtitle production, as well as a lead time reserved for the video store rental business (Media Practitioner 8).

OWNERSHIP AND STRUCTURE

Market dynamics can explain the structure of media ownership: Vancouver's Korean media are *immigrant media*, entirely owned by local immigrants based on local immigrant capital, unlike in L.A., where branches of Korea's major transnational media compete with immigrant media (see Chapter 4). Vancouver's three major newspapers were affiliated with either press conglomerates in Korea or their L.A. branches: *The Vancouver Korean Press* with *The Chosun Ilbo*, *The Korea Daily* with *The Korea Daily L.A.*, and *The Korea Times* with *The Korea Times L.A.* Vancouver's All TV and Enjoy &TV were also affiliated with MBC/MBC America and SBS/SBS International, and TV Korea was with KBS/KBS America and YTN. All of Vancouver's outlets, however, are financially independent franchises; their affiliation is limited to content sharing only through licensing agreements.

As the volume of capital dictates, these immigrant media outlets are mostly mom-and-pop–type small businesses. The size of the media outlets can be classified by number of employees: large (more than 100 employees), medium (50–100), small (10–49), and micro (fewer than 10; based on Murray et al., 2007, pp. 152–153). According to this classification, Korean media outlets in Vancouver are small or micro, with the largest having approximately 15 employees and the smallest employing three employees (full- and part-time combined). Compared to media of other diasporic communities, Korean media are smaller than Chinese media and almost on par with South Asian media.[4] With a small variation by media type, the employees of Korean media comprise editors, reporters (part-time, full-time, interns), anchors, technicians, graphic designers, webmasters, subscription/marketing professionals, administration, and delivery people, among others. Weeklies tend to have a few freelance translators for local news translation.

SERVICE LANGUAGE AND FEES

All these Korean media are widely available and accessible in Vancouver – across all media types, online and offline, and under various ownership models and sizes – mostly for local Koreans rather than for members of the broader community or society. Language is the main barrier. In the print sector, all Korean newspapers are offered in Korean and are thus accessible only for Korean speakers. Unlike in L.A., where English editions of Korean-language media (e.g., "The Korea Times" English website [www.koreatimes us.com]) and English publications (e.g., *KoreAm Journal*, until recently) are available, no attempt has been made to offer English-language Korean print media in Vancouver. *The Bridge* was a business-focused weekly launched by a younger-generation publisher, but it was also published in Korean. There is, however, no economic barrier to access: all of these publications are available for free at major Korean locations such as the the shopping plazas consisting of predominantly Korean businesses on North Road, which demarcates Coquitlam and Burnaby (see Figure 3.1). During the time of study, *The Korea Times* was the only outlet that operated subscription services for door-to-door delivery. However, it was also available for free the next day at major distribution centres.

In the broadcasting sector, programs are more accessible for a broader audience. Although limited mostly to entertainment programs on over-the-air television, a few programs provide English subtitles. Owing to *hallyu* (the Korean Wave) and the popularity of Korean dramas, the subtitled programs attract non-Korean audiences (Media Practitioner 18).[5] Local and international news programs, especially the now-defunct TV Korea's *Korean News*, however, did not provide subtitles, thus limiting access to local Korean speakers only. Economically, broadcasting is less accessible: except for over-the-air programs, most of these programs can only be accessed on cable channels and are available to subscribers as part of their subscription packages (Shaw Multicultural Channel) or at an additional cost (All TV).

Availability and Accessibility on Three Dimensions

The overview above shows that Korean media are widely available in all media types online and offline but are accessible mostly for Koreans. In a relative sense, the broadcasting sector is more accessible, since it provides English subtitles, although this is limited to selected programs. This snapshot requires deeper exploration in order to identify the areas in which broader accessibility is possible or challenging to varying degrees. The

FIGURE 3.1 **Newspaper dispensers**

conceptual guidelines developed in Chapter 1 help explore the following questions: How are Korean media available and accessible as a community, a civil society, and a market? What are the rationales, strategies, or short-comings within each dimension, if any? The following sections discuss the relative strengths and weaknesses of each dimension in terms of availability and accessibility of Korean discourse to all members of society and the implications for an intercultural media system.

KOREAN MEDIA AS A COMMUNITY

There is no doubt that Vancouver's Korean media serve as a community of common locality and interest. The proliferation of media platforms and information sources online and offline inundate immigrants' daily lives and enable them to travel back and forth virtually between where they live and where they are from. Nevertheless, the benefit of these diasporic media is that they cater to the everyday needs of immigrants *here* in Vancouver. It is within this niche that local diasporic media effectively operate, filling the information void that mainstream media of *here* or *there* do not address. According to Lin and Song (2006, pp. 367–368), the primary role of diasporic media is providing "geo-ethnic storytelling" – that is, stories that are "geographically bound and concern primarily the happenings in the community" and are "ethnically or culturally relevant to a particular ethnic group." Indeed, geo-ethnic storytelling provides geographically dispersed Koreans throughout Metro Vancouver with the information that matters to their everyday lives – news about the local community (neighbourhoods or the city) or the nation, or about Vancouver's Korean community or the country of Korea. The general news about *here* is particularly important, especially for those whose English is too limited to resort to mainstream media. As one CSO (civil society organization) leader put it: "Korean newspapers are the only source of information about local news ... In Korea, we have friends, families, relatives, and colleagues. They are all information sources. But in Canada, we only have Korean newspapers" (CSO Leader 3).[6]

"Multilocality" and News About Here *and* There

News content is a good way to understand what matters to the community as a whole. News presented in Korean media is dialectic: that is, it is about both *here* (the country of settlement) and *there* (the country of origin), and it is both *universal* (the broader society) and *particular* (the Korean community). News stories that are relevant to Koreans *here* are carefully selected to assist them in living *here*. During the interviews, media practitioners generally mentioned that most of their production efforts and resources are dedicated to geo-ethnic news in order to produce more and better stories about *here*. A content analysis of 200 news items from the front page of each section of the three local Korean dailies (*The Vancouver Korean Press, The Korea Daily, The Korea Times*) and one Korean TV news program (TV Korea's *Korean News* on OMNI) in a constructed week in March 2010 was conducted to see if such efforts are manifested in news content. Table 3.1

Table 3.1

News origin by media type, Vancouver (%)

	Total	TV	Newspaper
	$N = 200$	$N = 61$	$N = 139$
Staff writers	34	8[a]	45[b]
Imported from Korea	38	28[a]	42[a]
Canadian media	8	15[a]	4[b]
Other	6	5[a]	5[a]
Absent/unknown	16	44[a]	4[b]

NOTES: Numbers in the table are rounded off. Each subscript letter denotes a subset of column categories whose column proportions do or do not differ significantly from each other at the .05 level.

shows that 34% of the news items are locally produced by staff writers while the rest are supplemented by various sources, including media in Korea and local mainstream media.[7] Local production is much higher for newspapers (45%) than for TV (8%). Furthermore, among the locally produced content (written by staff writers), 94% of items are about Canada: 66% are geo-ethnic news (42% for general local news and 24% for Korean community news) and 28% are national or provincial news (see Table 3.2). In other words, local staff writers write mostly about *here*.

News that Matters to the Korean Community

What, then, are the news topics that are available for local Koreans? What are the selection criteria? The interviewed Korean media practitioners ranked immigration/immigration law, economy, and education as the top three priority topics for Canadian news, and politics (e.g., general politics, Canada-Korean relations), economy, and education as the top three topics of imported news from Korea. This is more or less consistent with the findings of *The Korea Daily*'s online survey of its readers ($n = 136$). News topics that are the most popular among readers include Canada's politics and economy (41%), followed by Korean community news (36%), Korean politics and economy (29%), immigration policy (24%), and education (23%; A.H. Kim, 2010).

Some media practitioners interviewed mentioned that the main target for Canadian news is Korean immigrants who settle in Canada, whereas for imported news from Korea, it is "transnational Koreans" who are more socioeconomically and politically mobile between Canada and Korea; the

TABLE 3.2

Geographic focus of news items by news origin, Vancouver (%)

	Total	Staff writer	Imported from Korea	Other	Absent/ unknown
	$N = 200$	$N = 67$	$N = 76$	$N = 25$	$N = 32$
Local					
• Korean	9	24[b]	–	4[a]	–
• Other diasporic	2	–	–	4[a, b]	6[b]
• General	24	42[b]	5[a]	32[b]	22[b]
Provincial/state	6	9[b]	1[a]	8[a, b]	9[b]
National	14	19[b]	1[a]	24[b]	22[b]
International					
• South Korea	36	–	86[a]	8[b]	16[b]
• North Korea	2	–	3[a]	4[a]	–
• General	9	3[a]	4[a]	16[b]	25[b]
Absent/unknown	1	3[a]	–	–	–

NOTES: Numbers in the table are rounded off. Each subscript letter denotes a subset of column categories whose column proportions do or do not differ significantly from each other at the .05 level.

boundary between these two audiences, though, is often blurred (Media Practitioners 4 and 5). This categorization reflects the demographic diversity within the community, as discussed in the introductory chapter. For this reason, one of the main criteria for the choice of Canadian news topics is relevancy to settlement: how to settle and make a living in a new country. As one interviewee explained, "All immigrants have unstable lives; we are unfamiliar with our new society and have a hard time defining our lives. We need media that help us settle in a new society" (Media Practitioner 4). Another said: "We focus on economy first, how to survive; second, education, as it is the main reason for Koreans to come to Canada; and third, the promotion of the Korean community in mainstream society" (Media Practitioner 5).

The findings of the content analysis are consistent with these comments from media practitioners. Comparing the news topics by geographic location (local, provincial/national, and international news about Korea), the top three Canadian topics at a provincial/national level are indeed economy/ business (15%), migration/immigration (10%), and education (8%; see Table 3.3).[8] News about migration/immigration includes headlines such as

Table 3.3

News topics by geographic focus, Vancouver (%)

	Local	Provincial/ national	International (South Korea)
	N = 67	**N = 39**	**N = 72**
Sports	30[a]	5[b, c]	—
Politics (Parliamentary practices)	2[a]	13[b]	15[b]
Crime/violence	8[a]	8[a]	15[a]
Community (Korean diaspora)	18[a]	—	—
Education	5[a]	8[a]	6[a]
Health	2[a]	10[b, c]	4[a, c]
People	3[a]	—	8[a]
Economy/business (Korean enclave, Korea)	2[a]	—	10[b]
Religion	—	—	11[b]
Entertainment/entertainment industry	2[a]	—	8[a]
Weather/season/daylight savings	8[a]	5[a]	1[a]
Economy/business (general)	2[a]	15[b]	—
Migration/migrants/immigration/immigrants	3[a, b]	10[b]	1[a]
Employment news	—	5[a]	4[a]
Other	20	21	15

NOTES: Numbers in the table are rounded off. Each subscript letter denotes a subset of column categories whose column proportions do or do not differ significantly from each other at the .05 level.

"CIC, looking for your opinion on immigration policy" (*The Vancouver Korean Press*, March 19, 2010, A1) as well as some Korean-specific headlines such as "160,000 Koreans in Vancouver by 2031, a steady growth of immigration and birth rate" (*The Vancouver Korean Press*, March 10, 2010, A1). Politics (13%) and health (10%) are two other topics that are also frequently discussed at a provincial/national level, as exemplified by the headlines "HST starting in one month" (*The Vancouver Korean Press*, March 24, 2010, A1), "The toughest drinking and driving law in the country is about to launch in BC" (*The Korea Daily*, March 9, 2010, A1), and "41% of Canadians suffer from hyperlipidemia, according to Statistics Canada" (*The Korea Times*, March 24, 2010, A1). All of these topics are time sensitive and leaving them unpublicized through Korean media could cause some inconvenience in the everyday lives of local Koreans.

At a local level, local Korean community news (18%), which is rarely discussed in mainstream media, was most frequently discussed, as in "Time to build Korean Cultural Centre" (*The Vancouver Korean Press*, March 27, 2010, A1), "The 39th Korean Society election" (*The Korea Times*, March 24, 2010, A1), and "Korean folk singers, Yoon and Kim are coming to Vancouver" (*The Korea Daily*, March 16, 2010, A1). The geo-Korean news also included self-congratulatory stories about successful younger-generation Korean Canadians. Some examples are Eric Shim, a baseball player (Han, 2010a); James Choi, a tennis player (M.S. Kwon, 2010d); Soo Hwan Kim, a Catholic priest (M.S. Kwon, 2010c); Belinda Kim, Miss Universe Canada participant (M.S. Kwon, 2010b); and Andrew Kim, a musician (Y. Choi, 2011). Another important geo-Korean news topic is new immigrant/community service programs that are made available and regularly updated online and offline through newspapers' community bulletin boards (e.g., *The Vancouver Korean Press*'s "Vancouver Sarangbang," *The Korea Daily*'s "Gaeshipan," *The Korea Times*'s "Donghohae Dongjung," and "Town Dongjung") or the community calendars of online publications.

News about *there* concerns current affairs in Korea. It is not any news but news that is relevant to local Koreans. Consistent with comments by media practitioners during interviews, news about politics (15%) and economics (10%) is most frequently covered, as in "Forging overseas account reporting system" (*The Korea Times*, March 12, 2010, A1) and "Revenue Korea, investigation into tax evasion" (*The Vancouver Korean Press*, March 27, 2010, B1; see Table 3.3).[9] The coverage of Korea's new election law is another good example: the Korean Consulate General in Vancouver conducted a mock election with local Korean citizens (M.S. Kwon, 2010e; K.H. Lee, 2010c). News about there is relevant particularly to local Koreans who are more mobile between Korean and Canada, as one media practitioner pointed out:

> For Korean news, we focus on politics, the economy, and education. Economic news is particularly important for those who still have their properties or businesses in Korea. Education news is also important for those who will eventually return to Korea after their temporary education in Canada. They need to be updated about the changes in Korea's education system. (Media Practitioner 5)

The significance of the portion of news about *there* in diasporic media has been debated in terms of whether it demonstrates an attachment to the country of origin and isolation from the country of settlement (Murray et al., 2007; Lin and Song, 2006). This study found that in addition to news value, imported news about there is also financially beneficial for media organizations as a way to easily create new advertising space. According to interviews with media practitioners, individual articles, even entire pages or video segments imported from Korea, are "pre-selected" by the publisher/producer and inserted directly with minimal or no modification in the process of editing (Media Practitioner 13). Unlike news from local mainstream sources, these news items require no English-to-Korean translation and thus save production time.

Geo-Korean Storytelling and Cultural Translation

The most important part of the Korean media's community role is cultural translation – that is, ensuring that news is written using culturally relevant Korean idioms and a narrative (or storytelling) style with which Koreans are familiar. While news produced directly by staff writers is already culturally translated, news from local mainstream sources needs to be reproduced or culturally translated as part of English-to-Korean translation. Direct translation from English to Korean often does not work, since the story does not follow the usual story development with which Koreans are familiar and/or lacks historical background necessary for new immigrants to fully comprehend the story (Media Practitioner 2). Therefore, cultural translation often involves repackaging news items by translating and rewriting the original story (while retaining the facts) into the language and the type of narration (or story development) with which Korean audiences are familiar. It also involves providing background information or the history of the event. Mainstream audiences already know this background, so it is excluded in the original source, but (new) immigrants need to have it in order to understand the context. It is through this process of cultural translation that the news is contexualized and recontexualized. As one media practitioner said,

> We don't do direct translation. We initially tried, but it didn't read smoothly. The way of thinking is different. It is not the usual way of story development in Korean papers. Therefore, we read through the article once and rewrite it and cross-check for accuracy. If the news needs more background information, then we do desk research to provide background information. (Media Practitioner 2)

Finally, cultural translation involves the reframing of a storyline and re-focusing of news actors. For an event involving Koreans, the story's focus is often different in mainstream media than in Korean media. One example is a story about a truck accident in the city of Maple Ridge, a Vancouver suburb: a truck ran into a Japanese restaurant and killed two female customers, one of them Korean. The headlines of the *The Vancouver Sun,* a local mainstream newspaper, read: "Reduced charges from Maple Ridge sushi restaurant fatal crash anger mother" (Steele, 2009a), "Man found not criminally responsible for fatal sushi restaurant crash" (Steele, 2009b), "Driver in deadly crash into Maple Ridge restaurant wins release" (Steele, 2009c), and "Driver in deadly Maple Ridge restaurant crash to get released today" (Steele, 2010). In contrast, the headlines of *The Vancouver Korean Press,* a local Korean newspaper, read: "Maple Ridge Japanese restaurant, one of the two dead is Korean" (Moon, 2009), "Oh Hyeshim case found 'not guilty'" (Han, 2009a), and "Oh Hyeshim case assailant set free" (Han, 2009b). In other words, the focus of the story for *The Vancouver Sun* was Brian Irving, the truck driver and assail-ant, whereas that of *The Vancouver Korean Press* was Hyeshim Oh, the victim, who was Korean. It is within this whole process of customization of news specifically for local Korean Canadians that cultural translation is critical.

Availability and Accessibility in the Digital Era

Availability and accessibility of Korean media for local Koreans has in-creased in the digital era. The community role of these media is strength-ened through the formation of online communities on websites of Korean newspapers, assisting the process of integration. Table 3.4 shows the results of a content analysis of 80 user-posted threads on the online community bulletin boards of Vancouver's three dailies – "Vanchosun Community" (*The Vancouver Korean Press*), "Gaeshipan" (*The Korea Daily*), and "Community" (*The Korea Times*) – during a constructed week of March 2010. The most frequently posted topics were announcements from Korean community or-ganizations or immigrant service organizations (21%), followed by an-nouncements from leisure/hobby interest groups (20%), business/ads (20%), and Canadian life (19%). The topics under "Canadian life" include questions that arise during day-to-day life in a new country: "How to install Shaw [Canadian telecom company] digital phone" (Vanchosun.com, March 16), "Criteria to consider when selecting realtors" (Vanchosun.com, March 24), and "Looking for a rental in North Vancouver" (Vanchosun.com, March 25). The inquiries related to "Immigration" (4%) include citizenship/visa

TABLE 3.4

Discussion topics of online bulletin boards in Korean media, Vancouver (%)

Discussion Topics	Total
	N = 80
CSO/immigrant services	21
Leisure/hobby	20
Business/ads	20
Canada life	19
Immigration (citizenship, other)	10
Education	5
Health	3
Finance (bank, other)	1
Opinion/discussion	1

procedures or status: "Can we postpone citizenship test?" (Vanchosun. com, March 15) and "Interviews after a citizenship test" (Vanchosun.com, March 15).

Indeed, these are *universal* (related to the broader society) yet *particular* (specific to the Korean community) topics that matter specifically to local Korean immigrants. Inquiries are exchanged not only among readers but also between readers and local experts. The *Vancouver Korean Press*'s "Expert Q&A" makes experts from the local Korean community available in the fields of immigration, education, accounting, mortgage, health, and real estate and has them respond to readers' inquiries. Such "quick fix" mechanisms built into this online community, which address the daily concerns of immigrants in the process of settlement, are in line with and serve the interest of a universal agenda of immigration policies and also supplement the existing national and local settlement services such as SUCCESS (Sino United Chinese Community Enrichment Services Society), Options Community Services Society, MOSAIC, Immigration Services Society (ISS), and North Shore Multicultural Society.

Availability and accessibility for the broader community
Are Korean media available and accessible for the broader community? All this locally produced news about the local Korean community, as well as

imported news from Korea, is a rich resource for improving cultural literacy for a broader audience, if accessible. It is not only a window into local Korean discourse but also into Korea. As mentioned above, imported news from Korea is not any news but news that is relevant to local Koreans in the Canadian context. However, the language in which the content is produced is a barrier. Unlike in L.A., where some Korean media content are accessible through English editions (e.g., "The Korea Times" English website [www.koreatimesus.com]) or English-language publications and programs (e.g., the former *KoreAm Journal*, TVK24 channel 2), only a few English-subtitled entertainment programs on cable television are accessible for a broader audience in Vancouver. Neither locally produced nor internationally imported Korean news is fully available in English. The limited financial capacity to provide timely subtitles or translations of the content upon production or importation, and the limited involvement of the younger generation in Korean media production are the main factors that prevent making these available resources accessible for broader use. But this only addresses challenges from the diasporic media side. The gap between media policies and actual practices discussed in Chapter 2 adds challenges in broadening accessibility. As examples, the provision of subtitles is left to the discretion of diasporic media organizations and the cost to access English-subtitled Korean programs on cable is left to the discretion of a broader audience.

While their content is not accessible in and of itself, Korean media do reach out and participate in *intercultural* community events, often in collaboration with local Korean civil society organizations (CSOs). CSO-media joint efforts to organize and cover events during the time of study included fundraising events for those affected by the Haiti and Fukushima earthquakes and tsunami. In response to the Haiti earthquake, the Korean Society of B.C. raised over $60,000 from the community and, with matching government funding, delivered over $100,000 to Red Cross Canada (S.H. Choi, 2010a; M.S. Kwon, 2010a). Responding to the Fukushima earthquake and tsunami, the Korean Society collaborated with 10 diasporic community leaders (e.g., Chinese, Filipino, African) and organized a walkathon in May 2011 (S.H. Choi, 2011; H.J. Cho, 2011). Eunice Oh, president of the Korean Society at that time, mentioned that the event was not only a fundraising event for Fukushima but also "a venue for diverse minority communities to meet and mingle" (S.H. Choi, 2011).

Still another example is the annual Korean Heritage Day Festival. The 2010 festival was held in Blue Mountain Park in the city of Coquitlam in

August (see Figure 3.2). The year's theme was "Harmony," which highlighted the intercultural tone of the event. The event was open to everyone in the city regardless of ethnicity. The various performances and contests included Muse Ensemble, Vancouver Korean Dance Society, Gayageum (Korean Harp), Korean Idol Contest by Tom Lee Music, Sunhangdo (martial arts), Latin and Caribbean music, and a South Asian dance team (Y. Choi, 2010). Sponsored by TD Bank and with 20 businesses participating, the event was attended by local politicians such as the Honourable James Moore, minister of Canadian Heritage and Official Languages; Senator Yonah Martin; MLAs Harry Bloy and Douglas Horne; and Richard Stewart, mayor of Coquitlam (Y. Choi, 2010). These intercultural initiatives are perceived positively within the community as a means to assist intercultural dialogue. As one CSO leader put it:

> It's important for organizations to be more pan-ethnic ... Some of the Korean organizations prevent Korean immigrants from being integrated into mainstream society ... You get comfortable and that's your social network. You speak Korean and you argue in Korean, and you go to a Korean church. You become distanced and become farther and farther from the broader society and lose the momentum of integration ... So if the Korean organizations do something with the Chinese community or other communities, it will be a bridge for them to get to know other people and sort of broaden their horizons, so to speak. (CSO Leader 2)

KOREAN MEDIA AS A CIVIL SOCIETY

The role of media within civil society is helping the public engage in public discussion and influence government decision-making processes. Diasporic media are especially important in the processes of settlement and integration as they provide information for those who are unfamiliar with not only Canada's official languages but also with the civic/political system. This information helps new members of society learn to engage in civic matters in their neighbourhood, city, and the broader society and to participate in politics, if they wish.

It is also through diasporic media that members of the broader society are able to hear and become familiar with what matters to their Korean neighbours, if an appropriate mechanism is in place to facilitate this listening, as discussed in Chapter 1. This potential for the two-way flow of information

Figure 3.2 **Korean Heritage Day Festival, Vancouver**
Blue Mountain Park, Coquitlam, B.C., August 14, 2010. *Top to bottom:* Korean traditional food; martial arts demonstration by Sunhangdo; Title sponsor TD Bank. *Facing page:* Hyundai Motors display; Liberal Party booth; Liberal MLA Harry Bloy booth.

corresponds to Kymlicka's (2002, p. 289) argument on "conversation": Engaging in public discourse requires both speaking one's own opinions and listening and responding to those of others. Listening involves not only attending to the voices of a broader audience but also ensuring that one's own voice is listened to by that audience. Accessibility to Korean voices for a broader audience thus becomes a critical condition here. It is, however, important to distinguish *engagement* from actual *influence,* since the former should come first in order to achieve the latter. The civil society role of Korean media and the challenges and opportunities for broadening accessibility is the focus of this section.

Bridging the Community with Broader Public Discourse

Korean media practitioners consider engaging in broader public discourse important and are generally satisfied with what they offer to the community with limited resources. The level of engagement varies; although it is sometimes proactive, most of the time it is reactive. The case of *Korean* (a quarterly Korean magazine published during the time of study) exemplifies proactive journalism. In the article "Thanks anyways Vancouver Sun. Cough cough: Reading Vancouver Sun in Korean" (D.I. Lee, 2007, p. 70), with the main title in English and the subtitle in Korean, the publisher of *Korean* shares an anecdote about *The Vancouver Sun*'s multilingual service targeting for ethnocultural minorities. The story narrates how the publisher's excitement about a multilingual service finally being offered by a mainstream daily newspaper turned into dismay when he discovered that the *Sun* depended on a computer-assisted translation service. The publisher tested the service himself and determined the poor quality of translation, which translated the Korean equivalent of "Thanks anyways Vancouver Sun" to "Vancouver's sun appreciates. Whichever you are." Disappointed, the publisher extended his comments to *The Tyee,* Vancouver's leading alternative online news source (Zandberg, 2007), saying that the *Sun* had underestimated the technological limitations in its attempt to service ethnocultural minorities.

Most of the time, however, Korean media are rather reactive, with practitioners monitoring mainstream news sources every day as part of their daily work routine, paying special attention to coverage of immigrants in general and Koreans in particular. When they come across any news items in mainstream media that cover immigrants or Koreans inappropriately, Korean journalists discuss the issue in their own stories and inform the community. Some of the stories mentioned during interviews were related to a lack of cultural understanding on the part of mainstream media: for example, a story about the 2002 World Cup in Korea and how Korean teams were negatively portrayed; a story about Mongolian spots on Korean babies and how they are misunderstood as a case of child abuse; a story about Korean women wearing sun caps when they take a walk outside to protect themselves from UV rays and how the actual effectiveness of this was skeptically discussed; a story about the Vancouver Golf Course's prohibition on languages other than English and how that is related to the LPGA's decision on mandatory English use among the players; and finally, a story about investment fraud against local Korean immigrants and how it was framed as a religious issue (Media Practitioners 9, 10, 12, and 13).

Korean media discuss these controversial issues internally through their own coverage; however, they do not necessarily respond institutionally to mainstream media. Media practitioners simply do not believe that it is their role to take any action on an institutional level; they would expect the same from mainstream media. Instead, media practitioners present the issues for discussion and invite readers and CSO leaders to respond, if they wish to do so (Media Practitioner 5). Thus, in most cases, media practitioners would rather respond individually, as concerned citizens, than institutionally. They were aware of some cases in which readers had responded to mainstream media individually, although there is no recorded information on the outcome of such action.

Some controversies are not discussed at all. Depending on the topic, these kinds of blind spots can lead not only to the absence of a Korean voice in the broader public discourse, if these issues are not raised by CSOs, but also to the loss of a chance to be heard by a broader audience. One example of this is the Bruce Allen controversy. Bruce Allen, a radio personality and a member of the 2010 Vancouver Winter Olympic Ceremonies Committee, mentioned in an interview with B.C. radio station CKNW on September 13, 2007, that "if you're immigrating to this country and you don't like the rules that are in place, then you have the right to choose not to live here ... We don't need you here. You have another place to go. It's called home. See ya" ("MP files complaint," 2007). His faux pas invited a flood of responses from diasporic communities through their community organizations and media, as well as through mainstream media. In *The Vancouver Sun*, members of the South Asian community said that Allen had "dissatisfied" the community (Bikramjit Singh of the Khalsa Diwan Society of New Westminster) and called for his "resignation" from the committee (Harry Bains, NDP MLA), while in an interview with CTV, Raymond Chan, the Liberal MP for Richmond, called Allen's comments "deceptive inaccuracy" and "unacceptable," ("Rant clarified," 2007; "MP files complaint," 2007). There were, however, neither comments by Korean media nor a community-wide response from the Korean community. Interviews with Korean media practitioners revealed that awareness of the incident was, in fact, low.

Promoting Political Engagement

Korean media, however, are relatively more proactive in the promotion of political engagement. One media practitioner mentioned that the company's motto in 2010 was, in fact, to support and "raise" Korean politicians and that this could be pursued as a common agenda among media practitioners, not in the form of "agenda setting" but as a form of community-wide support (Media Practitioner 12). Korean media have experience in promoting political engagement through the election campaigns of Korean Canadian candidates, most notably that of Yonah Martin (Conservative Party) during the 2008 Canadian federal election. As a 1.5-generation Korean Canadian, Martin ran in the Korean-concentrated New Westminster-Coquitlam riding, aiming to be the first Korean Canadian member of Parliament.[10] Winning the election was not only her personal goal but also a long-time ambition for the community, after several failures of Korean Canadian aspiring politicians in Vancouver, Toronto, and Calgary between 1993 and 2007 (Y.W. Lee, 2007). The aspiration of diasporic communities to have someone from the community *out there* in mainstream political circles is manifest in their support for community candidates.

Martin became a community project and received unprecedented support from the Korean Canadian community. Media coverage during this time was particularly noteworthy. Yu and Ahadi's (2010, p. 62) content analysis of coverage of the 2008 Canadian federal election in Korean and English newspapers found that 21% of news items in Korean papers covered visible minorities, compared to 5% in English papers, and attention was often given to Martin on the front page. There was also an increase in local news production in Korean media during the election, in that 60% of election-related news items in Korean newspapers were written by staff writers, compared to 30% in the nonelection period (p. 62). A significant amount of citizenship education was also underway to elicit informed participation of new Korean Canadian voters by providing candidate profiles and information about where and how to vote (p. 62). The main message that came across from

Korean media was that the community can make a difference by exercising their voting rights: for example, headlines included "Let's elect the first Korean MP" and "Let's write a new Korean history" (p. 62).

Some community leaders, however, criticized the media's endorsement of Korean candidates, claiming that the community became "mindlessly partisan" regardless of party affiliation (CSO Leader 2). As evidence, a by-election a year after the 2008 federal election, demonstrated the same pattern when another call was issued for community support for a Korean Canadian candidate, this time running for the Liberal Party.[11] The candidate's dependency on Korean Canadian voters was again high: "the result depends on the 3,000 Korean-Canadian voters in my riding," said the candidate in an interview with *The Vancouver Korean Press* (M.S. Kwon, 2009a). Ethnic block voting is, however, not always easy to obtain. Political unity is hard to achieve because of what Võ (2004, p. 159) calls "love-resentment-envy" relations between and within the community. Media practitioners mentioned that there is a "why not me" attitude among community leaders, in that they think, "If that person can run in the election, I can do it too" (Media Practitioners 4 and 12).

Nonetheless, for the community as a whole, it is undeniable that Korean Canadian candidates contribute to increasing the community's interest in political participation overall. Although Martin failed in the election, her later appointment to the Senate was celebrated in that it was "a historical event for the community," something that is "beyond imagination" and "never happened even in the 100 years of Korean American immigration history in the U.S." (Media Practitioner 12). Her appointment also elicited interest in politics among the younger generation. Internship programs for future Korean Canadian politicians immediately followed (S.H. Choi, 2010c). The younger generation is also beginning to join in community leadership: the newly formed Korean Society of B.C. had two 1.5- and second-generation directors on the board during the time of study. This is a noticeable change, considering the focus of the C3 Korean Canadian Society (or "C3" for short, which formerly represented the Corean Canadian Society"), a prominent organization led by and for 1.5- and second-generation Korean Canadians since 2003. The organization mainly concentrates on solidifying foundations for this demographic by fostering Korean cultural heritage and assisting career development, rather than community-wide leadership. These two broad mandates are reflected in the programs run by the organization such as Camp Korea and the Leadership Conference (see www.c3society.org).

Availability and Accessibility for Broader Community Organizations
The civil society role of diasporic media is also strengthened through collaboration with multiethnic immigration settlement services. Although these services focus on settlement and thus may seem to strengthen a community role rather than a civil society role, Korean community workers at these organizations facilitate *intercultural* access to government programs for local Koreans, on the one hand, and to the Korean community for community interest groups such as nonprofit immigrant service organizations, on the other.

During the time of study, there were more than 70 Korean community workers employed with federal, provincial, or municipal immigrant settlement services in Metro Vancouver (e.g., SUCCESS, Options Community Services Society, MOSAIC, ISS, North Shore Multicultural Society; see the Korean Community Workers Network for the updated list which has contact information for 48 workers as of 2016.) Their main role is to make government services that are already available across cities (e.g., Coquitlam, Surrey, Vancouver) and service areas (e.g., settlement/ESL, employment, legal, business, counselling, mental health, families, schools by school district) known to the Korean community. Until recently, Korean CSOs have tried to provide some of these services through the mobilization of community resources mainly due to low awareness of these available government resources. One community worker mentioned that these services were almost unknown to Korean immigrants until the late 1990s, when Korean community workers joined these CSOs and started to collaborate with local Korean media to make the services known to the community (Community Worker 1). Within months of the introduction of this information, the number of calls to the worker's organization received from the Korean community increased from 10 to 400 per month:

> When I came and started as a Korean worker here ... nobody knew (name of the agency) ... The reason that (name of the agency) got suddenly well-known and all that was because I used media ... What I did was whenever I [did] workshops, group sessions, like tenants' rights or citizenship or whatever, I asked my volunteers to summarize all the workshop content, the notes ... That time (name of the newspaper) contacted me about the workshops so I gave them the notes, the summary of the workshops ... it was more than 10 workshops ... and then about four other newspapers contacted me ...

That was [in the] late 1990s ... [and soon] all the newspapers had my name. (Community Worker 3)

As part of their service to the community, most of the community workers interviewed have either contributed columns or been interviewed by local Korean media at least once, if not regularly, on various topics mentioned above (Community Workers 1 and 3). New service programs are made available and regularly updated online and offline through the community bulletin boards of newspapers (e.g., *The Vancouver Korean Press*'s "Vancouver Sarangbang," *The Korea Daily*'s "Gaeshipan," *The Korea Times*'s "Donghohae Dongjung" and "Town Dongjung") or the community calendars of their websites. *The Korea Daily*'s special column titled "Community Worker Relay Column" is another example. Beginning in June 2008, when the Korean Community Worker Network was still just an idea, Korean community workers collaborated with *The Korea Daily* to contribute articles on various immigrant issues and potential solutions such as employment, small business, and senior programs. Each article discussed the chosen issue using actual case studies and introduced corresponding available resources (e.g., government programs) and the author's contact information for further inquiries.

To serve the community better through networking, Korean community workers formed the Korean Community Workers Network (KCWN) in 2009. Funded through the United Way's Community Capacity Building Funds, the KCWN began as a network of Korean community workers based in the Coquitlam, Port Coquitlam, and Port Moody area and gradually expanded to include other cities (Community Worker 2). Through this network, Korean workers are able to optimize the benefits of services available across agencies through cross-agency referrals, if necessary. The members find the network useful, since there are many programs offered by different agencies, and "sometime we don't even know what other agencies offer" (Community Worker 3). The network also runs a "cultural competence workshop" for staff at public institutions (e.g., libraries, ESL schools, victim services) to educate these workers on Korean culture (Community Worker 3). Figure 3.3 shows the photos from a resource fair organized by KCWN for the Korean community in October 2010. Korean workers representing each agency – SUCCESS, Options Community Services Society, MOSAIC, and ISS – set up their agency booths and introduced service programs to local Koreans.

FIGURE 3.3 **Resource fair, Vancouver**
Cameron Recreation Complex, Burnaby, B.C., October 2, 2010

Collaboration between the KCWN and Korean CSOs was also underway. One of the benefits of this collaboration is a referral system. There is often an overlap of services organized by Korean CSOs, which can easily be coordinated by the agencies. As part of a joint initiative, the Korean Society of B.C. and ISS coorganized a seminar on the Canadian citizenship exam (S.H. Choi, 2010b).

Beyond providing these services to the Korean community, KCWN representatives provide access to the Korean community for broader community organizations so that they are able to attend to the issues that matter to the Korean community. In doing so, the representatives urge stronger connection and collaboration between Korean media and CSOs. Specifically, the workers suggest that the Korean media's coverage of Korean issues and the resulting community reaction can influence government decision-making that affects the lives of Koreans (Community Worker 2).

A case in point concerns a series of incidents of family violence in the Korean community in the past few years in Vancouver (e.g., 2004 Surrey family murder-suicide, 2007 Victoria family murder-suicide, 2008 realtor suicide, 2009 Coquitlam priest suicide). While all of these incidents were deeply related to financial problems, cases such as these are often reported merely as family violence (Community Worker 2). A more proactive and timely action by the Korean CSOs, such as setting up a crisis hotline as a preventive measure, could have provided the broader society with some context for these cases and may have elicited broader societal support for follow-up measures. In fact, one community worker mentioned that immigrant service organizations were monitoring Korean media at the time of events in order to check community reaction and take further action if needed. However, since there was no more coverage, the organizations did not put the case forward to the government to request assistance for further investigation. Therefore, some of these tragedies may have been averted if stronger ties among "collective actors" – as mentioned earlier – within the community had been in place and a timely collaboration between Korean media and CSOs had occurred. Indeed, commenting on the 2007 Victoria family murder-suicide, one community worker (Community Worker 2) suggested that if an event such as this had happened in the Chinese community, the Chinese media would have provided broad coverage of the story. Since the Chinese media in Vancouver has a loud voice, the mainstream media and the government would pay attention.

Availability and Accessibility for Broader Political Interest Groups

In general, interaction with government institutions is most visible during election times and is usually absent between elections. Yu and Ahadi's (2010) work revealed that during the 2008 election campaign, both Elections Canada and political parties approached Korean Canadian voters through the placement of ads in Korean media. The Jason Kenney controversy is another event related to political circles' sporadic interest in ethnic voters and diasporic media as offering venues by which to reach them. In 2011, Jason Kenney, former minister of Citizenship, Immigration, and Multiculturalism, was "called on to resign" by the NDP for having been involved, as a member of Parliament, in partisan fundraising to support the development of media strategies that target specifically Chinese and South Asian voters. Although the focus of the incident was Kenney's misconduct as a MP, rather than the partisan fundraising for a diasporic media campaign itself, the letter sent out by Kenney's office to Conservative MPs clearly demonstrated an act of conscious political attention focusing on diasporic communities as important voter bases to be won, as well as how diasporic media serve as a venue by which to communicate with their members. The letter stated: "There are lots of ethnic voters ... There will be quite a few more soon. They live where we need to win" (CBC News, 2011).

Given such sporadic attention, Korean media practitioners shared their frustration with the lack of recognition of diasporic media by the government, as echoed by one media practitioner (Media Practitioner 5):

> Does the government know about us? Does the government know what roles we can play? Does the government know what contributions we can make? How does the government understand us? How the government sees us makes a difference in their support ... If they know minority media can be a watchdog, monitoring government practices, it will be a different story. (Media Practitioner 5)

In other words, immigrant groups are information-rich. Immigration agencies, CSOs, and, most importantly, community media relay necessary information about *here* to assist immigrants' settlement and integration. It is the broader society, especially government, which is not adequately updated on such progress and constantly assumes that immigrant communities are isolated and uninformed about broader society and thus unable to be first-class citizens. This relates to the "politics of listening" and the struggle for recognition that Dreher (2009) discussed (see Chapter 1).

Nonetheless, more efforts to develop *intercultural* interaction that value *inbetweenness* of Korean media are emerging from both the Korean community and the government. The aforementioned Korean Heritage Day Festival, to which local politicians were invited, is one way to see the community's connection to local politics. It is perhaps an act of mutual interest that local politicians and the community try to keep each other in the information loop. The federal government has also started to pay attention to local Korean media, which is, in part, related to Yonah Martin's run for federal office in 2008 and the appointment as Senator in the following year. Former Prime

Minister Stephen Harper's selection of a media group to visit Korea is a good example. Harper made his first official visit as prime minister to South Korea and China in December 2009 and invited two of the three local Korean dailies from Vancouver – *The Vancouver Korean Press* and *The Korea Daily* – to join his media group. On receiving this invitation, the invited media outlets published self-congratulatory remarks that it was "the first time in Korean media history that the company was officially invited by the government" (*"The Korea Daily*, first," 2009) and that they were "invited by the Prime Minister's office to join a *Canadian* media group [emphasis added]" "First [Korean] media," 2009). Another example is a municipal-level initiative in Vancouver. To share the city's plan for current city issues (e.g., crime, homelessness, H1N1) and hear diasporic media's opinions, Vancouver's mayor, Gregor Robertson, held a media roundtable in 2010 with Filipino, Vietnamese, Indian, and Korean media practitioners (Han, 2010b).

KOREAN MEDIA AS A MARKET

Korean media are invaluable to local enclave businesses. The mutual dependency between media and these businesses suggests that diasporic media are both promoters and players within the local enclave economy: they are a window into immigrant small businesses and are also small businesses themselves. Ads placed with Korean media are a good reflection of the scope and scale of the local enclave economy and also of the revenue sources for Korean media. While Korean media have operated primarily within the local enclave economy, over-competition in a saturated market has required the development of new business models, including intercultural outreach to connect with the mainstream market. This can be of mutual interest, helping both mainstream and Korean media to survive in the dwindling media industry. This section explores the business venture side of the Korean media and discusses opportunities and challenges for broadening accessibility for cross-ethnic collaboration and competition.

Korean Media's Dual Play: Korean Media as Promoters of Small Businesses

Korean media are venues for local small businesses to promote themselves. The Korean business directories published by media and organizations list more than 2,000 Korean businesses, ranging from commercial services (e.g., auto/auto repair, bank/finance, beauty, restaurants, travel/accommodation, educational institutions) to professional services (e.g., accounting, law, health [medical clinics, pharmacies, etc.], immigration consulting).[12] Table 3.5 shows the types of advertisers in Korean media and reflects the scale of the local enclave economy. The advertisers are almost entirely Korean businesses (e.g., restaurants, beauty, auto/auto repair) or professional service providers/agents (e.g., Sutton Group real estate). It is only occasionally that major Korean transnational corporations (e.g., Korean Air, Hyundai, Kia, LG) or mainstream institutions (e.g., Toronto Dominion Bank) advertise in local Korean media. (See below for further details.)

Estimates of the size of the Korean advertising market vary by media owner and are in the range of $300,000 to $800,000 per month for the market total. The market is relatively small compared to the advertising market for Chinese print media in Canada, which is estimated to be $50 million, according to Szonyi (cited in Zhou et al. 2006, p. 51). One interviewee described the Korean market as one of "10 active media outlets (out of

TABLE 3.5

Advertisers by media type, Vancouver (%)

	Total	TV	Newspaper
	N = 474	N = 106	N = 368
Real estate agency/realtor	10	–	13[b]
Restaurant	9	18[a]	7[b]
Bank/finance	9	3[a]	11[b]
Hospital/clinic/pharmacy	9	12[a]	8[a]
Beauty	9	7[a]	9[a]
Auto/auto repair	8	8[a]	8[a]
Law	8	0.9[a]	10[b]
Immigration/consulting agency	7	6[a]	8[a]
Education	6	11[a]	4[b]
Media	4	2[a]	4[a]
Food	3	9[a]	2[b]
Travel agency/ transportation/ accommodation	3	0.9[a]	4[a]
Health product/pharmaceutical	3	2[a]	3[a]
Accounting	3	–	3[a]
Other	10	20	6

NOTES: Numbers in the table are rounded off. Each subscript letter denotes a subset of column categories whose column proportions do or do not differ significantly from each other at the .05 level.

approximately 20 outlets) ... and 500 active advertisers (out of 2000 businesses)" (Media Practitioner 3). These 500 small businesses use 10 active media outlets to make themselves known to the local Korean community. Conversely, these 10 media outlets depend on 500 local businesses to sustain their own businesses.

Korean Media's Dual Play: Korean Media as Small Businesses Themselves

As players (or small businesses themselves in the enclave economy), Korean media's dependency on these advertisers is high; however, the local enclave economy, and thus the advertising market itself, is small, with low and continually dropping advertising rates. Such a market situation is attributed to various factors. At a macro level, the enclave economy is dependent on the transnational economy. The ebbs and flows of temporary migrants (e.g., temporary students, "geese families") influenced by fluctuating currency rates unsettle the enclave economy, including media. The media boom in the first half of 2007, with six new entries, and the disappearance of an almost equal number of outlets during the 2008 economic recession show the level of instability in the market.

At a micro level, internal competition among mom-and-pop–type small media outlets is fierce. Media practitioners point out that there are simply too many media outlets within a small market, including those that appear and then disappear from the market soon after. These short-lived entries make the already unstable market even more unstable by splitting the market share or even shrinking the market size altogether, to a certain extent, since they often offer promotional rates to win advertisers instantly (e.g., dumping rate, free ads; Media Practitioners 6 and 13). The consequence is a further lowering of the already low overall rate. Obviously, once lowered, the rate is unlikely to bounce back, since advertisers become used to the new lower rate (Media Practitioner 6). The continuing economic recession and a resulting significant cut in the volume of ads by up to 30% or 40% makes this a double whammy and leads to a mounting outstanding balance as advertisers are unable to pay their bills. As one media practitioner commented:

> Those who do not have industry experience (either as reporters or administrators) launch newspapers and disappear soon after the launch ... They believe it is a good business and also guarantees a certain level of social prestige. Yet without enough financial

backing to sustain at least the first few years, it is difficult to survive. High operating costs with a small pool of advertisers is the main reason. (Media practitioner 13)

Another said:

> Those who are interested in starting a media business often come to me for consultation. I suggest not to, as financing it is like "filling a bottomless vessel." But they think I only say this just to stop them ... An increase in the number of media means more competition for ads. Consequently, it brings down the ad rates as well as the revenue and further leads to employee layoffs. Having less employees then brings down the quality of content or the number of copies printed ... Publishers must have enough operating capital in order to not be swayed by advertisers. But in reality, we are all small businesses. (Media Practitioner 6)

Some media practitioners also attribute this type of market instability to a lack of major stakeholders in the market. After all, both media outlets and advertisers are just small enclave businesses operating on small immigrant capital:

> We are all financially struggling in the economic recession. It is hurting Korean community businesses. It takes six months to one year to collect payments from advertisers, especially seasonal businesses such as travel agencies. In summer when business is good they pay some, but not at all in winter. Realtors pay only when they make sales; one realtor has not paid $15,000. Until those payments are in, I have to put my own money in to sustain the business. (Media Practitioner 6)

> Advertisers, just like Korean immigrants in general, are unstable in their own businesses so they advertise out of fear. They advertise because others do. And they also advertise with multiple media outlets, when one is enough, thus intensifying competition and pulling down the ad rates. During the economic recession, the ad rates went down by 20% to 30%. (Media Practitioner 4)

Limited revenue sources other than advertising are another contributing factor to economic instability. Revenue sources may be limited, but operating costs are high. While there is a move towards online publication, it is still predominantly offline media that require certain fixed operating costs: personnel, printing, and broadcasting/licensing fees, among others. For the print sector, the largest cost is printing, which accounts for 50% of overhead expenses, while personnel expenses remain at 20% to 30%. The circulation size varies by frequency of publication (dailies vs. weeklies). The print media outlets who provided circulation figures are in the range of 3,000 and 16,000 copies and approximately 20 to 80 pages per week (Media Practitioners 1, 4, 5, and 6). For the broadcasting sector, it is personnel expenses that account for over 50% of the total budget, on par with broadcasting fees paid to program providers (Media Practitioners 7 and 8). High broadcasting fees are a burden for many local producers; however, producers say that it is still cheaper than doing their own production. This is where the Canadian content rules become a burden rather than an incentive. A relative advantage compared to their L.A. counterparts is that Vancouver's independent producers are at least free from an airtime fee. As discussed in Chapter 2, Shaw Multicultural Channel provides free airtime to selected third-language producers.

The cost of all this must be covered through advertising. Other than All TV, which also generates revenue from subscriptions, all media services depend largely on advertising.[13] As mentioned earlier, all of Vancouver's Korean newspapers are free, a unique characteristic of Vancouver's Korean media that sets them apart from L.A.'s Korean media. Indeed, among Korean media practitioners, Vancouver is known to be the only market where free newspapers are expected, even though the socioeconomic standard of readers is higher than any Korean community in North America (Media Practitioners 9, 10, and 12). The consequence of such a tradition is greater dependency on advertising.

Availability and Accessibility for Broader Industry Stakeholders

In this climate of over-competition in an already saturated market, intercultural capacity-building beyond the Korean community, one of many survival strategies tried over the years, is a breakthrough for many media outlets. On a positive note, this inevitable market factor pushes previously in-group oriented (or self-sufficient) Korean media outlets to develop *intercultural* media strategies that go beyond the Korean community. Although many of the strategies are still in the discussion stage and are more ad hoc than constant, intercultural attempts are becoming more visible. The volume of ads from non-Korean businesses is still minimal, but securing more is definitely a priority business strategy for many Korean media outlets. This effort is consistent with the community's outreach to the local economy such as the Korean Heritage Day Festival – the 2011 event sponsored by Toronto Dominion Bank.

Generally, intercultural partnerships serve various purposes and can be discussed in two different dimensions: institution (mainstream vs. diasporic) and purpose (content vs. ads). These two dimensions intersect at different junctures for different purposes. In the institutional dimension, Korean media reach out to mainstream businesses for content and to other diasporic businesses for advertising. For content, Korean media have a number of different sources from which to draw for local "hard news," sources such as government offices (Canadian and Korean), corporate communications/PR offices, local branches of Korean corporations, the Canadian Press, and personal networks. Local sources for soft news, however, are still limited, and media practitioners thus need to reach out further to secure a constant flow of content. In fact, there have been a few cases of licensing agreements between Korean and mainstream print media (Media Practitioners 3 and 13).

Case 1: The Canada Express

One of the pioneers of licensing agreements with mainstream media is *Canada Express*. As a weekly specialty paper founded in 2007, it is known to the Korean community as a "translated paper," since it made it possible for local Koreans to read mainstream papers (mostly *The Vancouver Sun* and *The Province*) in Korean. This was possible through the landmark licensing agreement between Canwest and *Canada Express*. After years of persistent negotiation, the company won exclusive licensing and gained access to Canwest's 11 newspapers across Canada (Murray et al., 2007, p. 20).[14] Conversely, the exclusive rights to *Canada Express* meant an automatic restriction on the use of any Canwest news items for all other Korean media outlets. Indeed, immediately on finalizing the agreement, Canwest took action to protect its licensee by sending out a formal letter to all Korean newspapers, informing them about the agreement and advising them not to use any Canwest news items from then on. All of the print media practitioners interviewed acknowledged that they had received the letter. Reaction to the exclusive licensing varied (Media Practitioners 5 and 6). According to the interviews with Korean media practitioners, some were fully aware of copyright restrictions and have been practicing fair use of external sources. Others have become more conscious of and cautious about using Canwest items since the exclusive licensing. Regardless of the responses, it is undeniable that the event was a wake-up call for many Korean media:

> The exclusive licensing does not affect our operation. We get enough from CP [Canadian Press] and we have in-house content. We received the letter and responded that we won't use their content. (Media Practitioner 5)

> (Name of company) has received the letter. We have limited our use ever since. As long as the news sources are properly cited, such as "according to *The Vancouver Sun*," there is nothing illegal about using their news items. But photos can be a problem. We do not use their photos ... No Korean media can remain sustainable by paying the licensing fees. (Media Practitioner 6)

Although not directly related to Korean media, similar intercultural strategies surface from mainstream media with an intention to "tap into Canada's thriving ethnic media readership" (Zandberg, 2007). The aforementioned case of *The Vancouver Sun* and its attempt to offer online multilingual services in 2007 is a good example. Another case that followed on this was CBC BC's development, in 2008, of a Chinese-language news service. According to the organization's news director, Liz Hughes, the goal was "to have as many people as possible see it" (Hermida, 2008). Unlike *The Vancouver Sun*'s "machine translations," CBC provided "human translations." Journalists at Radio Canada International translated the stories chosen by staff at the Vancouver newsroom (Hermida, 2008). Although both programs have been discontinued, these cases suggest a growing interest in third-language communities among mainstream media and signal potential crossover to the diasporic market in the future.

Yet in the prolonged recession, the diasporic market is also seen more as a market to downsize than to tap into. Mainstream media have started to withdraw their intercultural strategies. One example that impacted Korean media is the case of TV Korea's *Korean News* at Rogers's OMNI. It was part of a multilingual daily news broadcast, along with Cantonese, Mandarin, and Punjabi. The program was first moved to unfavourable time spots and then finally removed altogether in 2011. The first shift was in August 2009. The airtime for the half-hour *Korean News* changed from a 7:30 a.m. start to 9:00 a.m. (with reruns at 3:30 p.m.), with no change to the number of days (Tuesday through Saturday). What took over that time slot was a rerun of Cantonese News (which aired weeknights at 5:00 p.m. and 11:00 p.m.). A significant change followed a year later, in September 2010, when *Korean News* was downsized from five days to three days (Saturday at 9:00 a.m. with reruns on Sunday at 7:00 a.m. and Monday at 9:00 a.m.). This change made *Korean News* virtually a weekly news service and decreased the total airtime by 70%, from 5 hours to 1.5 hours. The change occurred during a period of transition for OMNI BC during which OMNI joined Citytv, a part of Rogers Broadcasting Limited, in August 2010. This case is not unrelated to the overall decline of the diasporic media sector. The revenue for ethnic and third-language specialty services fell from $73 million in 2008 to $70 million in 2009. It was only in 2010 that the revenue picked up again, to $78 million (CRTC, 2011). Later, in 2015, Rogers discontinued OMNI's multilingual daily news entirely, one of the measures taken to resolve its financial problems (Houpt, 2015).

Availability and Accessibility for Diasporic Industry Stakeholders

In market terms, Korean diasporic media have relatively more *intercultural* interaction with other diasporic media than with mainstream media. Tapping into enclave businesses of other diasporic communities seems to be an easy first step for intercultural marketing. One media practitioner's company hired a marketing manager of Chinese ethnicity exclusively for Chinese marketing, in order to better appeal to Chinese clientele (Media Practitioner 5). This was an effort to eliminate a barrier of double translation (to English and then to Chinese) and approach clientele with their own cultural idioms. Many of the media practitioners interviewed still say, however, that intercultural marketing has a long way to go. Korean advertisers

TABLE 3.6

Origin of advertisers by media type, Vancouver (%)

	Total	TV	Newspaper
	$N = 474$	$N = 106$	$N = 368$
Korean diaspora	84	52[a]	94[b]
Korean transnational corporations	1	–	2[a]
Other diasporic communities	1	–	2[a]
Mainstream	13	48[a]	3[b]

NOTES: Numbers in the table are rounded off. Each subscript letter denotes a subset of column categories whose column proportions do or do not differ significantly from each other at the .05 level.

are trying to tap into the Chinese market, but the same flow into the Korean market has not been seen (Media Practitioner 2). Chinese advertisers tend to prefer short-term, more or less ad hoc trials and then withdraw their advertising if there is no immediate return. After all, they are also small enclave businesses.

The volume of ads from mainstream and other diasporic communities thus generally remains marginal in the overall output for the majority of Korean media outlets. Other than election periods, when political institutions approach diasporic media in order to engage ethnic voters (Yu and Ahadi, 2010), Korean media generally have weak ties with non-Korean advertisers. Table 3.6 shows the origin of advertisers by media type. Over 80% of ads are from Korean enclave businesses, and this rate is higher (94%) if it is restricted to newspapers only. The remaining 6% of the newspaper ads are placed by transnational corporations from Korea or by mainstream or other diasporic businesses. The portion of mainstream ads for television (48%) is inflated. Almost 50% of the ads on OMNI's TV Korea are from so-called mainstream advertisers (e.g., Bank of Montreal, London Drugs, Safeway, P&G, L'Oréal). However, these advertisers sponsored OMNI and not TV Korea.

Aside from ad hoc trials, some long-term initiatives to market Korean media's brands have been also implemented. *The Korea Daily*'s newspaper dispenser at SkyTrain stations is a good example. The company set up its own dispensers under a contract with TransLink (Metro Vancouver's transportation authority). This was one of the company's intercultural initiatives to promote the company's brand within the broader society. *The Korea Daily* was the only Korean newspaper available at SkyTrain stations during the time of study. Another intercultural outreach, also by *The Korea Daily*, was sponsorship of the annual Richmond Summer Night Market (now called International Summer Night Market or Panda Market). Operated and organized by Lions Communications Inc. since 2008, the market ran on weekends (Fridays, Saturdays, Sundays, and holidays) from May to October (now September) in Richmond, one of the most vibrant Chinese enclave cities (www.pandamarket.com), during the time of study. The market started small in the late 1990s, with only 70 booths at the Continental Centre in the city of Richmond (M.W. Lee, 2006). Now it is the venue for approximately 250 booths and attracts an average of more than 30,000 local Vancouverites of all ethnicities (50% Chinese and 50% non-Chinese) on one weekend night (M.W. Lee, 2006; J.O. Kim, 2009). *The Korea Daily* joined the Summer Night Market as a media sponsor in 2009 and as a coorganizer in 2010 and added the "Korean Festival" to the program, which included Korean performances and a cooking demonstration (K.H. Lee, 2010a, 2010b).

Conclusion

There is no doubt that Korean media in Vancouver serve as a community, civil society, and market for the Korean community. The dialectic nature of diasporic media – *here* and *there*, *universal* and *particular*, and *in-between* and *intercultural* – is manifest in every role these media play. As a community, Korean media deliver news about *here* (from local Korean community news to national news) and *there* (news about Korea) that is relevant to local Koreans in their everyday living in Vancouver. Adding to their relevancy is Korean media's cultural translation and eye-level interpretation of *here* in the idioms that Koreans are familiar with, which helps new immigrants better understand *here* and enhances cultural literacy. Thus, it is through this niche information, unavailable in mainstream media, of both *here* and *there* that the contribution of Korean media emerges. Digital transitions further enhance availability and accessibility for the Korean community: online communities that have formed on local Korean print media websites facilitate dialogue among local Koreans and provide "quick fix" solutions in the process of settlement and integration.

Korean media also function as a civil society. Indeed, this is "the reason diasporic media were born" and it is a role "imposed on immigrant media" (Media Practitioner 10). Mobilization of the community in support of Korean Canadian candidates during elections, as well as the provision of customized information for new citizens on how to participate in elections *here*, encourages informed political participation. From outside, these media may be seen to be promoting an ethnic political bloc (*particular*), yet the intention is rather geared towards pushing for recognition within the broader society (*universal*). Finally, Korean media are a window into the Korean enclave economy and are simultaneously enclave businesses themselves. Since these media are business entities susceptible to the ups and downs of the transnational and local economies, survival strategies are critical. Among the innovative business strategies they have tried is intercultural outreach, which is timely and necessary in a saturated local enclave advertising market.

Nonetheless, in terms of an intercultural media system, Korean media are largely *media for local Koreans* rather than *media for all*, as their content is provided mainly in the Korean language. Korean media are committed to "geo-Korean storytelling" and only in a limited way to "neighbourhood storytelling" across communities or multicultural storytelling within the broader media system, as Ball-Rokeach's communication infrastructure theory envisioned. Korean media are certainly a window into the broader society for the Korean community, but they are a window into the Korean community only for certain interest groups rather than for the general public. Thus, these media may contribute to enhancing the cultural literacy of local Koreans but not, as of yet, that of a broader audience to the same extent.

The Korean community in Vancouver is a young diaspora with a lack of sociocultural and economic capital in the diasporic community, and so the struggle for increasing the availability and accessibility of Korean discourse for the broader society occurs at the intersection of prioritizing service to local Korean immigrants over intercultural outreach, on one hand, and the political economy of the media industry, on the other. A hopeful sign is that *in-between* and *intercultural* outreach efforts are emerging. As a community, Korean media collaborate with local Korean CSOs in organizing community events such as the Annual Korean Heritage Day Festival, where they network with local residents, politicians, and businesses. Participation of these interest groups through various sponsorships also indicates the recognition of mutual benefits. Furthermore, governments and political groups also approach Korean media, although this is visible mostly during election periods. In the market, more attempts at intercultural outreach to mainstream institutions as well as to other diasporic communities surface as part of survival strategies.

The next chapter looks at the case of Korean media in L.A. Examining how the locality and ethnicity play out in a different geographic context will help tease out city-specific and ethnicity-specific factors relative to Vancouver and will lead to deeper discussion in Chapter 5.

4
Korean Diasporic Media
.... in Los Angeles

Overall, L.A.'s Korean media resembles those of Vancouver in their three-dimensional role as a community, a civil society, and a market. What differentiates Korean media in L.A., however, is the presence of transnational media branches that are in direct competition with locally developed immigrant media in the enclave market. A constant flow of content and financial aid from their Korean headquarters grant greater competitiveness to transnational branches over immigrant media, which tend to source content through their own local production or partnership with media outlets in Korea that are not related to the headquarters of these transnational branches. This complexity, which is manifest in the everyday production and distribution of Korean discourse, influences the community, civil society, and market roles of these media outlets. This chapter looks at how this dynamic plays out in terms of availability and accessibility of Korean media on these three dimensions within and across communities.

Availability and Accessibility of Korean Media: An Overview

NUMBER OF MEDIA OUTLETS

Along with civil society organizations (CSOs), alumni networks, and churches, media constitute an important component of Korean diasporic communication infrastructure. L.A.'s Korean media are by far the most vibrant among all Korean diasporic media operating in North America.[1] All of the North American regional head offices of transnational Korean media conglomerates are located in L.A.: KBS America (Korea Broadcasting System), MBC America (Munhwa Broadcasting Corporation), SBS International (Seoul Broadcasting System), *The Korea Times* (*Hankook Ilbo*), and *The Korea Daily* (or *JoongAng Ilbo*).[2] As well, multicultural media, such as LA18, compete with transnational media branches in the same market, as do locally developed immigrant media such as TVK24, Radio Korea,

Koreatown Daily, Korea Herald Business (or *Herald Kyungjae*), *Sunday Journal, The Koreana News U.S.A.* (or *Koreana News*), and *The Town News*.[3]

Lists of Korean media are available through various online/offline Korean business directories.[4] The total number of media outlets, approximately 50 to 100, varies according to source. This variation is attributed to the different geographic focus of the directories: some have a focus as broad as all of California (Southern and Northern California combined), while others focus on individual major ethnoburbs or on L.A. and Orange Counties. In addition, all of these lists include religious media outlets, which account for 20% to 30% of the total. Thus, if a more conservative figure is drawn from these rather comprehensive lists by focusing on outlets that are nonreligious and easily available and accessible in L.A., there were approximately 30 active outlets during the time of study. These include four dailies, four weeklies, 10 television services, and three radio services. The actual number, however, may not be meaningful, as was pointed out by the media practitioners and CSO leaders interviewed, since the market takes the form of a two-horse race, led by the major transnational branches and followed by a distant few local immigrant media. The discussion in this section is based on those active media outlets.

HISTORICAL TRAJECTORY

The history of Korean media in L.A. is a short one compared to that of the Latino and other Asian communities.[5] The two major dailies, *The Korea Times* and *The Korea Daily* (the branches of transnational Korean newspaper conglomerates), were established in 1969 and 1974, respectively. L.A.'s Korean media sector saw more entries in the following two decades. The launch of weeklies, TV, and radio in the 1980s included *Sunday Journal* (1982), *Korean Sunday News* (or *Joogan Yunyue*) (1984), Korean Television Enterprise (now KBS America, 1983), and Radio Korea (1989). KBS America heralded the entry into the broadcasting sector among the three branches (along with MBC America and SBS International) in the early 1990s. With these new entries, the community had all genres of media by the late 1980s: TV, radio, dailies, and weeklies.

The real growth of Korean media in L.A. came in the 1990s and 2000s with the simultaneous entry of new outlets and expansion of existing outlets. Some of the outlets launched in the 1990s were *KoreAm Journal* (1990), MBC America (1991), SBS International (1992), Radio Seoul (1992), KTAN-TV (1993), *The Town News* (1994), *Kyocharo* (or *Kyocharo Daily* or

Korean Consumer Daily, 1998), *The Koreana News U.S.A.* (1998), and *Daily Sports Seoul U.S.A* (or *Sports Seoul U.S.A.,* 1999). The start-up of Radio Korea was timely. Launched just before the 1992 L.A. riots, Radio Korea played a critical role during this time of crisis (more details in the following sections). A horizontal expansion of *The Korea Times* (as a media corporation) is also of note during this period. With the launch of Radio Seoul and KTN-TV, *The Korea Times* formed a multimedia platform well ahead of its competitors. (Note that KTN-TV ceased service in January 2013; see *The Korea Times L.A.* [2013].) In addition, media ownership by a 1.5-generation Korean American was also notable during this period, with the launch of *KoreAm Journal,* a monthly magazine published in English by James Ryu. (Note that the journal also published its last edition in 2015 and is now an online hub, "Kore Asian Media" [http://kore.am]).

The 2000s saw further growth, with the addition of TVK24 (2005), TV Korea (2005), *Korea Herald Business* (2005), JBC AM1230 (2007), *Koreatown Daily* (2007), LA18 Prime Time Local News (2009), SKDTV (2009), *The Daily Ilgan Plus* (or *IS Ilgan Plus,* 2010), and MVIBO.com (2011). Among these entries, the "first 24-hour Korean network available nationwide as a digital basic service," is especially notable (TVK24, n.d.). It is also the first free Korean-language channel available on major cable networks such as Comcast, Time Warner, and Cox (TVK24, n.d.). In contrast to the three major transnational television branches (KBS America, MBC America, and SBS International), the company was built on local capital and managed by a 1.5-generation Korean American CEO, Eric Yoon. Another television entry was LA18's Prime Time Local News. LA18, , which was then the largest Asian television network in the United States since 1988, formed an in-house Korean news team to start a Korean-language news program in 2009. The station used to relay only imported Korean programs but added Korean news to the existing line of Chinese and Vietnamese news programs (la18. tv). (Again, as noted in Chapter 2, LA18 cancelled its international programming format in July 2017, replacing it with English infomercials.) In addition, after the transition to digital in 2009, Seoul Korea Digital TV (SKDTV), an immigrant-owned television service in partnership with the Maeil Broadcasting Network (MBN) in Korea, was initially launched on Channel 44.3 (where KTN-TV is) and then moved to LA18's digital channel, LA18.9. (Note that SKDTV also no longer exists.)

With regard to the expansion of existing outlets Radio Korea launched TV Korea (now RKTV) to offer a Korean version of *National Geographic* through

DirecTV. *The Korea Daily* (as a media corporation) also entered the radio market with JBC AM1230 which made *The Korea Daily* a multimedia group and set up competition with the existing Radio Korea and *The Korea Times*'s Radio Seoul. After four years, however, JBC discontinued the service in March 2011 to start the television business ("JBC radio," 2011). *The Korea Daily* also launched *The Daily Ilgan Plus*, a free daily, in 2010. Lastly, local immigrant media *Daily Sports Seoul U.S.A.*, launched *Koreatown Daily*, a newspaper that focuses on Koreatown news, in 2007.

This historical trajectory demonstrates a development pattern consisting of two phases: the formative phase in the 1970s and 1980s (the launch of various types of media) and the growth and expansion phase in the 1990s and the 2000s (the launch of more of each media type). Each period had a balanced entry of all media types, allowing room for new entries to settle and compete with the existing ones. Unlike Vancouver's Korean media, where print is dominant, the relatively relaxed regulations in the broadcasting sector in L.A. may have contributed to the growth of Korean television services. As discussed in Chapter 2, the cable and satellite sectors in the United States are not considered broadcasting and are thus unregulated. Indeed, these are the sectors in which Korean services in L.A. are abundant.

Ownership and Structure

As noted earlier, L.A. Korean media operate based on three types of ownership: branches of Korean transnational media conglomerates, locally developed immigrant media, and multicultural media (as part of the multicultural programs). Korean ownership in over-the-air broadcasting is absent: all Korean broadcasters are program providers through brokerage offering services by purchasing airtime from licence holders. The transnational television services may be capable of ownership financially but are not eligible for ownership because of equally strict regulation to that of Canada. One known attempt to purchase a television station failed because of the Federal Communications Commission's foreign ownership regulation (Media Practitioner 23). Other television services either operate in the cable sector (TVK24) or are not owned by Koreans (LA18's Korean-language news).

The presence of all three types of media organizations across various sources of capital produces organizations in a variety of sizes and organizational structures. Using the same scale of comparison as in the analysis of

Vancouver above – large (more than 100 employees), medium (50–100), small (10–49), and micro (fewer than 10) – L.A.'s Korean media outlets are primarily available in a few dominant, large outlets, followed by small and micro outlets. Overall, large outlets are in the range of more than 100 employees and include the two transnational dailies (*The Korea Times* and *The Korea Daily*) and an immigrant radio station (Radio Korea). The small and micro outlets include other dailies and weeklies. Media practitioners frequently mention that the size of media outlet determines the market share.

Operational structures vary by media type, that generally include editors; producers; journalists and reporters (part-time and full-time); anchors; technicians; graphic designers; webmasters; subscription, marketing, and sales professionals; administration; and delivery personnel. In addition to local reporters, some outlets also have regional correspondents in other parts of the United States or from Korean headquarters. Large and small media outlets tend to have separate departments and teams by news genre or type of work: editorial desk, national desk, local desk, business desk, political desk, newsroom, production department, transmission department, and marketing/business/sales department. Each department manages smaller work teams. In contrast, micro outlets tend to have individuals representing each of these teams or departments. Proportionally, weeklies tend to have a higher emphasis on marketing and sales and on administrative personnel than reporters. A few outlets, in fact, operate with only two to three reporters; this is quite common for small and micro outlets, regardless of media type.

SERVICE PROGRAMS

Korean media make available various genres of programming, from news to entertainment. Among these genres, local news is the most important, since it is one of the very few regular programs that is locally made. During the time of study, six different outlets in L.A. offered seven daily local evening news programs: KBS America (KBS America News), MBC America (MBC News Tonight), SBS International (SBS Evening News), KTN-TV (KTN News), TVK24 (TVK News Wide and TVK News English Edition), and LA18 (Prime Time Local News; see Table 4.1).[6] There is a good reason for this variety: local news serves both editorial and market purposes. Editorially, local news contributes to the integrity of media institutions. As one media practitioner put it: "It is not a broadcasting station if there is no newsroom" (Media Practitioner 23).[7] Korea's 2009 election law, which ex-

TABLE 4.1

Korean news schedule by outlet, Los Angeles, March 2010

	KBS America	MBC America	SBS International	KTN-TV	TVK24	TVK24	LA18
Description	KBS branch	MBC branch	SBS branch	The Korea Times TV	Local immigrant media	Local immigrant cable TV	Asian television
Local news	KBS America News	MBC News Tonight	SBS Evening News	KTN News	TVK News Wide	TVK News English Edition	Primetime News
Cable	Time Warner ch. 159/Cox ch. 473 (M–F 20:00–20:15) Time Warner ch. 14/ Cox ch. 31 (M–F 20:00–20:24)		Time Warner ch. 603 *Not available in L.A.		Time Warner ch. 158 (M–Sat 20:00–20:50)	Time Warner ch. 158 (M–F 23:00–23:20)	Time Warner ch. 18 (M–F 20:00–20:30)
Terrestrial digital	KXLA ch. 44 (M–F 20:00–20:24)	KSCI ch. 18.3 (M–F 20:50–21:00)		KXLA ch. 44.3 (M–F 20:00–20:30; Tu–Sat 08:00–08:30 [rerun])			KSCI ch. 18.1 (M–F 20:00–20:30)
Satellite	TANTV 1 (Tu–Sat 08:00–08:30; M–F 22:15–22:30)		TANTV 3 (M 20:00–20:40; Tu–F 20:00–20:30; Tu–Sat 00:00–00:40)				
Imported news	KBS News 9 KBS Sports News	MBC News Live MBC News Today (Sat)	1. SBS Sports News 2. SBS News 3. SBS Korean Int'l News	MBN Live Today	YTN News Wide		MBC News LiveSBS Korean Int'l News

Cable	Time Warner ch.159/Cox ch.159 (M–Sun 21:00–21:50) Time Warner ch.14/Cox ch.31 (M–Sun 21:00–21:35)	Formerly Time Warner ch.650 through Hanmi Cable	Time Warner ch. 603 *Not available in L.A.	Time Warner ch.158 (M–Thu 20:50–21:50; F 20:50–21:30; Sat 21:15–21:30; Sun 21:15–21:50)	KSCI ch. 18.1 (M–F 20:30–21:30) KSCI ch. 18.3 (M–F 21:00–21:30)
Terrestrial digital	KXLA ch.44 (M–Sun 21:00–21:35)	KSCI ch. 18.3 (M–F 21:00–21:30)	3. KSCI ch.18.1 (M–F 20:30–21:30)	KXLA ch. 44.3 (M–Sun 20:30–21:40)	
Satellite	TANTV 1 (M–F 22:30–22:45)	TANTV2 (M–Sat 19:00–19:40; Sun 19:00–19:15)	1. TANTV 3 (Tu–F 20:30–20:40; Sat 20:50–21:02) TANTV 3 (Sat 20:10–20:50; Sun 20:15–20:30)		
Online archive	http://www.kbs-america.com/reruns/news (formerly http://www.mvibo.com)	http://www.mbc-america.com/default/MBC_News_tonight.php	http://www.sbs-int.com/program/news_detail.aspx?id=1585	http://www.tvk24.com/bbs/board.php?bo_table=subo4_newswide&menu_id=4	

NOTE: This is a summary of the program schedules for Korean news in March 2010, compiled by the author.

tended voting rights to overseas Koreans, added further significance to local news production, especially for transnational branches, which offer a venue for providing necessary information to eligible Korean voters. As one media practitioner said, "If there had been no change in Korea's election law, the (names of companies) would not even have considered local news production" (Media Practitioner 23). Three of the six local news programs (MBC News Tonight, SBS Evening News, LA18 Prime Time Local News) were launched in 2009, the year the election law was passed.

Marketwise, local news is what earns a media outlet a local reputation and helps tap into the local enclave market. Transnational media branches pursue localization in order to be financially self-sufficient, and local news is known to attract the most advertising. As one media practitioner put it:

> Broadcasting without a news desk is less influential, even if you have prestige that comes along with the name brand such as (name of company) or (name of company) ... We show that we are with the local audience and that we pay attention to the difficulties of local Koreans and report on their issues. Then, the Korean community wants us more ... They invite us to events, etc ... Also, one of the reasons for growing news production is that it contributes to ad revenue. (Media Practitioner 26)

The local news was available in short or long form, in a range of 10 minutes (MBC News Tonight) to 50 minutes (TVK News Wide). In parallel, the six television outlets offering daily local news programs also aired unedited imported news programs from Korea via various platforms. KBS America distributed its imported news from its headquarters (e.g., KBS News 9) via all platforms (terrestrial, cable, and satellite). MBC America and SBS International also used LA18's digital channels to distribute their imported news programs from their respective headquarters (e.g., MBC News Live, SBS 8 News). In addition to television news, three radio channels delivered news a minimum of three times a day (morning, noon, and evening). The radio evening news segments were lengthy, ranging from two (Radio Seoul and JBC) to three hours (Radio Korea). With all of these news services, it is fair to say that the Korean community was news rich.

GEOGRAPHIC SERVICE AREAS

Geographically, in addition to *The Korea Times* and *The Korea Daily* operating branches in major cities across North America (see Introduction), Korean media are widely available in the major ethnoburbs, especially in L.A. and Orange Counties. While the majority of active media outlets are located in the city of L.A., some are also found in the major ethnoburbs, such as *The Town News* in the city of Garden Grove in Orange County, which services – but is not limited to – Orange County Koreans. Major dailies (*The Korea Times, The Korea Daily, Daily Sports Seoul U.S.A.*) also make themselves available by operating distribution centres in Orange County. The media outlets without a distribution centre still make their products available in major Korean locations through their own delivery system.

SERVICE LANGUAGES AND FEES

In terms of accessibility for a broader audience, most of these services are provided in Korean, with limited subtitled over-the-air programs (e.g., drama, documentaries). KBS America, for example, provides English subtitles to 82% of KBS World programs ("KBS offers Spanish," 2008) but only for entertainment programs. No subtitles are provided for everyday local evening news. Nonetheless, in a relative sense, English service is far more advanced in L.A. than in Vancouver. Until 2011, TVK24 offered a 30-minute English news program, targeting younger-generation Korean Americans. (Potential factors that led to the failure of English news programs are discussed in the following section.) The print sector is also relatively more accessible. An example is *The Korea Times*, which also produces an English website that can be accessed via *The Korea Times*'s homepage (www.koreatimes.com) or directly (www.koreatimesus. com) (see *Korea Times L.A.*, n.d.-e). The following sections discuss these options in detail. For services fees, only over-the-air programs are available for free, the rest being pay services available for cable and satellite subscribers either as part of their subscription packages or for an additional charge. The section below on Korean media as a market discusses it in detail as part of the revenue structure. The market competitiveness of cable and satellite services in the digital era is further discussed in Chapters 5 and 6. All online and offline publications are available for free except the two major dailies, *The Korea Times* and *The Korea Daily.*

Availability and Accessibility on Three Dimensions

A snapshot of the Korean media sector in L.A. shows that Korean media are available and accessible to varying degrees. A deeper exploration of the degree of availability and accessibility as a community, a civil society, and a market is necessary to understand the strengths and weaknesses of Korean media on each dimension. An important question to address in the case of Korean media in L.A. is whether the source of capital (or ownership) makes any difference, specifically when immigrant media and transnational media branches (hereafter "transnational media") are compared. Does it make a difference in who they serve and how they serve? What are the implications for availability and accessibility of Korean media for local Koreans as well as for a broader audience? Although the function of media may not be clear-cut by ownership, it is an important question to ask to explore ethnicity-specific and city-specific factors.

KOREAN MEDIA AS A COMMUNITY

"Multilocality" and News About Here *and* There

The community role of diasporic media is primarily to provide national and geo-ethnic news that is both *here* and *there,* and both *universal* and *particular,* with cultural translation to those who depend largely on Korean media. As discussed in Chapter 3, geo-ethnic news constitutes "ethnically or culturally relevant" and "geographically bound" news, from local city news to Korean community news and from general local events to immigrant settlement information (Lin and Song, 2006, pp. 367–368). Geo-ethnic storytelling by L.A.'s Korean media can be more geographically grounded than in Vancouver: While L.A.'s Korean communication infrastructure is anchored in Koreatown, media outlets also branch out to major ethnoburbs, servicing Korean clientele in those areas.

Similar to Vancouver's Korean media, most of the production efforts and resources of L.A.'s diasporic media are dedicated to national and geo-ethnic news. Although the absolute quantity may be small, these locally produced items make their way to the A section or to the front page of each section of newspapers and to the headlines of television and radio. One media practitioner described the importance of the location of a news item:

> The section weight is more important than the absolute quantity as a whole. The A section has the most dedication, investment, and revenue-generating space. Thus, it is more important to compare section by section than the absolute quantity in total. This is because people tend to read the A section, plus one more section, and disregard the rest. A small article in the A section and a big article in the B or C section aren't comparable. What matters to Koreans

TABLE 4.2

News origin by source of capital, Los Angeles (%)

	Total	Local immigrant media	Transnational media	Multicultural media
	N = 1,593	N = 459	N = 1,027	N = 107
Staff writers	38	45[a]	36[b]	30[b]
Imported from Korea	22	19[a]	26[b]	–
U.S. media	6	9[a]	6[a]	9[a]
Other	1	2[a]	1[a]	–
Absent/unknown	32	27[a]	31[a]	61[b]

NOTES: Numbers in the table are rounded off. Each subscript letter denotes a subset of column categories whose column proportions do or do not differ significantly from each other at the .05 level.

and matters to the U.S. in general goes into the A section. (Media Practitioner 31)

A content analysis of 1,593 television, newspaper, and radio news items (see Table 4.2) showed that 38% of the total output is locally produced and the rest is supplemented by news imported from either Korea (22%) or elsewhere (40%).[8] Interestingly, the difference is visible when compared by source of capital.[9] The z-test of comparing column proportions further shows that immigrant media tend to produce more news locally by staff writers (45%) than do transnational media (36%) and multicultural media (30%) and depend less on imported news from Korea (19%) than do transnational media (26%). By media type, newspapers tend to produce more news locally (55%) than do radio (39%) and television (28%).

If geographic focus is compared by news origin, a clear division of labour between local production and international imports is evident. Eighty-six percent of the news produced locally by staff writers focuses on national (27%) and geo-ethnic (54%) news – with a similar distribution between general local news (27%) and Korean community news (27%) – and significantly less coverage of international news (12%; see Table 4.3). Again, similar to Vancouver's Korean media, staff writers generally write about *here*. Imported news from Korea (from Korean headquarters or news agencies such as Yonhap News Agency), however, focuses mainly on Korea (52%) and other parts of the world (29%). Most news from local mainstream media (e.g., *Los*

TABLE 4.3

Geographic focus of news items by news origin, Los Angeles (%)

	Total	Staff writers	Imported from Korea	U.S. media	Other	Absent/ unknown
	$N = 1{,}593$	$N = 605$	$N = 355$	$N = 100$	$N = 23$	$N = 510$
Local						
• Korean	11	27[d]	—	1[a,b]	9[c,d]	3[a,c]
• General	16	27[d]	0.3[c]	10[a,b]	—	17[a]
Provincial/state	6	5[b]	1[c]	8[a,b]	—	9[a]
National	31	27[c]	12[b]	69[a]	—	43[d]
International						
• South Korea	17	6[b]	52[c]	4[a,b]	4[a,b]	10[a]
• North Korea	2	0.3[a]	5[b]	1[a,b]	22[c]	1[a]
• General	15	6[a]	29[b]	6[a]	65[c]	17[d]
Absent/unknown	1	3[b]	0.3[c]	1[a,b,c]	—	0.2[a,c]

NOTES: Numbers in the table are rounded off. Each subscript letter denotes a subset of column categories whose column proportions do or do not differ significantly from each other at the .05 level.

Angeles Times, Associated Press) also focuses specifically on U.S. national news (69%).

Similarly, when geographic focus is compared by source of capital (TV only) – local immigrant (TVK24), transnational (KBS, MBC, SBS, and KTN-TV), and multicultural television news (LA18) – the focus is clear.[10] Overall, multicultural television is the most U.S. news–oriented (94%) compared to local immigrant (80%) and transnational television (63%; see Table 4.4, top). The coverage of general local news (23%) is particularly high in multicultural television as compared to local immigrant and transnational television. The coverage of state news (news about California), however, is highest in local immigrant television (15%), compared to transnational (6%) and multicultural (5%) television. Most importantly, the coverage of imported news from Korea is the highest in transnational television (17%) and almost nonexistent in local immigrant (1%) and multicultural (3%) television.

In comparing local and transnational newspapers (Table 4.4, bottom), local immigrant newspapers (*Koreatown Daily* and *Korea Herald Business*) are again significantly more U.S. focused than transnational newspapers

TABLE 4.4

Geographic focus of news items by source of capital: TV and newspapers, Los Angeles (%)

Geographic focus	Total	Local immigrant media	Transnational media	Multicultural media
TV only	N = 501	N = 157	N = 237	N = 107
Local				
• Korean	14	9[a]	14[a, b]	22[b]
• General	14	11[a]	12[a]	23[b]
Provincial/state	9	15[a]	6[b]	5[b]
National	39	45[a]	31[b]	45[a]
International				
• South Korea	9	1[a]	17[b]	3[a]
• North Korea	1	0.6[a]	2[a]	—
• General	15	19[a]	17[a]	3[b]
Newspapers only	N = 232	N = 258	N = 2,174	
Local				
• Korean	20	19[a]	21[a]	
• General	9	9[a]	9[a]	
Provincial/state	6	3[a]	7[a]	
National	29	43[a]	25[b]	
International				
• South Korea	25	9[a]	31[b]	
• North Korea	0.4	—	1[a]	
• General	7	10[a]	6[a]	
Absent/unknown	3	7[a]	2[b]	

NOTE: Numbers in the table are rounded off. Each subscript letter denotes a subset of column categories whose column proportions do or do not differ significantly from each other at the .05 level.

(*The Korea Times* and *The Korea Daily*). Seventy-four percent of the total news output is dedicated to news about *here*, compared to 62% for transnational newspapers. Conversely, local immigrant media dedicate only 9% to news about Korea, compared to 30% for transnational media. Such a contrast in geographic emphasis between immigrant and transnational media is attributed to editorial direction and access to Korean news items, among other factors. Obviously, it is transnational media that are more Korea-oriented and have easier access to Korean news items, through their own company headquarters. (See below for further discussion.)

News That Matters to the Korean Community
With these differences in content and news source, what news topics are available for local Koreans? Again, the "relevancy to the Korean community and the interest of Koreans" is one of the most important criteria, as commonly mentioned by the interviewed media practitioners. A comparison of news topics by news origin showed a clear division of labour between news produced by staff writers and that produced by external sources. Table 4.5 shows that other than the regularly included sports, stock market, weather, and traffic information, staff writers focus largely on the Korean enclave economy and businesses (9%) and on community news (9%). Headlines include "The food truck Kalbi enters the OC market" (*The Korea Daily*, March 12, 2010, K1), "Forever 21 ranks 2nd among L.A.'s top 50 minority corporations" (*The Korea Times*, March 16, 2010, D1), and "Korean American Coalition, an official not-for-profit partner of the LPGA" (KBS America, March 12, 2010). Aside from these topics, immigration (5%) and education (5%) are two topics frequently discussed: "Increase in immigrant settlement in medium- and small-size cities" (KBS America, March 15, 2010), "California lays off 22,000 teachers and staff" (TVK24, March 15, 2010), and "Arizona's new immigration law" (Radio Korea, April 24, 2010). The U.S. sources (e.g., *Los Angeles Times, U.S.A. Today, The Washington Post,* CNN), in contrast, provide news related to economy/business (17%), crime/violence (12%), and sports (12%). For sports news specifically, only 34% (50 out of 148 items) of stories are locally produced by Korean media; the rest are supplied by U.S. and Korean sources (12% each). Note that "Toyota recall" was a national hot-topic event during the time of study, thus separated from generic news topic categories in order to understand the degree of attention it received from Korean media.

News about *there* from Korean sources, on the other hand, provides stories about crime/violence (10%), international/bilateral politics (9%), and international/bilateral economy (5%): "Google, criticized for closing its China office" (SBS, March 23, 2010) and "North Korea increases rent of diplomatic offices by 20%" (*The Korea Daily*, March 12, 2010, B1). The coverage of acts of terror (40%) and crime/violence (16%) was unusually high, which can be attributed to a major murder case during the time of sampling and also to the sinking of a South Korean warship that occurred on March 26, 2010, killing 46 soldiers. Some of the headlines are "Major disaster in the west sea, the sinking of Korea's warship Chogae" (*The Korea Daily*, March 27, 2010, A1/A2), "Internal explosion or external attack? 46 are missing"

TABLE 4.5

News topics by news origin, Los Angeles (%)

	Total	Staff writers	Imported from Korea	U.S. media	Other	Absent/ unknown
	N = 1,593	N = 605	N = 355	N = 100	N = 23	N = 510
Sports	9	8[a]	12[b]	12[a, b]	4[a, b]	8[a, b]
Acts of terror	8	2[a]	21[b]	1[a]	9[b, c]	7[c]
Crime/violence	7	4[b]	10[a]	12[a]	9[a, b]	8[a]
Economy/business (general)	7	5[b]	5[b]	17[a]		10[c]
Transportation/traffic	7	15[c]	0.6[b]	2[a, b]	4[a, c]	2[a, b]
International/bilateral politics	6	5[a]	9[b]	2[a]	22[c]	6[a, b]
Politics (Parliamentary practices)	6	4[b]	5[b]	6[a, b]	4[a, b]	9[a]
Economy/business (Korean enclave, Korea)	5	9[c]	3[a, b]	1[a]	9[b, c]	2[a]
Weather/season/ daylight saving	4	11[b]	0.8[a]	–	–	0.4[a]
Community (Korean diaspora)	4	9[a]	–	6[a]		0.2[b]
Education	4	3[b, c]	1[c]	5[a, b]	4[a, b, c]	6[a]
Stock market	3	2[a, b]	5[b]	–	–	3[a, b]
Migration/migrants/ immigration/ immigrants	2	3[a]	–	3[a]	4[a]	3[a]
International/bilateral economy/business	2	0.5[a]	5[b, c]	2[a, b]	13[c]	1[a]
Toyota, other recalls	2	0.8[b]	0.8[b]	8[a]	–	3[c]
State/city politics	2	1[b]		2[a, b]		5[a]
People	2	2[a]	2[a]	2[a]	–	2[a]
Entertainment/ entertainment industry	2	1[b, c]	0.3[c]	3[a, b]	–	4[a]
Natural disasters	2	1[a, c]	1[c]	4[a, b, c]	9[b]	2[a, c]
Health	2	2[a]	2[a]	3[a]	–	1[a]
Real estate	2	2[a, b]	0.6[b]	1[a, b]		2[a]
Politics (election)	2	0.8[a]	3[b]	1[a, b]	4[a, b]	2[a, b]
Other	12	12	14	7	4	13

NOTES: The numbers in the table are rounded off. Each subscript letter denotes a subset of column categories whose column proportions do or do not differ significantly from each other at the .05 level.

(*The Korea Times,* March 27, 2010, A1), and "Chonanham being recovered" (Radio Korea, April 12, 2010).

Although relevancy to the community is a priority in the selection of news about Korea, factors such as content licensing arrangements also have a role to play. Immigrant media or broadcasting outlets tend to select item by item from affiliated sources, whereas transnational newspapers select page by page from the headquarter's publication of the day to construct a 15-page "Korea Section" (or *Bonkookpan*). This Korea Section is, in fact, unique to Korean transnational newspapers and shows that the absolute quantity of news about there alone is not a good indicator of home orientation. The Korea Section is also related to the political economy of news production rather than a genuinely higher interest in the country of origin. One media practitioner explained it this way:

> It is a section seen only among Korean press. *The L.A. Times* or *La Opinión* does not have, for example, a Mexico Section. However, this section serves a financial interest by creating extra ad spaces. Thus, to the question of whether or not higher coverage of news about Korea means higher interest in Korea than America, it is difficult to say that the paper is more Korea-focused because of that. (Media Practitioner 31)

Nonetheless, the Korea Section is not free of internal criticism with respect to editorial direction:

> Is (name of person) from here? Why do we even talk about him here? We have Korean news for recently immigrated people or for visitors. However, we need to empirically find out the ratio of our readers, the proportion of those who have lived here for over five years. I believe those who have lived here over five years are not too interested in Korean news ... Another reason we need Korean news is to create more ad spaces. (Media Practitioner 28)

Geo-Korean Storytelling and Cultural Translation

Similar to Vancouver's Korean media, news about *here* is made available through cultural translation. News stories are culturally translated or repackaged, using cultural idioms that are familiar to Koreans and providing background information (history or contextual references), if necessary, for those who are unfamiliar with the chronology of events because they are new to the country. As A.Y. Chung (2007, p. 51) argues, Korean media have served to provide "culture-friendly information on both homeland and American events, along with tips on how to promote educational and economic goals." It is through this process of selection and translation that the news is filtered and contexualized by local Korean media practitioners and made available to a Korean audience.

National and geo-ethnic news is produced or reproduced differently depending on the news origin. The general local news is produced directly by staff writers through on-site reporting, telephone interviews, or press releases. One of the important criteria for on-site reporting is the event's relevancy to the local Korean community. For example, the so-called metro news of one of the newspapers reports on the activities and decisions made at city and county halls that are relevant to Koreatown (Media Practitioner 29). The U.S.–Korea events that are taking place in either L.A. or Korea (e.g., a U.S. politician visiting Korea, U.S.–Korea FTA talks) are also considered newsworthy for on-site reporting (Media Practitioner 30).

National and geo-ethnic news is also reproduced in the process of cultural translation. The stories of broader interest are recontexualized to highlight the geo-ethnicity: "Healthcare reform is a good example. We narrate it based on 'our standards.' Americans think differently. We focus on what will happen to seniors' Medicare and prescription drugs, how much we have to pay at our income level, etc." (Media Practitioner 26).

Similarly, one of the un-bylined news items on the Census narrates that "the response rate of the city of Los Angeles *that includes K-town* (emphasis added) was 11%" (KBS, March 24, 2010). Another un-bylined news item reads:

> The Census questionnaire has been mailed out to 120 million households today. The Census questionnaire includes ten questions in English that ask name, race, and gender, among others. *If you need a questionnaire in Korean, please call a free Korean-language service, 1-866-955-2010* [emphasis added]. (TVK24, March 15, 2010)

The ethnicity-specific, Korean community news is produced by local reporters. According to one media practitioner, the news about the Korean community as a whole or Koreans as individuals allows Korean media to serve an advocacy function:

An *L.A. Times* reporter once asked me if our company is the same as *The L.A. Times*. I asked in return, what is the difference? I think differently now. We have a community advocacy function. It is undeniable that "the skin is nearer than the shirt." It is what we are born for. Our priority is to tell our own stories that involve the Korean community. That is what determines our news value. We want to tell our stories, celebrate our victories, and encourage our children's achievements, which mainstream media never discuss. We recognize them and give credit to ourselves. Mainstream society cannot understand our unique problems ... We talk about those problems; sometimes we criticize and other times we sympathize. (Media Practitioner 38)

Indeed, Korean media discuss "our stories" and "our victories," which mainstream media have never been known to celebrate. Examples include headlines such as "Professor D. I. Kim's students won an award at the traffic safety symposium" (Radio Korea, April 9, 2010) and "Korean female student elected the new student body president of Northwestern University" (JBC, April 21, 2010). The appointment of Sung Kim as the U.S. ambassador to South Korea in June 2011 was also widely discussed in L.A.'s Korean media (N.Y. Kim, 2011a). TVK24's *Story G* is yet another venue that features successful Korean Americans in a documentary format. During the time of study, a story about Sonia Kim Été, CEO of the Academy of Couture Art, a fashion design school in L.A., was broadcast (TVK24, March 14, 2010). Korean media also rebroadcast coverage of Korean Americans spotlighted in mainstream media. For example, the *Los Angeles Times*'s article on "Forever 21's Stylish Sisters" covered two daughters of Mr. D.W. Chang, CEO of Forever 21 (K.H. Chung, 2010). Although Asian studies scholars often criticize the reinforcement of "model minority" stereotypes (Min, 2006a; C.J. Kim and Lee, 2007; L. Cheng and Yang, 1996), the recognition of model Koreans is part of the "immigration ideology" – that is, "the belief that America is the land of opportunity in the initial stages of immigration unlike native-born minority groups" (A.Y. Chung, 2007, p. 61).

Besides news, an important part of geo-ethnic information is the classifieds, which Korean immigrants often use to find employment and access business opportunities. Min's (2001) study confirms that Korean immigrants often find employment through personal networks or ads in Korean diasporic newspapers. Indeed, the classified sections of *The Korea Times* and

The Korea Daily are sizable, not much smaller than the A section: 16 pages of classifieds compared to 28 pages of the A section in *The Korea Times,* and 20 compared to 26 in *The Korea Daily.* The classified section contains information on, for example, employment, real estate, and rent/leases. The downside of the so-called ethnic classified, however, may be that Koreans tend to limit their search to the options listed in Korean newspapers. This often results in "ethnic facilitation" – having kin or coethnic labour in the workforce – which leads to "industrial clustering," overrepresentation in some industries and underrepresentation in others (Light and Bonacich, 1988, p. 179).

Availability and Accessibility in the Digital Era

Availability and accessibility of Korean media as a community is ever more prominent in the digital era. Most active online discussion boards are formed on the "Open Lounge" (or *Yulinmadang*) of *The Korea Times* and the "ASK U.S.A." (or *ASK Mikook*) forum of *The Korea Daily.* These two are distinct in terms of the type of information discussed. While the former facilitates an exchange of philosophical ideas or critiques (see *Korea Times L.A.,* n.d.-c; "Open Lounge" is categorized as "opinion" in Table 4.6), the latter focuses on technical issues in the process of settlement and integration, such as the U.S. social security administration, immigration/visa, law, education, finance, U.S. life, and health (*Korea Daily L.A.,* n.d.-a). Similar to Vancouver's Korean media, local experts are available to respond to technical questions raised by readers. *The Korea Daily* either selects its own "*Korea Daily* Recommended

TABLE 4.6

Discussion topics of online bulletin boards in Korean media, Los Angeles (%)

Discussion topics	Total
	N = 244
Immigration (citizenship, other)	28
Law (crime, divorce, labour/commercial, other)	18
U.S. life	16
Opinions	13
Finance (bank, other)	12
Education	9
Health	4
Medicare/social programs	1

NOTE: The numbers in the table are rounded off.

Experts" for one-on-one consultation or encourages experts to register themselves as an "ASK U.S.A Expert."

A content analysis of 244 online threads during a constructed week of March 2010 found that the average daily postings of all four local Korean dailies – *The Korea Times, The Korea Daily, Koreatown Daily,* and *Korea Herald Business* – ranged from 30 to 50 threads, mostly generated from *The Korea Daily* (see Table 4.6). Topics related to immigration (28%) are discussed most, followed by law (18%), U.S. life in general (16%), opinion (13%), and finance (12%). Some examples of immigration-related topics are re-entry permits, work permits as international students, and citizenship applications. The average hit frequency of the 244 items was 284 (with the highest being 2,450 hits and the lowest being 11 hits). Looking at the top five most-read topics, again, issues relating to immigration dominate, reflecting a sizable floating population within the Korean community, as discussed in the introductory chapter. The first thread (hit frequency = 2,450) asked if it is possible to get a visa reissued when the person has stayed in the United States for two years as an alien student and can be transferred to a high school in Korea.

In addition, over 50% of these questions were answered by multiple people, both experts (52%) and nonexperts (51%). The nonexperts were those who wished to share their own personal experiences and expertise with others. The readers who posted their questions also responded to the comments (20%), asking follow-up questions or simply expressing their appreciation to those who responded to their questions. In all of these threads, the main language of discussion was Korean (95%), although some experts did occasionally respond in English to questions asked in Korean (5%). Interestingly, unlike the hyperlocal discussion in Vancouver, L.A.'s online community invites national and international (about Korea) discussions among Koreans across the United States and Korea, although these are still marginal in terms of the number of threads. Within the 244 posts, the origin of those from outside of L.A. and from Korea account for 36% and 3%, respectively.

Availability and Accessibility for the Broader Community

English Editions

As noted above, the news locally produced and internationally imported from Korea is a rich resource for a broader audience to improve cultural literacy. It is a window into both Korean community and Korea. In particular, imported news about Korea is not any news but news that is relevant to the U.S. context and so is useful for a broader audience. But how accessible is this rich resource for this broader audience?

Unlike Korean media in Vancouver, *intercultural* initiatives have regularly been attempted in L.A., although they have been often short-lived. One of the earliest attempts was *The Korea Times English*, led by K.W. Lee, in the form of a one- or two-page insert into the Korean-language print edition. The short lifespan of this initiative is owed to the limited appeal to advertisers and the high operational costs. Interviewed media practitioner recalled that it was simply too challenging to convince management, as well as advertisers, to support an English edition when the readers were entirely first-generation immigrants. Operating an English edition team of perfectly bilingual staff with journalistic training was another challenge. When New America Media asked one Korean newspaper to contribute articles, the company rejected the offer for the same reasons (Media Practitioner 38).

Nevertheless, trials have continued, and in 2013, *The Korea Times* launched *The Korea Times in English* online, which can be accessed via *The Korea Times*'s homepage (www.koreatimes.com) or directly (www.koreatimesus.com). This service takes the form of an independent English website rather than a compatible bilingual website in which the same news stories are available in two different languages. A separate content analysis would be needed to understand the degree of local production (i.e., the volume of stories written by local staff writers) for this website. For now (as of 2017), stories appearing in the sites' various sections contain a mix of predominantly Yonhap News Agency and *New York Times* articles and some (outdated) locally produced news written by staff writers – bylined as "(name of reporter) – *The Korea Times*, Staff Reporter."[11] Further research is needed on the users of this website to understand its impact: Are users predominantly Korean Americans or others? Why are these users accessing the site? A deeper understanding of the site's users will help in strategizing to broaden the accessibility for a wider audience. Following in the footsteps of *The Korea Times, The Korea Daily* also launched an English website (www.koreadailyus.com) in 2016 (see *Korea Daily L.A.*, 2016).

Besides the efforts by the first-generation media, *in-between* and *intercultural* initiatives by the younger generation also continue. *KoreAm Journal,* a monthly magazine, was first published in English in 1990 by a 1.5-generation publisher, James Ryu, and was mandated to serve as a venue for Korean Americans; it ceased publication in December 2015 (see Kore Asian Media's "About Kore" and "What is Kore?"; V. Kim, 2015). Some of the topics included in the March 2010 edition are "(Another) KA booted from Pyongyang," "This season in reality TV – Asians abound!" and "Peeking into Korea's historic past." The magazine also provided "Community Pages" for Korean American organizations to post their activities: the Korean American Bar Association (KABA), Korean American Coalition (KAC), Korean American Community Foundation (KACF), Korean Churches for Community Development (KCCD), and Korean Cultural Center of Los Angeles (KCCLA), among others. The magazine was also one of the hyperlocal ethnic media linked to LA Beez when it was in service (see Chapter 2). The *Los Angeles Times* reports that one of the reasons for the closure of *KoreAm Journal*, according to the publisher, James Ryu, is a failure to attract advertisers, who "preferred Korean-language publications, thinking English-speaking second-generation Korean Americans would be captured by their mainstream media product pitches" (V. Kim, 2015, para. 10). Unfortunately, V. Kim notes, "the folding of KoreAm as a magazine comes at a time when second-generation Korean and Asian Americans are more visible than ever" (para. 13).

In the broadcasting sector, the initiatives targeting 1.5- and second-generation Korean Americans suggest a potential for broadening accessibility for a wider audience, although some improvement of these efforts is desirable. One example is TVK News English Edition. Discontinued as of 2011, it was a 20-minute English-language daily news program (23:00–23:20, Monday to Friday). An analysis of news content found a potential reason for the failure: the needs of the target audience were not addressed adequately. Table 4.7 compares the geographic focus of TVK News Wide (Korean-language news) and TVK News English Edition (English) and shows that both Korean- and English-language programs focus predominantly or entirely on U.S. news: over 80% of news is general U.S. news. Such a focus on *here* may be a merit for Korean-language news, since most audience members are first-generation immigrants, but not for the English edition, since the target audience of that edition has multiple news sources to resort to. Only 15% of news in the English edition is about the Korean community, and there is no news about Korea, when these two areas of coverage may really be the information that the target audience is looking for and that could provide a window into the Korean American community, as well as Korea. If English news programs produced by Korean media are to be accountable to their supposed target audience, the geographic focus of news stories needs to be differentiated from Korean-language news.

TABLE 4.7

Geographic focus of news items by language: TVK News Wide (Korean) and TVK News English Edition, Los Angeles (%)

		Total	Korean	English
		N = 203	N = 157	N = 46
Local	• Korean	10	9[a]	15[a]
	• General	19	11[a]	48[b]
Provincial/state		17	15[a]	26[a]
National		37	45[a]	11[b]
International	• South Korea	1	1[a]	–
	• North Korea	0.5	0.6[a]	–
	• General	14	19[a]	–

NOTES: Numbers in the table are rounded off. Each subscript letter denotes a subset of column categories whose column proportions do or do not differ significantly from each other at the .05 level.

Intercultural community events

While news content has limited accessibility for a broader audience, Korean media often go beyond the Korean community and initiate intercultural projects to connect with the broader community. *The Korea Daily's* annual Anabada Flea Market is a good example.[12] Attended by 20,000 people of diverse ethnicities, the market celebrated its fifth year on March 24, 2010, during the time of study (Hwang, Moon, and Chang, 2010). Among those represented were the Latino and African American communities, making the 2010 market a "pan-community event," according to *The Korea Daily* (S.J. Park, 2010). In-Sung Choi (2010), the JBC news chief, suggested that the Anabada market may help break down the "invisible wall" that exists between the various diasporic communities, considering the in-group orientation of the Korean community and the underrecognition of the Korean American market among mainstream corporations. Choi commented that the market was a positive move "for Koreans who find intercultural cooperation and interaction difficult, for mainstream corporations who are surprised by the development and the size of Korean community, and for Latino neighbors who feel distant from their Korean neighbors." A total of 150 sponsors and retailers participated in the event, along with more than 30 public and private corporations and institutions (e.g., PepsiCo, McDonald's, White Memorial Hospital), who supported not only the flea market but also the organization of a job fair and a free medical clinic for local residents ("Anabada market," 2010).

The annual L.A. Korean Festival is another example of community outreach. The 37th festival (September 30 to October 3, 2010) was attended by 20,000 people, including local politicians such as Tom Labonge, city councilman; Carmen Trutanich, L.A. city attorney; and J.P. Hong of the One Nation Party (*Hannaladang*). Sponsored by local Korean and mainstream corporations (e.g., Hyundai Motors, Kia Motors, Toyota, Prudential, McDonald's), the festival organized a variety of events, including performances by Korean pop music (K-pop) stars and local sports and art groups, foods, and parades (J.H. Kim, 2010). The highlight of the event is *The Korea Times*'s annual Korean Parade. The parade proceeds through Koreatown and is joined by local and overseas politicians, corporate representatives, and local residents.

The Korean communities in the major ethnoburbs also organize their own Korean festivals. During the time of study, these included the 27th Orange County Korean Festival (October 8–10, 2010), the 2nd Inland Korean Festival (December 4, 2010), and the 2nd Irvine Korean American Day Festival (January 15–16, 2011; Moon and Lee, 2010; Moon, 2010; J.W. Lee, 2010). According to the organizing committees, the purpose of these festivals is to promote these communities' Korean heritage to the younger generation and to the broader society through various events: non-Korean K-pop contests, kimchi-making demonstrations, and Korean traditional music performances (Moon, 2010). Some of the festivals are also transnational, inviting a sister city or a "friend city" to participate in some way. The Irvine Korean festival, for example, invited a calligrapher from the city of Seocho in Korea, its friend city, to join the festival (Moon, 2010).

Intercultural communication and campaigns

Intercultural outreach is a trend that is not limited to Korean media outlets. Koreatown–wide community initiatives are undertaken to reach out to the broader community. One example is the "We Speak English" campaign, organized by the Consul General of the Republic of Korea in L.A. in early 2010 to revitalize the Koreatown economy and to internationalize Korean cuisine (M.K. Shim, 2010). Consulate General J.S. Kim pointed out that there was widespread perception of Koreatown being very Korean and of Korean businesses generally exhibiting low levels of English (e.g., no English menu, no English-speaking employees; J.H. Lee, 2010b). Intended to attract non-Korean customers, the consulate office initially distributed 500 "We Speak English" stickers for businesses in Koreatown to place on their doors, with

2,000 more to follow, in collaboration with the Korean Federation (J.H. Lee, 2010b). It was, in fact, the second such initiative by the consulate office: its "Revitalizing K-town Economy" campaign in 2008 was sponsored by *The Korea Times* and had more than 20 Korean CSOs participating (E.H. Lee, 2008).

A related example is a workshop on successful marketing strategies for Asian restaurant owners, held on June 4, 2011, at the Wilshire Grand Hotel. Recognizing a lack of cultural understanding in dealing with customers of ethnicities other than their own, the Koreatown Youth and Community Center (KYCC) invited a consultant to speak on various franchising and marketing strategies, from PR to employee training (Y.S. Kim, 2011b). Indeed, Asian restaurants often fail to expand, even with high competitiveness and growth potential, because they focus too much on taste and price, when the key to success is providing a pleasant "dining-out experience" to customers through friendly service (Y.S. Kim 2011b).

Koreatown businesses responded to these initiatives by switching business signs from Korean to English or to a mix of Korean and English to attract non-Korean customers (J.M. Kwak, 2010). A majority of the signs in Koreatown have long been only in Korean. One of the motivators for this switch was the popularity of all-you-can-eat barbecue restaurants in Koreatown, which have attracted non-Korean customers and increased the demand for English signs and menus. With the change, the businesses, in fact, have seen an "increase in non-Korean customers" (J.M. Kwak, 2010). In parallel, the City of L.A.'s 2009 language requirement for signs added impetus to having a 50/50 ratio of Korean to English language signage (J.M. Kwak, 2010). Still another initiative to make the Koreatown community more interculturally friendly was a Visitor Information Center in Koreatown, initiated by the Korean American Chamber of Commerce of Los Angeles (D.Y. Chung, 2011). The absence of such a service, together with representative Korean landmarks, has been pointed out as a barrier to intercultural outreach. Other than Korean restaurants, there are no venues for Koreatown tourists to experience Korean heritage. The Dawooljung (Korean Pavilion Garden), the only landmark, has been undermaintained due to budget shortfalls (S.J. Lee, 2011).

KOREAN MEDIA AS A CIVIL SOCIETY

The civil society role of diasporic media goes beyond providing culturally translated geo-ethnic storytelling. It also involves helping the public engage in public discussion and influence government decision-making processes.

A series of interethnic encounters has contributed to strengthening political consciousness among Korean community members and leaders and has led to actual engagement in broader public discourse. During the 1992 L.A. riots, for example, the English edition of *The Korea Times* worked closely with *Los Angeles Sentinel,* an African American newspaper in the city, facilitating dialogue between the two communities through an exchange of articles and editorials (E. Chang and Diaz-Veizades, 1999). Internally, Korean media collectively functioned as a venue for first-generation Koreans (whose English was not sufficient to join public debates) to stay informed during the riots. As one media practitioner said:

> The 1992 L.A. riots is a good example of how mainstream media manipulate the situation and frame the story artfully as a Korean-African-American conflict ... Mainstream media collaborate to serve the interest of the country. That is why it is important to have our own channels. (Media Practitioner 23)

Founded just before the riots, Radio Korea is particularly well-known for its contribution. Thanks to the nature of the medium, Radio Korea was able to provide real-time news on the development of the riots, thus saving the lives of many Koreans in affected neighbourhoods and helping mobilize the community for peace rallies (Min, 1996). Such active engagement of Korean media in inter- and intra-community debates is a sign of healthy democratic practice. However, whether engagement is part of everyday practice or is more or less ad hoc, limited to only national hot-topic events such as the L.A. riots, is worth investigating. This section looks at the role of Korean diasporic media as a civil society.

Bridging the Community with Broader Public Discourse

I. Kim (1981, p. 185) argues that Korean media function as "a powerful means of provoking, leading, integrating, expanding and enlightening some selective community values or opinions." Korean media practitioners are generally satisfied with the level of response to political controversies and the promotion of political engagement within the given resources (Media Practitioner 23). Just like Vancouver's Korean media, monitoring local and national mainstream media is part of the daily routine. When mainstream media inaccurately or negatively portray Koreans, Korean media respond immediately to correct errors or do background research to report the rationale for these portrayals. As one media practitioner recalled, "We found degrading remarks about Koreans in a story of (name of company). We complained and received a letter of apology" (Media Practitioner 28). Another media practitioner remembered an incident in which a diasporic newspaper used a photo of the North Korean national flag to represent South Korea (Media Practitioner 31). This ombudsman role of Korean diasporic media continues to ensure the accurate portrayal of Koreans and Korea in mainstream media:

> These [roles] are important, because mainstream media are often biased. The Virginia Tech incident is a good example. Korean media have a responsibility to let mainstream society know that this is not representative of the Korean community. Korean media also have a responsibility to raise awareness of the misrepresentation of Koreans, for example, in museums and textbooks. (Media Practitioner 23)

In addition to the diasporic media's engagement with day-to-day issues, hot-topic events and issues are, of course, covered. These never stop in L.A., especially issues at the intersection of race and geo-politics involving conflicts among various ethnocultural groups over geographic space. Some of these are long-term projects that span years, while others are more time-sensitive or temporary. In either case, Korean diasporic media contribute to forming community discourse during such events. The three hot-topic events discussed in this section are the redrawing of the Koreatown boundary, the rearrangement of the Koreatown electoral district, and the designation of the Preserve America Community.

Case 1: The Redrawing of the Koreatown Boundary

Historically, Koreatown overlaps "contested boundaries" of the

> four biracial and multiracial regions, including several highly clustered Asian-Latino spaces extending from Koreatown eastward into West Covina; one overlapping Asian-Black section around the Koreatown-West Adams border; one White-Asian area on the northern periphery of Hollywood; and a small multiracial area consisting of African Americans, Latinos, and Asian Pacific Americans. (Oliver and Grant, cited in A.Y. Chung, 2007 p. 53)

Certainly, the redrawing of the Koreatown boundary involved debates about the traditions and tensions in the area.

The discussion began in December 2008, when the Bangladeshi community proposed to build "Little Bangladesh" in the middle of Koreatown on 3rd Street (Yoo, 2010). Conflicts of interest continued to surface, since there were overlaps in the claimed boundaries by various interest groups, including the Koreatown Boundary Committee, Wilshire Center Koreatown Neighborhood Council, P.I.C.O. Neighborhood Council, and Councilman Tom Labonge (Yoo, 2010). Specifically, the overlap between the Koreatown Boundary Committee and the P.I.C.O. Neighborhood Council included the area where the El Salvador community had wished to develop an "El Salvador Business Street" (D.Y. Chung, 2010b). In the end, the Koreatown Boundary Committee – led by C.Y. Lee, director of the Korean American Federation – suggested that Koreatown retain the original boundary, which had been officially approved by the City of L.A. in 1980 (D.Y. Chung, 2010a). However, after a series of public hearings, in August 2010, the City of L.A. approved the smallest boundary among all the options that had been proposed. This new boundary stretches from Vermont Avenue to Western Avenue (east to west) and from 3rd Street to Olympic Boulevard (north to south). The City also approved "Little Bangladesh" on 3rd Street within Koreatown (D.Y. Chung, 2010a).

Case 2: Rearrangement of the Koreatown electoral district
Another relevant event was the rearrangement of the Koreatown electoral district. Electoral districts are rearranged based on the results of every census. In 2001, Little Tokyo, Chinatown, and Filipinotown secured their towns as single electoral districts, while Koreatown remained split (A.Y. Chung, 2007, p. 52). Indeed, among the 15 ridings, Koreatown overlaps four of them: the 10th and 13th ridings in the centre of Koreatown, the 4th on the west end, and the 1st on the east end ("Long-term strategy," 2015). Consolidating Koreatown into a single riding has long been a community project, since it is considered "a basic condition for consolidating Koreans' political power" ("Long-term strategy," 2015). As one CSO leader put it, "If the district is formed, it will be easier for Korean Americans to run for councilman and later for state member ... That is what we want" (CSO Leader 5). Korean representation in the political milieu is not absent, but it is also

not strong. According to the Korean American Democratic National Organization (KADNO), there are approximately 50 elected or appointed Korean American politicians in the United States, including Sukhee Kang, mayor of the City of Irvine, and Joseph Cho, former mayor of the City of Cerritos and city councilman (N.Y. Kim, 2011b). Brad Lee, president of KADNO, adds a positive spin: "It is encouraging that the number [of Korean American politicians] is growing quickly" (N.Y. Kim, 2011b). Nonetheless, there is still no Korean representation in Congress, whereas there are 42 African Americans, 26 Hispanics, and 10 Asians (D.S. Kim, 2011). Thus, this new electoral district is considered a means to move a step closer to this goal.

To proceed with this project, the Korean community formed a committee in 2001 to prepare for the 2010 Census. The aim was to consolidate four congressional districts and two senatorial districts that currently oversee Koreatown into a single electoral district (A.Y. Chung, 2007; Y.S. Kim, 2011a). As the results of the 2010 census came out in early 2011, the committee involving Korean CSOs – such as the Korean American Coalition (KAC), the Koreatown Youth and Community Center (KYCC), the Korean American Democratic Committee (KADC), and KADNO – held a public hearing and introduced a proposal for a new Koreatown electoral district. The proposed district stretched from Hoover Street to Crenshaw Boulevard (east to west) and Freeway No. 10 and Melrose Avenue (south to north; Y.S. Kim, 2011a). Despite the committee's efforts, the proposal was rejected and Koreatown remains split. As a response, the committee filed a petition with the federal court to have the decision invalidated. Nonetheless, in February 2015, even the petition was rejected, and the next opportunity to pursue is in 2022, when the new census will come out ("Long-term strategy," 2015).

Ethnic block voting, however, has challenges of its own, as discussed in Chapter 3. Added to the "love-resentment-envy" trend (Võ, 2004, p. 159) among candidates, another barrier for the Koreatown district is that it is in large part a commercial hub rather than an ethnoburb where Korean Americans actually reside. Over 50 percent of Koreatown residents are in fact Latinos (Yu et al., cited in Min, 2006b, pp. 236–237). The geographical dispersion of the Korean population works against the potential synergy Korean Americans expect from a single Koreatown district. Still another barrier to block voting are individualistic approaches to politics. Dong-suk Kim of the Korean American Voters' Council (KAVC) points out that Korean Americans tend to enter politics individually and seek community support later, whereas Jewish American politicians, for example, enter politics with full community support already behind them (S.M. Kim, 2011). A similar pattern is found in terms of campaign support. Koreans tend to support politicians – Koreans or non-Koreans – individually rather than as a community; thus, raising a community voice for a collective political agenda is difficult to achieve. As one media practitioner put it:

> All major government bureaus monitor (name of company) ... U.S. politicians raise funds through fundraising parties. So far Koreans have supported them [politicians] individually rather than as a community as a whole. It may be effective for delivering an individual agenda, but not for raising a community voice ... Koreans account for only 0.7% of the U.S. population, and have no single electoral district to represent Korean voters. There is no Korean American in the Congress. Collective action is important. (Media Practitioner 30)

Case 3: The Designation of the "Preserve America Community"
Still another relevant case is the designation of Koreatown as a "Preserve America Community" by the Advisory Council on Historic Preservation (ACHP). Founded in 2003, the Preserve America program is a federal initiative which designates communities that "protect and celebrate their heritage, use their historic assets for economic development and community revitalization, and encourage people to experience and appreciate local historic resources through education and heritage tourism programs" (www.preserveamerica.gov). The designated communities are eligible to apply for up to $250,000 in federal grants to develop sustainability programs and are allowed to use the "Preserve America Community" signage for the promotion of their community (Seo, 2009c). Koreatown was designated in 2009 as one of 845 "Preserve America Communities," along with the historic Filipinotown (Seo, 2009b). The designation came a year after that of Little Tokyo, Chinatown, and Thai Town in early 2008 (Ha, 2009).

In all of these three cases – the Koreatown boundary, the Koreatown electoral district, and the Preserve America program – an interesting commonality is the intimate interplay between geo-politics and race, which illustrates the struggle to secure a geographic boundary of an ethnic enclave. This boundary is further extended as a means of asserting political leadership within those boundaries. At the centre of these claims, there is invisible ethnic rivalry: some rivalries are conflict-ridden, while others are mutually supportive. If the Koreatown boundary and electoral district projects involved a conflict of interest among ethnocultural groups over Koreatown, the Preserve America program is mutually rewarding, since these communities earn official recognition of their cultural heritage. As multiethnic and political as these cases are, the involvement of multiethnic organizations, interest groups, and residents in the decision-making process is common. In all of these cases, Korean media played a critical role in engaging the Korean community in these processes by covering the development of the events closely and also organizing forums for discussion, whether independently or in collaboration with CSOs, and contributed to collecting community opinions. Examples of the latter are roundtables organized by *The Korea Daily* on the future of Koreatown (J.H. Lee, 2010a) and on the redrawing of the Koreatown boundary (Seo, 2009a). Local community leaders representing Korean or Koreatown CSOs such as KAC (Korean American Coalition), academics, and a city commissioner were invited to discuss these topics.

Promoting Political Engagement

Diasporic media in L.A. play a role in promoting political engagement regardless of the source of capital. In most cases, the outlets with more stable capital tend to take the lead in major geopolitical and interethnic community projects. One example is the 2011 Korean American Political Conference (June 2–4, 2011) held in L.A. Celebrating its 42nd anniversary of publication, *The Korea Times* organized the conference, hosted by the World Korean Political Council, the Korean American Leadership Foundation, and the Bright World Foundation (S.M. Kim, 2011). The conference, the first of its kind, allowed Korean American politicians to discuss the agenda for Korean American political advancement and was attended by more than 100 current and past politicians and 500 community members (S.M. Kim, 2011). According to Dong-suk Kim of the Korean American Voters' Council (KAVC), the ultimate purpose of this conference was to support Jun Choi, former mayor of the City of Edison, New Jersey, in his run for Congress (S.M. Kim,

2011). *The Korea Daily* also organized roundtables of a similar nature. One example is a roundtable for Korean American politicians in Southern California (Lim, 2010). Attended by five Korean American politicians, including two current and former Korean American mayors in Orange County, the event focused on issues concerning voter registration and campaigns, and supporting and networking with other diasporic communities (Lim, 2010).

Proactive political engagement is a trend found among Korean Americans. They have a strong presence in the local neighbourhood councils that oversee Koreatown, such as the Wilshire Center Koreatown Neighborhood Council, the P.I.C.O. Neighborhood Council, and the Downtown Council (Media Practitioner 29). The Wilshire Center Koreatown Neighborhood Council is the largest among the 100 neighbourhood councils in the city and shows the highest Korean representation. Among the 26 directors, over 90% were Koreans, including 1.5- and second-generation Koreans, during the time of study. Through this involvement, Koreans participate in the city's decision-making process on initiatives that matter to Koreatown, such as pipeline construction in Koreatown (Media Practitioner 29).

Availability and Accessibility for Broader Community Organizations

In all of these three cases – the Koreatown boundary, the electoral district, and the Preserve America designation – the collaboration between media and local Korean CSOs, especially the younger-generation CSOs, is noteworthy. While first-generation Korean media and CSOs consolidate the community internally, the younger-generation Korean Americans and the CSOs they lead reach out to the broader society. Examples of 1.5- and second-generation–led organizations include social service organizations such as the Koreatown Youth and Community Center (KYCC) and Korean Health, Education, Information, and Referral Center (KHEIR), and advocacy groups such as the Koreatown Immigrant Workers Alliance (KIWA), Korean Resource Center (KRC), and National Korean American Service and Education Consortium (NAKASEC). Some of these organizations are sizable in terms of their annual operating budgets. For example, the KYCC had an annual operating revenue of U.S.$4 million in 2008, generated from grants, public support, and fundraising, among other sources. The organization is also backed up by a board of 14 directors from various industries and of various ethnocultural backgrounds (KYCC, 2008).

What sets younger-generation organizations apart from those of the older generation is their intercultural focus on geography rather than ethnicity.

All of these younger-generation organizations serve all residents of the Koreatown area, regardless of ethnicity, who are in need of their respective services (e.g., youth for the KYCC, labour for the KIWA, health for the KHEIR). Serving such a broad clientele, compared to the former focus on only Koreans in Koreatown, is the organizations' response to the changing demographic composition in the Koreatown area, as discussed earlier. Indeed, the KYCC and the KIWA even changed the first word in their organizational name from "Korean" to "Koreatown" in the 2000s, in order to highlight the service location rather than the ethnicity of service clientele (A.Y. Chung, 2007). As one representative of the multiethnic organizations put it:

> We are not ethnic-specific; we are more geographic-specific ... That is our philosophy, to really focus on the K-town area ... The K-town area is very unique and different from many other suburban areas ... I believe if you are a service organization that receives government grants, you have to be really geographically focused. (CSO Leader 2)

These organizations collaborate among themselves as well as across CSOs originating in other ethnocultural groups, such as Para Los Niños, the Organization of Chinese Americans (OCA), and the Little Tokyo Service Center, on common issues such as immigration, education, and development (CSO Leader 3). In promoting their projects, these organizations reach out to both Korean and mainstream media such as the *Los Angeles Times* and ABC, as well as to Asian and Latino media such as *La Opinión,* in order to reach multiethnic clientele (CSO Leaders 2 and 5):

> What is important is ... we recognize the importance of one another and work together ... In the past five to ten years, we have partnered with many different organizations ... We don't do anything new or try not to ... We share resources and subcontract ... for counselling work, education, environmental [initiatives] such as tree planting. (CSO Leader 2)

The involvement of the younger generation in community work did not come naturally. The 1992 L.A. riots were the landmark event that acted as a call for help to the U.S.-raised and -educated 1.5- and second-generation

Korean Americans and marked the beginning of their involvement in community work. The younger-generation professional leaders acted as frontline spokespersons for the community, providing Korean American views to the broader society on the causes and effects of the riots. Their contributions were particularly important, since they responded to the "white conspiracy hypothesis" that surfaced in the post-riot discourses (Min, 1996, p. 104). Despite the riot's connection to broader socioeconomic and racial issues present in the United States, media staged it as a Korean–African American conflict. ABC repeatedly played images of Soon Ja Du, a Korean grocery owner in South Central, shooting Latasha Harlins, an African American customer, and of Rodney King being beaten by police on the night of outbreak of the riots – the two incidents that many believed to be the cause of the riot (Min, 1996, p. 104). ABC's *Nightline* featured only African American leaders, "encouraging them to criticize Korean merchants without any Koreans being represented" (p. 105).

Korean Americans responded to this media coverage by sending complaints via letters and telephone calls, arguing that ABC was "biased, unbalanced, and sensational" (Min, 1996, p. 105). The complaints led ABC to prepare a follow-up show that focused on the Korean community (p. 105). Angela Oh, a second-generation Korean American defence lawyer, appeared on *Nightline* to voice the Korean community's opinion, which eventually "created a space for others to fill the political vacuum within the community" (Park, 1994, p. 200). Oh was quickly joined by 1.5- and second-generation Korean American service and political organizations such as the KAC and KYCC and by professional groups such as the Korean American Bar Association of Los Angeles and the Korean American Legal Advocacy Foundation (Min, 1996).

For the community as a whole, the 1992 L.A. riots had a few important implications. First, a power shift from the "old guard" led by first-generation immigrants to the younger generation is worth noting (E.J.W. Park, 2001, p. 278). While the first-generation immigrants vented their frustrations only through local Korean-language media, which had "little impact on the mainstream discourse" (p. 276), the younger generation could alter the mainstream discourse by participating in the intercultural dialogue. Second, the power shift suggested a division of labour in the community during the crisis. While the old guard consolidated the community by organizing a community crime-prevention patrol called "Tae Kuk Bang Bum Dae" (Min, 1996, pp. 155–157), the younger generation reached out to the broader public sphere by organizing rallies and writing letters to the editors of local mainstream newspapers, among other tactics. Third, the ways in which the old and young generations interpreted and reacted to the event showed a clear difference in understanding interethnic relations. While the older generation directed their anger towards the African Americans who participated in the riots, owing to their past experience with the African American community, the young generation directed their anger towards the police and the mainstream media that negatively exacerbated the situation by staging a Korean–African American conflict (Min, 1996).

Availability and Accessibility for Broader Political Interest Groups

Mainstream government officials and politicians also join in the Korean American discourse, especially during election periods, in order to gain support from the Korean community. Their interest often synchronizes nicely with the community's intent to create a path to mainstream politics by supporting local politicians. In such cases, Korean media provide a bridge for intercultural dialogue by covering stories about and delivering the voices of local politicians to the Korean community. Mainstream politicians may provide internships to qualified Korean Americans or support community projects such as the Koreatown electoral district (Y.H. Chang, 2009; S.J. Yang, 2011). In other instances, they join the debates hosted by Korean media. One example is the Los Angeles city attorney candidate debate organized by TVK24 on May 4, 2009, prior to the May 19 L.A. city attorney election. The two candidates, Carmen Trutanich and Jack Weiss, were invited to the debate, which was moderated by Christopher Lee, an L.A. city attorney (see Figure 4.1).

KOREAN MEDIA AS A MARKET

Korean media fill various self-directed and prescribed roles, both socio-cultural and political. Multiple roles for Korean media are possible, however, only if they survive as business entities in an increasingly competitive market. As in Vancouver, Korean media in L.A. are both promoters of and players within the local enclave economy – a window into immigrant small businesses and simultaneously enclave businesses themselves. One difference between the two cities is the presence of transnational media branches in L.A., which create a certain dynamic not present in Vancouver. This section discusses the relationship of immigrant and transnational media with the local enclave economy and their combined influence on availability of

FIGURE 4.1
L.A. city attorney
candidate debate,
Los Angeles
Wilshire Plaza
Hotel, L.A.,
May 4, 2009

and accessibility to Korean media for local Korean businesses as well as for broader industry stakeholders.

Korean Media as Promoters of Small Businesses
According to *The Korea Times L.A.*'s Korean Business Directory 2008–2009, there are more than 20,000 businesses in the five major Korean ethnoburbs of L.A., Orange, San Diego, San Bernardino, and Riverside Counties (*Korea*

Times L.A., n.d.-b), and 67% of these businesses (equivalent to 13,509) are located in L.A. County (E.H. Lee, 2010).[13] An analysis of those 20,000 Korean businesses suggests a shift in enclave businesses from traditional small businesses to professional businesses. In 2010, over 50% of these businesses were professional businesses such as hospitals and law offices, and accounting offices, signalling a "rearrangement of Korean businesses" from traditional labour-intensive immigrant businesses to professional, high profit–yielding businesses (E.H. Lee, 2010).[14] The growth of hospitals is most significant, with an increase of 100, which brings the total number of Korean hospitals in the analysis to 2,100. It is, in fact, the most flourishing business category in the community, followed by real estate agencies/realtors (1,650), restaurants (1,265), schools/academies (798), and automobiles (761; E.H. Lee, 2010). Businesses such as dry cleaners, shipping, and insurance, however, decreased by 5% to 10% during the economic recession (E.H. Lee, 2010). All of these businesses are main advertisers in Korean media.

The type of ads that appear in Korean media is one way to understand the overall Korean enclave economy and the economic integration of Korean immigrants. Table 4.8, based on a content analysis of ads, shows that auto/auto repair (12%) is most visible, followed by banking and finance (11%); restaurants (9%); travel, transportation, and accommodation (6%); and law agencies (6%). Locally oriented services such as restaurants (12%), law agencies (7%), and entertainment and sports events (5%) tend to prefer immigrant media, whereas transnational services or trading products such as travel agency, transportation, and accommodation (collectively, 9%) tend to prefer transnational media. Technology and telecommunication (17%), shopping malls and retailers (9%), media (8%), and government (6%) tend to prefer multicultural media over immigrant and transnational media. Note that government ads account for only 1% each for the latter two media types.

Consistent with the above-mentioned analysis, ads for Korean-owned financial institutions such as the Saehan Bank, Nara Bank, Central Bank, and Wilshire Bank, and medical institutions such as the Western 3rd Medical Center and Jaseng Center are noticeably present. These ads indeed demonstrate the transition in the Korean enclave economy from labour-intensive to professional businesses. Real estate agencies/realtors are also important clientele, although the actual proportion of total ads is small (as shown in Table 4.8). One of the leading agencies was spending $700,000 to $800,000 a year on advertising at the time of study (Media Practitioner 28). Transnational advertisers include regional branches of the Korean transnational corpor-

Table 4.8

Advertisers by source of capital, Los Angeles (%)

	Total	Local immigrant media	Transnational media	Multicultural media
	$N = 2{,}338$	$N = 1{,}087$	$N = 1{,}161$	$N = 90$
Auto/auto repair	12	14[a]	11[b]	6[b]
Bank/finance	11	13[a]	10[b]	9[a, b]
Restaurant	9	12[a]	7[b]	1[c]
Travel agency/transportation/ accommodation	6	4[a]	9[b]	1[a]
Law	6	7[a]	5[b]	–
Health product/ pharmaceutical	5	4[a]	5[b]	8[b]
Alcohol	4	2[a]	5[b]	9[b]
Beauty	3	3[a]	4[a]	–
Entertainment/sports event	3	5[a]	2[b]	–
Insurance	3	3[a]	4[a]	3[a]
Organization event/ announcement	3	3[a]	4[a]	2[a]
Technology/ telecommunication	3	2[a]	3[b]	17[c]
Supermarket	3	4[a]	2[b]	–
Shopping mall/retailer	3	2[a]	3[a]	9[b]
Media	3	2[a]	3[a]	8[b]
Electronic	3	3[a]	3[a]	–
Hospital/clinic/pharmacy	3	1[a]	4[b]	7[b]
Education	2	0.9[a]	3[b]	6[b]
Apparel/shoes/accessory	2	3[a]	1[a]	–
Furniture	2	2[a]	2[a]	2[a]
Real estate agency/realtor	1	0.3[a]	3[b]	–
Government (national)	1	1[a]	1[a]	6[b]
Other	8	9	8	8

NOTES: Numbers in the table are rounded off. Each subscript letter denotes a subset of column categories whose column proportions do or do not differ significantly from each other at the .05 level.

ations mentioned earlier, such as Korean Air, Kia Motors, and Bekseju America Inc. Direct importation of unedited transnational ads is quite common; the ads designed for audiences in Korea are used in L.A. for the local Korean audience (e.g., Bekseju).

Korean Media as Small Businesses

Korean media are also business ventures themselves, with enclave and transnational businesses as their clientele. According to interviews with media practitioners, estimates of the market size vary by outlet, ranging between $2,000,000 and $10,000,000 per month. Interestingly, small outlets (mostly immigrant media) tend to underestimate the overall size of the market, as they believe their share of the market is equivalent to the size of the entire market itself. By market share, the media practitioners interviewed generally estimated that transnational media branches take the majority of market share even though these outlets, by number, account for only 30% to 40% of the total number of media outlets. Backed up by a constant flow of content and transnational capital from headquarters, the transnational branches are able to surpass competing local immigrant media for shares of the market. Among these branches, the major dailies (approximately 60% of market share) take the lead, followed by TV, radio, weeklies, and the rest. According to one media practitioner, the market share has been consistently apportioned in this way since the 1980s:

> Do you think the advertising market is big? It is not, actually. There is no actual difference in terms of the volume of ads we did in the 1980s, in the 1990s, and what we do now ... (Name of company) made some difference. More new entries to the market also made some difference. However, the ads from K-town are all restaurant ads. Therefore, the overall volume may have increased; the actual share is the same. (Media Practitioner 37)

Thus, media outlets experience market competition differently depending on the size of the outlet. Media practitioners of the large outlets tend to say that the market has been "stable," since dailies dominate the market (Media Practitioner 28). Indeed, L.A.'s Korean media market experienced a boom of weeklies in the 1970s and 1980s (which occurred in Vancouver in the 1990s and 2000s) and has now entered a settling period. The small and micro media outlets, on the other hand, say that the market is still "unstable" with constant ebbs and flows of new entries, usually of similar small-size outlets. According to one media practitioner:

> The market is still volatile. Former employees left the company and opened up new outlets of their own. However, they did not survive for long. One went out of business after its first edition, and the second one after six months, and the third one after one and a half years. New entries offer lower rates or free ads. However, they cannot sustain themselves. They think it is easy. (Media Practitioner 39)

Despite the lopsided competition, high operating costs and limited revenue sources render all Korean media in L.A. dependent on advertising. Indeed, for many small outlets, expenses often exceed revenues. Looking first at operating expenses across the media outlets, personnel expenses account for approximately 50% of the total expenses. Other expenses vary by media type. For print media, printing and printing material costs are the second-greatest expense, accounting for 30% to 50% of direct expenses. Although most of the print media outlets publish both online and offline, the dependency on offline print publication is still high. Considering the number of pages for major publications, printing costs can take up a good portion of direct expenses. According to the author's count during the time of study, *The Korea Times* and *The Korea Daily* published from 140 to 180 pages from Monday to Saturday. The weekly total for the other two dailies (*Koreatown Daily* and *Korea Herald Business*) and the weeklies (e.g., *Kyocharo* [or *Kyocharo Daily* or *Korean Consumer Daily*]) ranged from 70 to 200 pages, with those that published three times a week at the higher end.

For television and radio, the dominant expense is airtime and/or broadcasting fees (to licence holders and content providers). Cable channels, for example, cost approximately $400,000 a month to operate for only three to four hours a day of airtime (Media Practitioner 38). Thus, only those media outlets that are financially strong can afford this expense. The high airtime fee is certainly a burden for many producers. As one media practitioner put it, "Increasing airtime fees upon every renewal in fact has pushed many out of the market ... What we are basically doing is getting money from the local enclave market and giving it to the licence holders" (Media Practitioner 24). The digital transition that started in 2009 opened up new opportunities for new entries. A digital 24-hour channel is available for approximately one-tenth of the analogue airtime fee. The lower airtime fee is the upside, but the higher content fee to fill 24 hours of programming is the downside. Thus, unless the media outlet has secured a constant flow of content, it is a challenge to budget for the increased hours. Some digital channels, in fact, have disappeared soon after startup. "It is quite common," said one media practitioner. "They think the television business is easy so they start it and then disappear overnight" (Media Practitioner 38).

Expenses are high but revenue sources are generally limited, depending on ownership and source of capital. The revenue sources for transnational media branches are relatively more dispersed, ranging from content sales to national and local advertising and subscriptions, whereas immigrant media depend almost entirely on local advertising (Media Practitioner 27). Based on a content analysis of 2,338 ads from L.A.'s 13 Korean media outlets, advertising accounts for up to 45% of space.[15] The proportion of advertising varies by media type: print media tend to dedicate proportionally more space to advertising than does broadcasting. When the ads on the front page of each section of the newspapers were counted, the four dailies dedicated from 35% to 45% of their total space to ads, with the highest being *The Korea Daily* (45%), followed by *Korea Herald Business* (43%), *Koreatown Daily* (41%), and *The Korea Times* (38%). For television, the ads account for 21% on average out of the total evening news time: KTN News, 29%; LA18 Prime Time Local News, 26%; KBS America News, 20%; TVK News Wide, 17%; TVK News English Edition, 12%; and MBC News Tonight, 10%.[16] For three radio evening news programs, ads account for 25% on average: Radio Korea, 30%; JBC, 24%; and Radio Seoul, 22%.

Dependence on local businesses, especially enclave businesses, is overwhelmingly high for all Korean media in L.A. regardless of the source of capital (see Table 4.9). Nearly 80% of the ads are from local Korean businesses. Multicultural media have a relatively smaller portion of local Korean businesses (63%) than immigrant media (77%) and transnational media (78%); however, this is compensated for by a relatively higher portion of mainstream businesses (22%). The overall proportion of mainstream ads, at 6%, may be small, but the revenue generated from that 6% is incomparable to that from the local Korean business: "In actual dollars, the mainstream ads will probably account for 50% of the total ad revenue. A few local enclave ads are equivalent to one mainstream ad" (Media Practitioner 32). Mainstream advertisers include transnational corporations (e.g., Verizon, McDonalds, State Farm, Toyota), government (e.g., Census, iWatch), and local professional services (e.g., Richard Hoffman, lawyer).

TABLE 4.9

Origin of advertisers by source of capital, Los Angeles (%)

	Total	Local immigrant media	Transnational media	Multicultural media
	N = 2,338	N = 1,087	N = 1,161	N = 90
Korean diaspora	77	77[a]	78[a]	63[b]
Korean transnational corporations	16	15[a]	17[a]	11[a]
Other diasporic communities	–	–	0.1[a]	–
Mainstream	6	6[a]	5[a]	22[b]
Absent/unknown	1	2[a]	0.3[b]	3[a]

NOTES: Numbers in the table are rounded off. Each subscript letter denotes a subset of column categories whose column proportions do or do not differ significantly from each other at the .05 level.

Other sources of revenue include subscriptions. All of the transnational media branches are paid services. *The Korea Times* and *The Korea Daily* are the only paid newspapers in the market: 75 cents at the newsstand or $22 per month by subscription. Figure 4.2 shows the newspaper dispensers available on the streets of Koreatown, one of the ways to purchase these papers if not subscribed. In the broadcasting sector, KBS America, MBC America, and SBS International are available on cable and satellite (e.g., Time Warner, Cox, Comcast, DirecTV, Dish Network) and are paid services, since they are available as part of subscription packages or at an additional fee only to subscribers. During the time of study, for example, Dish Network's Tiger Pack, which contained seven Korean-language channels (Arirang TV, BTN [Buddhist], JSTV [Christian], KBS World, ONGAMENET, The Golf Channel, and WOW-TV), was offered at an additional $19.99 (Dish TV U.S.A. n.d.). KBS World was included in Dish Network's basic pack, Dish America ($24.99 monthly as of 2011; for 2017 prices, see Dish Network, n.d.). The DirecTV's KoreanDirect, which provided 10 Korean channels (MBC, MBC Every1, SBS, SBS Plus, EBS, YTN, CTS, National Geographic Channel Korea, Radio Korea, and TAN TV), was also offered at an additional $26.99 per month – $31.99 if the Golf Channel was included (see KoreanDirect n.d.). Only those programs that were offered on digital over-the-air for three to four hours a day were free: for example, KBS World, on KXLA Ch. 44, and MBCD (MBC America's digital channel), on LA18.3.

FIGURE 4.2 **Newspaper dispensers, Los Angeles**
(From left to right) Street in K-town, unspecified local free daily, *ilgan Sports USA* (or *IS ilgan Sports*), *The Korea Times*, and *The Korea Daily*

In contrast to transnational media, the local immigrant media are almost all free. All dailies (*Koreatown Daily, Korea Herald Business*) and weeklies (e.g., *Sunday Journal, The Koreana News U.S.A.* or [*Koreana News*], *The Town News*) are available free at major Korean locations. TVK24's two channels, TVK1 and TVK2, are included as basic channels in the local cable network packages of Time Warner, Champion, Charter, and Cox and are available to their Southern California subscribers at no additional fee (TVK24, n.d.). Radio channels are available free 24 hours a day on AM frequencies: Radio Korea (AM1540), Radio Seoul (AM1650), and JBC (AM1230), until it was discontinued in February 2011.

Availability and Accessibility for Broader Industry Stakeholders

Intercultural Business Partnerships

As discussed, competition for Korean media outlets is mainly internal, and this internal competition in a saturated market pushes in-group–oriented Korean media to the broader market. Intercultural capacity-building beyond the Korean community has been attempted as one of many revenue-generating strategies over the years. A business partnership with the *Los Angeles Times* is especially noteworthy. Both *The Korea Times* (since 1999) and *The Korea Daily* have a long history of partnership with the *Los Angeles Times*. Both newspapers provide the *Los Angeles Times* Sunday edition to their subscribers (*Korea Times L.A.*, n.d.-a, and *Korea Daily L.A.*, n.d.-b). The partnership between *The Korea Times* and the *Los Angeles Times* is particularly strong. *The Korea Times* has established a joint delivery system with the *Los Angeles Times*, which is more cost effective than operating an in-house delivery system of its own or outsourcing delivery. Other types of collaboration include joint coverage of the 1988 Seoul Olympics and access to a photo archive. *The Korea Times* and the *Los Angeles Times* jointly developed a one-page promotional insert to promote local businesses. Also, as part of its community service, the *Los Angeles Times* opened access to its photo library to *The Korea Times* at no fee, with the condition that the photos be properly cited and permission be obtained from the section head prior to use. Along with the *Los Angeles Times*, *The Korea Times* also has ties with *The New York Times*. In the past, also as part of its community service, *The New York Times* offered training sessions to *The Korea Times*'s reporters on news production, although the sessions were more ad hoc than regularly scheduled. This partnership continues today through content sharing; *The Korea Times*'s website (www.koreatimes.com) has a separate tab leading to selected *New York Times* articles (in English, *Korea Times L.A.*, n.d.-d).

Nonetheless, media practitioners are somewhat unsupportive of, if not outright skeptical about, mainstream-diasporic partnerships. Some see these efforts more as marketing strategies in the form of customer service than as filling an actual need for mainstream content. Content partnerships are limited by two main factors: professional ego and the aspiration for a local Korean narrative instead of "their narrative" (Media Practitioner 26). As one media practitioner put it, "We do not want to ask a favour of mainstream media for content" (Media Practitioner 37). Another reason for skepticism is the fact that the flow of content from headquarters' international bureaus or news agencies is already sufficient (Media Practitioner 25). U.S. news (which is considered international news to Korean headquarters and news agencies but considered national news to Korean diasporic media in L.A.) is constantly provided by those sources and can be used with minor or no cultural translation, unlike mainstream news items:

> We have no intention of increasing local news through content sharing with mainstream media ... It is their news and their point of view ... We want to produce our own narratives. If we were to increase the local portion, we would rather include diverse views present in the U.S. [other than mainstream views]. (Media Practitioner 26)

The Seoul office has an international news department. It covers U.S. news. We use those items. We are the L.A. office so we focus on here. The (name of a province in Korea) office does not cover the Blue House. It is the Seoul office's job. (Media Practitioner 25)

U.S. Ad Team

On the market side, Korean media outlets are more dependent on mainstream advertisers than on other diasporic community advertisers, although in total, non-Korean enclave ads (such as nonsmoking, teacher recruiting, and Census ads) account for only six percent of the total, as the findings of a content analysis of the surrounding ads confirmed. Media practitioners collectively mentioned that there should be more mainstream ads, since they generate more revenue due to a higher rate. Furthermore, mainstream ads are the only breakthrough in the highly saturated enclave market (Media Practitioners 36 and 39). The economic recession has convinced the previously in-group–oriented media owners that the enclave economy is no longer self-sufficient. As a response, intercultural initiatives are emerging, such as a "U.S. ad team" or "foreign ad team" (where "foreign" means non-Korean) that is geared towards mainstream marketing (Media Practitioner 32). Second-generation Korean Americans usually lead the team:

Currently 99% of the ads are from Korean enclave businesses. Reaching out to mainstream advertisers is the only possible breakthrough. Right now, we have one [ad] from (name of company) and another one from a (name of company) ... Because the Korean population is big here, they want to advertise with [a] Korean newspaper ... What they care about most is geographic coverage. (Media Practitioner 39)

Conclusion

Korean media are indeed a community, civil society, and market for the Korean community in L.A. As a community, Korean media offer culturally translated news about *here* that helps Korean immigrants make sense of locality in the process of settlement and integration. In the digital era, the community role is further strengthened through online communities formed on the websites of print publications to provide "quick fix" solutions to particular concerns and to supplement a universal agenda of immigration settlement and community services. As a civil society, Korean media not only work as a community watchdog, monitoring mainstream media to correct misrepresentations of Koreans and the Korean community, but also mobilize the community to articulate *particular* Korean discourse on various *universal* urban geopolitical issues and push for political recognition in a broader political circle. As a market, Korean media are an indispensable part of the enclave economy as a promoter of other enclave businesses and employment, and they are simultaneously enclave businesses in and of themselves.

What differentiates L.A.'s media landscape from that of Vancouver is the dominance of transnational media branches, which sets up a competitive structure between transnational media and local immigrant media that is both economic and editorial. Economically, the two-horse race, led by leading transnational media branches, creates lopsided competition in which local immigrant media are inevitably in a vulnerable position in terms of content and financial mobilization. Editorially, transnational media branches' higher emphasis on news from and about Korea characterizes editorial direction and suggests a pervasive influence of Korea on Korean diaspora. A heightened emphasis on news about Korea in recent years is owed to Korea's new election law, passed in 2009. Now that overseas Korean citizens are eligible to vote, local Korean media assist them in making informed decisions and exercising their new rights.

Nonetheless, it is the financially strong media organizations, usually transnational media branches, that are capable of, and indeed are at the forefront of, *in-between* and *intercultural* initiatives and serving as media for all. As a community, initiatives such as "The Korea Times" English website (www.koreatimesus.com) and *The Korea Daily*'s Anabada Flea Market contribute to broadening availability and accessibility of Korean discourse for a broader audience. As a civil society, Korean media organize debates and roundtables to mobilize the community on various urban geopolitical issues that involve Koreatown (e.g., redrawing the Koreatown boundary and Koreatown electoral district). As a market, an in-house U.S. ad team is often formed to aggressively approach mainstream advertisers, including governments. Notably, many of these initiatives involve younger-generation Korean Americans. The division of labour in which first-generation media and CSOs look after internal communication while the younger generation reaches out to the broader society for intercultural communication works effectively. In a relative sense, these synergies are more substantial in L.A. than in Vancouver and are possible models that Vancouver's Korean media could emulate.

5
Locality, Ethnicity, and
.... Emerging Trends

In multicultural societies consisting of members from diverse ethnocultural and linguistic backgrounds, cultural literacy is an important precondition for optimal functioning of the community, civil society, and market. It is a foundation on which a common history can be built. Among the ways cultural literacy is improved, an *intercultural media system* in which mainstream and diasporic media are not only *available* to but also *accessible* for all members of society is particularly important. This system allows for voices from diverse communities to be adequately created, circulated, contested, and cultivated in everyday discourse and for all members of society to experience a full sense of belonging and have sufficient cultural literacy to make informed democratic choices.

This book focuses on diasporic media. Broadly, it examines how multicultural cities, diasporic communities, and their media help us to understand the media system of a multicultural society and the potential contribution of diasporic media for building an interculturally engaged media system. In doing so, it focuses on the extent to which diasporic media and the discourse these media produce are available and accessible for not only members of diasporic communities but also members of the broader society. This perspective is new. Earlier studies have focused primarily on the autonomous roles of diasporic media within their respective communities, with little attention to their role within the broader society. Certainly, there is more to learn about the autonomous roles of diasporic media, especially when considering how changes brought about by new media technologies and the participation of the younger generation in media production, among other factors, have continually expanded the role of diasporic media within and beyond diasporic communities in the past decades.

This same reason renders the understanding of the role of diasporic media within the broader society equally important. Diasporic media are not only a communicative space for diasporic communities; they also function as an indispensable part of the broader community, the public sphere, and the media industry, as discussed in previous chapters. Despite the transformation of diasporic media, however, the persisting perception within the arenas of policy, media industry, and academia, as well as the public sphere, is that diasporic media are "media *only* by, for, and about ethnic communities" (Yu, 2015, p. 133). Such conceptual or substantial marginalization of diasporic media as *media for the Other*, rather than *media for all*, makes existing diasporic media options underutilized and unnecessarily limits the opportunity for all members of society to be adequately exposed to multiple discourses from diverse communities. This continues when sufficient exposure is increasingly important for cultural literacy and the full exercise of citizenship in a multicultural society.

From this perspective, building an intercultural media system requires collective efforts from government, media sectors, industry associations, and academic institutions. The final two chapters address the key areas of this collective effort. This chapter revisits the case of Korean media and discusses the necessary efforts of and expectation for diasporic media. The final chapter returns to the policy discussion outlined in Chapter 2 and suggests areas in need of attention and relevant policy support.

The focus of this chapter is on how multicultural cities, their Korean communities, and Korean diasporic media produce both a creative dynamic and a tension in building an intercultural media system. Availability and accessibility are governed by multiple factors: immigration and media policies, demographics, the history of immigration, the development of communication infrastructure within diasporic communities, the language in which the content is produced (ethnic languages vs. English), the level of public awareness and promotion of diasporic media, and access costs, among others. This chapter specifically focuses on identifying the city-specific and ethnicity-specific factors that individually and collectively pose challenges and opportunities for broadening accessibility of Korean discourse for broader society – on the one hand, factors that are driven by locality, and on the other, Korean-specific factors that are commonly found among Korean media regardless of their locality. What are the contributions of Korean media in building an intercultural media system? Who are the key agents? And what more can be expected?

This chapter also addresses emerging new factors that add creative synergy to improving intercultural dialogue. In all of the efforts discussed here, the twofold focus is on two-way communication between diasporic communities and the broader society and the role of diasporic media in facilitating that dialogue.

Locality: City-Specific Factors

IMMIGRATION HISTORY AND YOUNGER-GENERATION LEADERSHIP

The communication infrastructures of the Korean communities in Vancouver and L.A. reflect the demographic diversity of the Korean populations in those cities and the populations' response to different characteristics of the city. As discussed in Chapter 2, L.A.'s Korean community has a relatively longer immigration history than Vancouver's does. In L.A., the earlier peak of immigration, stemming from the 1965 Immigration and Nationality Act (A.Y. Chung, 2007; K. Lee, 2000; Min, 2006b; Martin, 2005), resulted in a relatively larger proportion of younger-generation Koreans than in Vancouver (26%, compared to Vancouver's 17%) and, conversely, a smaller proportion of first-generation Koreans.

Within the Korean media sector, the stronger presence of younger-generation Korean Americans in L.A. is manifest in the creation of media specifically by and for this generation, such as the now-defunct *KoreAm Journal* and TVK24 – media that positively contribute to increasing the potential for wider distribution of Korean discourse beyond the Korean community. This sets L.A. apart from Vancouver, where only sporadic similar attempts have been made, such as the short-lived *Bridge*. Media practitioners interviewed in Vancouver expect to see more initiatives by and for the 1.5- and second-generation, both in Canada and the United States, owing to a generational shift in media ownership: first-generation Korean media owners are passing their businesses down to their children (Media Practitioner 8).

The longer immigration history of L.A.'s Korean community and the complicated racial relations in the United States also have resulted in more interracial and interethnic interactions – some positive and others negative. This particular experience grants extra significance to Korean media as a way to express diverse voices and consolidate community action. Historically, the middleman minority position of Korean merchants in the local economy, with no prior experience and knowledge about U.S. race relations, has often left them vulnerable in challenging interracial interactions (Min, 1996; E. Chang and Diaz-Veizades, 1999).[1] One example of this, mentioned in Chapter 4, is a Korean–African American conflict in which a Korean grocery owner in South Central, Soon Ja Du, fatally shot Latasha Harlins, an African American customer. Along with Rodney King's case, this incident was believed by many to be the cause of the 1992 L.A. riots (Min, 1996). The interracial tension continues today, as is manifest in various Koreatown projects, such as the redrawing of the Koreatown boundary and consolidating Koreatown as a single electoral district (see Chapter 4).

In many of these interracial relations, the younger-generation Korean Americans and their leadership through their Koreatown–located advocacy groups, such as KAC and KIWA, are worthy of attention. As discussed in Chapter 4, there is a clear division of labour across generations. That is, while the first-generation media facilitate dialogue among first-generation Koreans, the younger generation facilitates the intercultural dialogue between the Korean community and the broader society – specifically, mainstream media. Their approach to this dialogue is more *universal* than *particular* (or diasporic) and is also *in-between* and *intercultural* through attention to overall structural issues underlying racial relations rather than to ethnic-specific frustrations.

This type of approach is common in the younger generation's leadership of community activities; indeed, it is one of the notable differences from older-generation leadership in Koreatown. The younger-generation leaders tend to forge pan-ethnic leadership by focusing on geography rather than ethnicity, serving Koreatown residents in general rather than Koreans in particular. Certainly, it is a new form of ethnic enclave, advancing the former notion of "place of stigma" to "neighbourhood of hope," changing a place of ethnic segregation within the urban geography to a site of cross-ethnic and intercultural collaboration (Murdie and Skop, 2011, p. 64). The transition is not unrelated to the younger generation's attention to the unique characteristics of Koreatown. Unlike many other ethnic enclaves, where members of the community own businesses as well as establish their residences, Koreatown comprises mainly Korean-owned businesses but non-Korean residents. This distinction has indeed been a barrier for many Korean community projects, as discussed in Chapter 4. The younger generation's pan-ethnic leadership and service to *all* residents contributes to turning barriers into opportunities.

As discussed in Chapter 1, Ball-Rokeach's communication infrastructure theory looks at the relationship among residents, diasporic media, and community organizations to understand the possibility for the communication infrastructure serving as a civil society. While understanding each of the components that constitute the structure is important, the case of the Korean community suggests that identifying key agents in each component and understanding their roles for community projects is equally important. For the Korean community's internal communication, the first-generation media and civil society organizations (CSOs) provide a space for *particular* expression. For the Korean community's intercultural outreach and communication with the broader community, it is the younger-generation media and CSOs and their *universal* agenda that contribute to broadening both the availability and accessibility of Korean discourse for the broader society. As this division of labour demonstrates, cross-generational ties and synergy is critical for young diaspora like the Korean community and can maximize community efforts in broadening availability and accessibility of Korean discourse and building a functioning civil society within and across communities. Such collaboration is desirable in Vancouver's Korean community, in which younger-generation leadership in community projects is, at the time of writing, relatively weak.

TRANSNATIONAL MEDIA BRANCHES: FRIENDS OR FOES?

The longer immigration history of the Korean community in L.A. vis-à-vis Vancouver has generated a longer history of Korean media in L.A. Indeed, Korean media in L.A. pioneered Korean diasporic media in North America, beginning in the late 1960s with *The Korea Times* (or *Hankook Ilbo*, est. 1969) and followed a few years later by *The Korea Daily* (or *JoongAng Ilbo*, est. 1974). The different phases of development – the formation period in the 1970s and 1980s, followed by the growth and expansion period in the 1990s and the 2000s – saw a balanced entry of all media types, allowing room for new entries to settle in and compete with the existing ones. At the centre of this development are transnational media branches. The significance of the Korean immigrant population in L.A. – as the largest Korean diaspora in North America – provided enough reason for Korean media conglomerates to set up their branches in this city. In addition, the branches were considered as a route to the American market, as mentioned during the interviews (Media Practitioner 24).

The consequences of these branches being established have been both positive and negative. In contrast with the heavy concentration in the print media sector in Vancouver, a relatively balanced growth in all media types in L.A. is one of the positive consequences. This allows Korean media to be available and accessible in all media types for local Korean immigrants. Furthermore, the contribution of transnational media branches to many intercultural projects in all three dimensions – community, civil society, and market – is another positive outcome (see Chapter 4). Although these intercultural initiatives have involved not only transnational media but also financially strong immigrant media organizations, the leadership of the former is certainly visible. "The Korea Times" English website (www.koreatimesus.com) is a notable contribution, after years of continuous trial and error. The annual Korean Heritage Day, sponsored by *The Korea Times,* and the annual Anabada Flea Market, sponsored by *The Korea Daily,* are also important contributions that help promote the presence of the Korean community in greater L.A. On the market level, the so-called U.S. ad team is another step forward. Although it is a survival strategy developed from years of overcompetition in a saturated enclave market, initiatives such as this one certainly broaden accessibility to the Korean enclave economy to broader industry stakeholders.

The downside of this situation is transnational media's orientation towards Korea. As the content analysis found, there is certainly more emphasis in transnational media on news about and from Korea compared to immigrant and multicultural media (see Chapter 4). The transnationalization of Korean politics and economics (e.g., Korea's election law) and the potential influence on Korean American politics and economics is present. Despite the fact that the diverse audience segments and information needs demand a certain degree of *Korea influence,* the overwhelming preoccupation with matters concerning Korea raises concerns among Korean media practitioners, as expressed by one media practitioner:

> In the future, we need to focus on promoting Korean American identity, instead of providing general information ... to provide direction on how to settle in America ... Korean media so far have focused on Korean politics ... Koreans here know about Korean politics more than Koreans in Korea do. That is wrong ... Even the entertainment section covers mostly Korean celebrities ... What is the relevance? Publishers' attitudes need to change. (Media Practitioner 35)

Another downside is the competition between transnational media branches and locally developed immigrant media, with the latter inevitably in a weaker or also-ran position. Competition for advertisers (primarily

local enclave businesses) is inevitable, and the dependency on the local enclave market is high regardless of source of capital. As discussed in Chapter
4, 77% of L.A.'s ads are generated from enclave businesses. By medium,
newspapers in L.A. have a high dependency on enclave businesses (88%),
with a much smaller proportion of mainstream ads (6%). As one media
practitioner put it, "We have 13 television services in a one million dollar
market. Is it realistically possible to operate with $50,000 a month?" (Media
Practitioner 28).[2] One consequence is staff layoffs as part of cost-saving
strategies. Then the dominoes start falling: a shortage of human resource
overloads an individual's share of work, which consequently challenges the
commitment to investigative journalism (Yu, 2017b).

Vancouver's Korean media market, on the other hand, was formed much
later than L.A.'s. *The Korean Canadian News* (est. 1983) and *The Vancouver
Korean Press* (or *The Chosun Ilbo Vancouver Edition*, est. 1986) were launched
in the 1980s, when L.A.'s market already had all media types in place (dailies
and weeklies, television, and radio). Vancouver's Korean media are entirely
immigrant owned, mainly by those who immigrated in the post-1986
Business Immigration Program period. Thus, if L.A.'s market competition is
between immigrant media and transnational media branches, Vancouver's
competition is among immigrant-owned media in the print sector.
Vancouver's Korean media are also mainly print media. The relatively
smaller amount of immigrant capital (compared to the transnational capital
of L.A.'s Korean media) has led to an overconcentration in the print media
sector, which requires a relatively smaller initial investment. Underregulation
of the print sector provides additional motivation to immigrants. As a result,
Vancouver's Korean media market saw a boom of weeklies in the 2000s, with
six new weeklies launched in the same year (2007), although only a few of
them survive today. Such a heavy concentration in one media sector is certainly a concern, since more fierce competition is likely to put availability
and accessibility of Korean discourse at risk. Intercultural initiatives are not
absent in Vancouver but are often indirect, manifesting as community events
rather than media content. English-language media such as L.A.'s "The
Korea Times" English website and TVK24 are not yet available in Vancouver.

Transnational media branches do not exist in Vancouver, although the
prospect cannot be dismissed. As one Vancouver media practitioner said,
"All immigrant media services may not be able to be sustainable down the
road, since Korean broadcasting companies set up their own branches in
North America and create competition against the immigrant services ...

They are going to eat us up" (Media Practitioner 7). Thus, Korean Canadian producers feel a need to prepare for the possible transnational expansion into the Canadian market through localization and specialization. Measures being considered or underway include partnering with Korea's cable channels to secure content (which is what immigrant media in L.A. are doing), developing geographically specific programs, and expanding into media-related businesses such as equipment sales.

Ethnicity: Ethnicity-Specific Factors

Although the historical particulars may be different in the two cities, both the production of Korean discourse as a factor of the sociocultural capacity of media institutions and dependency on the enclave market are consistent regardless of locality. It is important to note, however, that these similarities are the result of the dynamic interplay of various factors rather than being entirely attributable to ethnicity.

MEDIA PREDOMINANTLY BY AND FOR FIRST-GENERATION KOREAN IMMIGRANTS

Although L.A.'s Korean community has a relatively larger proportion of the younger generation, both L.A. and Vancouver communities are first-generation–dominant diasporas whose high dependency on the mother tongue characterizes the Korean enclave in general. The We Speak English campaign in Koreatown, discussed in Chapter 4, is one example that illustrates the level of integration of Koreatown in L.A.'s urban economy. Koreatown, the economic hub of the Korean enclave economy, has been self-sufficient over the years mainly through in-group, in-language clientele. Thus, within the broader urban geography of the city of L.A., Koreatown is a sociocultural and economic space used mainly by ethnocultural populations rather than broadly by *all*. More than thirty years after the official designation of Koreatown, the community is finally pursuing an intercultural marketing campaign to respond to the general perception that Koreatown business owners and employees speak limited English.

Thus, it is not surprising that Korean media are predominantly Korean-language media by and for Korean immigrants. Except for younger-generation media in L.A. such as the former *KoreAm Journal* and TVK24 Channel 2, all active Korean media during the time of study produced content in the Korean language, and the producers and audiences of those media were predominantly Korean immigrants. A natural consequence is that the emphasis is more on delivering news about *here* to the community than de-livering Korean community news to the broader society, although the latter is never dismissed. Limitations exist either way, attributed to factors that include the level of producers' cultural literacy – that is, knowledge about *here* (Yu, 2016a).[3] In Vancouver, for example, a majority of outlets are owned by those who arrived in the 1990s and 2000s, owing largely to the 1986 Business Immigration Program (see Chapter 2). As I have argued elsewhere (Yu, 2016a), the lead time between media owners' immigration to Canada and the start-up of their media business is between 5 and 22 years. The lead time is shorter for the post-1986 immigrants than for the post-1967 immi-grants. It is even shorter for staff reporters who began their current or for-mer employment almost immediately upon their immigration to Canada. In other words, they started to engage in news production when their cul-tural literacy was still low and they themselves were immigrants still in the process of integration. Related to this lack of cultural literacy is official lan-guage proficiency. A lack of bilingual reporters in Korean diasporic news-rooms is common. Certainly, the level of cultural and language fluency of journalists does influence how much and how well they deliver news about here to the community and news about the community to the broader soci-ety (Yu, 2016a).

Nonetheless, it is also true that nearly 50 years of Korean media history in North America has produced media practitioners of established tenure in the local Korean media sector – an average of nine years for Vancouver and 13 years for L.A. (Yu, 2016a). In other words, the Korean media have re-tained media practitioners who are integrated into the broader society and are capable of cultural translation, although some are still skeptical about this claim. In *Becoming Intercultural,* Y.Y. Kim (2001, p. 77) argues that "rela-tively stress-free ethnic communication experiences" can delay the process of cultural adaptation by limiting the "opportunities to participate in the social communication activities of the host environment"; however, ethnic media can "facilitate cross-cultural adaptation in the initial phases as long as the coethnics involved are themselves well adapted." In other words, if the media practitioners (journalists and senior management who are involved in news production) are themselves well integrated into the broader society, diasporic media can contribute to intercultural dialogue and civic engage-ment. Certainly, young diasporas have their own limitations in making their discourse available and accessible for audiences within and beyond their respective communities. This shortcoming makes collaboration within the community – especially between the first generation and the younger generation, as well as between media organizations and community organizations – critical.

RELATIONSHIP WITH MULTIETHNIC CSOs

The role of "collective actors" (Gamson, 2001, p. 68) is especially important for diasporic communities, since immigrants as individuals have limited sociocultural and linguistic capital with which to take action, even if they wish to. For diasporic discourse to reach the public sphere effectively, whether to influence broader public discourse or policy decision-making processes, diasporic media may act independently or in collaboration with CSOs to collect community opinion and speak on behalf of the community. Again, Ball-Rokeach's theory of communication infrastructure is useful here to understand the level of institutional connection that works towards building an intercultural media system.

While English editions and other intercultural initiatives were conscious efforts by diasporic media organizations in both cities, multiethnic civil society organizations have emerged rather organically. As discussed in Chapters 3 and 4, Korean media's relationship with these multiethnic organizations seems to be generally more productive than that with the community's own CSOs. In Vancouver, Korean community workers at immigrant settlement agencies take leadership roles in providing immigrant settlement services to the Korean community, either through providing service-related columns to Korean media or through the organization of events such as resource fairs (see Chapter 3). This involvement is critical in the absence of Korean CSOs that are capable of providing all of the necessary settlement services. The Korean Society of B.C. only occasionally provides ad hoc services, and the organizations led by the younger-generation Korean Canadians focus largely on sociocultural issues of their own rather than on settlement services for immigrants. These workers also serve as a liaison between the Korean community and interest groups in the wider community by broadening access on each end and facilitating communication. In L.A., the equivalent organizations are headed by younger-generation Korean Americans and cater to the needs of all Koreatown residents, as mentioned earlier. Again, collaboration with multiethnic organizations contributes to broadening availability and accessibility of Korean discourse for the broader society. All of this collaboration further reminds us of the importance of similar efforts to engage with multiethnic news sites such as the "Alhambra Source," an online hyper-local multilingual space discussed earlier, to amplify Korean discourse in the broader society. Instead of young diasporic media trying to commit to both internal and intercultural communication, collaboration with multiethnic media initiatives can be considered in order to create a positive synergy to multiply public discourse.

RELATIONSHIP WITH KOREAN CSOS WITHIN THE COMMUNITY

Korean media's collaboration with first-generation Korean CSOs is not absent in either Vancouver and L.A. but seems to lack cohesion. Community leaders express difficulties in community-level collaboration, even while admitting that Koreans are generally "very nationalistic ... pure race ... [a mentality of] we and us and ourselves only" (CSO Leader 2). Such a discrepancy is, in fact, consistent with the findings of a Korean community study conducted for the City of Vancouver, Canadian Heritage, and MOSAIC in 2000 as part of the City's Community Profile/Needs Assessment Project. The report identified "divisions in the Korean population" and "a lack of a sense of community" (Martin Spigelman Research Associates, 2000). In response to this, community leaders pointed out several factors, including different times of arrival in Canada and varying socioeconomic levels, the increasingly transnational nature of settlement, and a generation gap between first-generation and Canadian-born second-generation Koreans. In other words, there are divides within the community along socioeconomic and generational lines. Conflicts between old and new immigrants, economically privileged and underprivileged, and first-generation and 1.5- and second-generation are manifest at both the individual and institutional levels:

> We see fragmentation between old immigrants who came with nothing versus new immigrants with money who play golf every day ... And there are 1.5- and second-generation immigrants who don't really speak Korean ... Some Korean student organizations are fragmented by Korean language ability, those who can speak Korean versus [those] who can't. (CSO Leader 2)

Similarly, in pursuing these community projects in L.A., Korean media collaborate frequently with CSOs. Although some interactions are productive while others are conflict-ridden, as part of the overall communication infrastructure, Korean media and CSOs are in a mutually supportive relationship. CSOs are good news sources for media (Media Practitioner 28), and media are important communication routes for CSOs to promote their activities. In fact, for not-for-profit organizations that depend on public and private funding, media coverage of their activities is an important part of funding applications: "I think every year, we have about 300 to 400 media hits ... It is pretty much every day" (CSO Leader 3). The frequency of coverage is one thing, but the tone of coverage is another. As one CSO leader put it, "Negative coverage in Korean media affects private funding. For example, (name of company) never sponsors any organizations that are related to either any specific religion or community conflicts" (CSO Leader 5). CSOs thus proactively cultivate media relations by organizing "media roundtables" to share and educate Korean media on the agendas they pursue (CSO Leader 3). One example of this kind is a roundtable organized by the Korean Resource Center (KRC) titled "Effects of the California Budget Crisis on the Korean-American Community," on March 16, 2011. Such a collaboration is, in fact, the most desired form of collaboration, as mentioned by journalists during interviews.

One barrier to media–CSO collaboration mentioned during the interviews is a divided sense of belonging *here* (Media Practitioners 25 and 32). One *Korea Times* columnist stated the problem clearly: "Korean Americans are silent during the U.S. election but loud during the Korean election for which they have no voting rights" (Yeo, 2008).[4] For first-generation Koreans, it is Korea's politics, more than U.S. politics, that they pay attention to. Interestingly, though, the reactions to Korea's new election law vary. For some Korean community leaders, voting rights in Korean elections mean regaining first-class citizenship (Korean citizenship) – the symbolic significance of which may not be an overstatement, considering the prevailing perception of overseas Koreans as "second-class citizens" (Yu, 2016a, p. 9). After the law was enacted, some community leaders were pleased that a "long-cherished wish has finally been obtained" and expected "policies for overseas Koreans from the Korean government" to improve "overseas Korean rights" (N.Y. Kim, 2009):

> 1.5- and second-generation Koreans are more interested in political issues. The actual audience of our news, however, is relatively less interested in political issues ... Instead, they are interested in what is happening in K-town and what is on sale in which Korean market.

We prioritize news accordingly ... 1.5- and second-generation Koreans watch mainstream news ... Compared to ABC, CBS, and CNN, our capacity to cover mainstream accidents or events is just inadequate. (Media Practitioner 25)

Some other CSO leaders and media practitioners, however, think otherwise, anticipating further fragmentation of the Korean community between Koreans versus Korean Americans (CSO Leader 6). The issue is likely to heat up if election campaigning (advertising and speeches) through overseas Korean media is allowed. A bill was brought before the National Assembly of Korea on motions in 2011 (C.S. Kim, 2011), and the legal provisions on election campaigning through digital means, announced by the National Election Commission the following year, allows Korean candidates to advertise to overseas voters through Internet home pages, email, and Internet media advertising (S.K. Kim, 2012).

Relationship with mainstream media

In both cities, interaction with mainstream media is limited. Other than formal interactions related to content licensing and agreements, the day-to-day interaction between Korean and mainstream journalists consists of more or less random calls for a quick reference check or on-site interactions at press conferences. Mainstream journalists contact Korean journalists sporadically when they need more information on Korean-related incidents. Inquiries include information about people – usually about those who were involved in local incidences – or issues about North Korea (e.g., nuclear proliferation) or South Korea (e.g., Pyungchang's lost bid for the winter Olympics; Media Practitioners 5 and 6). These sporadic interactions pose a concern for cultural translation on the part of mainstream journalists. As discussed in Chapters 3 and 4, cultural translation is one of the key merits of Korean media; and it depends on Korean journalists' cultural literacy about Canada and the United States (Yu, 2016a). If the same logic is applied to mainstream journalists, it raises a question of how much and how well multicultural reporting (or diversity reporting) is done in mainstream newsrooms. As evidence of this, a Vancouver Korean journalist recalls that during the time of the murder-suicide case of a Korean family in Victoria discussed in Chapter 3, the journalist was contacted by mainstream reporters and asked about potential cultural implications, even though the incident was about family violence related to financial difficulties (Media Practitioner 10).

Similarly, L.A.'s Korean media interact with mainstream media on an issue-by-issue basis, mostly on issues that involve the misrepresentation of Korea or the Korean community in mainstream media, as mentioned earlier. Mainstream media approach Korean media mostly for a quick reference on events "that are big enough to be of interest to the broader society" (Media Practitioner 38). Examples include the cases of Euna Lee, a South Korea–born American journalist who was detained in North Korea in 2009, and Yuna Kim, a South Korean gold-medal figure skater in the 2010 Vancouver Olympics (Media Practitioners 21 and 28). In the case of Euna Lee, a CSO leader recalls that ABC reporters were stationed in one of the CSOs in Koreatown for 24 hours to follow the story's progress (CSO Leader 5). In addition to these events, a local Koreatown event that received mainstream media attention was the conflict with the Bangladeshi community over the Koreatown boundary (Media Practitioner 28).

Indeed, diasporic-mainstream media collaboration has proven challenging for many reasons, from institutional rivalry to institutional indifference (Ramirez, 2011; Rong, 2015). Nevertheless, benefits to both parties are clear: "It's a way to expand your talent base," according to Manny Garcia, executive editor of *El Nuevo Herald* (Ramirez, 2011, para. 3). Not many mainstream newsrooms are equipped with multicultural language ability and cultural literacy to cover diverse stories. Of equal importance, diasporic media are often understaffed and in the process of sociocultural integration. A lack of human resources, both in absolute number of reporters and the number of bilingual reporters with adequate cultural literacy, is one of the barriers for broadening availability and accessibility of Korean discourse within and across communities.

As discussed earlier, Korean media in Vancouver, for example, are mostly mom-and-pop, small business–style companies of fewer than 15 employees. Dailies are on the higher end in terms of number of employees, whereas weeklies are on the lower end, often operating with a bare minimum staff of an editor, a reporter, a graphic designer, and a delivery person; in some cases, a company consists of one person who plays all of these roles. Similarly, in L.A., a lack of human resources is a constant problem: "We are a community paper with an understaffed structure" (Media Practitioner 31). The number of items for which each reporter is responsible on an average day varies by media type and size of outlet, ranging from three to ten items. "I write ten articles per day," said one media practitioner. "We cannot expect depth of information with this level of workload ... Our chief editor, however, encourages us to write at least one or two feature articles a week" (Media Practitioner 32). Another interviewee noted, "In order to be politically active, we should be able to engage in the debate. We simply do not have that capacity" (Media Practitioner 37). When one of the Korean dailies was approached by New America Media, a network of ethnic media organizations in the United States, and asked to contribute stories, it had to turn the offer down because of a lack of human resources, even though it was a chance for Korean discourse to be distributed beyond the Korean community (see Chapter 4).

That said, diasporic-mainstream media collaboration helps fill that gap. A recent *New York Times* story demonstrates the synergy between diasporic and mainstream media on an individual level. In 2015, Sarah Maslin Nir, a reporter at *The New York Times,* published "The price of nice nails," a 7,000-word story about labour exploitation of nail salon manicurists in New York City (Nir, 2015). Interestingly, diasporic media in the same city had been covering this story for more than a decade without reaching a broader audience. The story finally reached mainstream media when a story pitch by Rong Xiaoqing, a reporter at *Sing Tao Daily,* a Chinese language newspaper, was picked up by Nir (Rong, 2015). Nir's story – translated into Korean, Chinese, and Spanish – reached local and global readers. According to Elisabeth Goodridge, deputy editor with the Metro desk at *The New York Times,* "readers based in South Korea" were visiting the newspaper's website for the first time: "We are overwhelmed by the reaction, and on every single metric we were so pleased" (Bech, 2015, para. 6). Is this something we can expect more of when an intercultural media system is in place? Perhaps, and maybe even more creative and innovative synergy can be anticipated.

Of course, not all collaborations are successful. Nonetheless, in all cases, networking seems to be critical on this playing field. As emphasized by Kai Wright, then editorial director of Colorlines.com: "A lot of stuff is based on relationships. And editors of ethnic-based media are less likely to have relationships with the editors of ProPublica or wherever" (Ramirez, 2011, para. 9). Indeed, it took Rong at *Sing Tao Daily* 12 years of persistent investigative reporting efforts to produce meaningful synergy with Nir at *The New York Times.* This suggests that Korean media whose publications are produced almost entirely in their own ethnic language, like Rong's *Sing Tao Daily,* face enormous challenges in collaborating with mainstream media. Yet intercultural networking is essential for broadening accessibility for a broader audience.

The Emerging Trends: The Korean Wave, YouTube, and Cultural Literacy

Korean diasporic media now face a new phase. Among many factors, the Korean Wave (or *hallyu*), which is spreading in North America, is one. As many media practitioners interviewed for this study agreed, more and more non-Korean audiences have tuned into their programs as Korean drama and K-pop have increased in popularity in North America. For so-called K-pop fans, Korean diasporic media provide a way to stay connected to K-pop celebrities. In fact, a survey conducted by YA Entertainment, a major Korean drama distributor in North America, found that over 90% of Korean drama viewers were not Korean (Chen, Nguyen, Bernick, and Chen, 2006). The Korean Wave reached its peak when Psy's *Gangnam Style* became a YouTube sensation in 2012, attracting two billion views overall (Associated Press, 2014). All of these external factors – none of which feature diasporic production – contribute to promoting Korea in North America and improving the cultural literacy of North Americans about Korea. For availability and accessibility of diasporic media, this new dynamic creates a new path to reach out to the broader society and diversify public discourse.

THE KOREAN WAVE

The Korean Wave characterizes the popularity of Korean cultural products spreading from Asia to North America and Europe. The views on the genesis of this phenomenon vary. D. Shim (2006) dates it back to the late 1990s, when two Korean dramas – *What is Love All About* and *Stars in My Heart* – aired consecutively in 1997 (and re-aired in 1998) and 1999 through China Central Television (CCTV) and earned great popularity. Ryoo (2009, 139), on the other hand, points to 2004, when *Winter Sonata,* a South Korean television drama series, became "something of a frenzy," starting in Japan and spreading across Asia. The political economy of Asia in general and the cultural industries in particular at the turn of the century explains the context of such a spike. In general, Asia was going through an unprecedented economic crisis, and for countries like South Korea, a bailout from the International Monetary Fund (IMF) was inevitable. For the cultural industries, this meant a preference for cheaper programs among Asian buyers, and Korean programs were a perfect alternative to high-priced Japanese ones (D. Shim, 2006).

What preceded the economic crisis was the liberalization of the cultural industries across Asia, which essentially threw the doors open for these industries. In Korea, the cultural industries experienced unprecedented freedom. The level of censorship decreased dramatically after the 1993 inauguration of President Kim Young-sam, the first civilian to lead the government after more than 30 years of military leadership (S. Kwon and Kim, 2013). Further deregulation occurred during the subsequent Kim Dae-jung administration (1998–2003), with the relaxation of constraints on foreign firms and an increase of funding opportunities for domestic firms, from KRW5 billion in 1994 (under the Kim Young-sam administration) to KRW640 billion (S. Kwon and Kim, 2013).

China, following Deng Xiao Ping's "four modernization policy" in the 1980s, also liberalized the film and television industries in the early 1990s (J. Yang, 2012). The relationship between "modernization" and "ideological control" is discussed as a useful parameter to examine changes in the cultural industries in China including the import of Korean cultural products (Leung, 2008, p. 58; J. Yang, 2012). In Taiwan, the liberalization of the market led to the liberalization of the cultural industries. Under pressure from the United States, a new copyright law and cable television law were introduced in 1992 and 1993, respectively (J. Yang, 2012). The latter opened the market for foreign programs to take up to 80% of total airtime and consequently increased the demand for foreign programs to fill this time. Korean programs were not adopted immediately for political and cultural reasons – including the establishment of a Korea-China diplomatic relationship and the perception in Taiwan of Korean cultural products being backward (J. Yang, 2012). However, in 2000, the success of the Korean drama *Fireworks* revaluated Korean cultural products.

As the Korean Wave spread in Asia and beyond, the Korean cultural industries became preoccupied with exporting their products abroad. The industries saw a giant leap forward in total sales, from U.S.$600 million in 2001 to U.S.$3.22 billion in 2010 (S. Kwon and Kim, 2013, p. 518). In 2010, the export of Korean programs alone totalled U.S.$187 million, and among all genres, drama accounted for 88% (equivalent to U.S.$133 million; Republic of Korea, Ministry of Culture, Sports, and Tourism, 2011).[5]

YouTube and Psy's *Gangnam Style*

The Korean Wave peaked with Psy's YouTube sensation, *Gangnam Style*. Korea's so-called idol groups, such as Girls' Generation and Super Junior (S.M. Entertainment), have had global appeal, manifest in international fandom spanning continents. Nevertheless, Psy is second to none, with his video being a record-setting sensation. According to the *Financial Post*, "no other video comes close to *Gangnam* on the streaming service's list of top videos" (Leong, 2014). Within three months of its debut (July 15, 2012), the song became the "most 'liked' video in YouTube history" and "topped charts worldwide" (Brady, 2012). Also within less than six months, it became "the first video to have over one billion views on YouTube" and was "watched seven to 10 million times a day on average" ("PSY's 'Gangnam style' hits one billion," 2012). Indeed, in November 2012, the video had surpassed Justin Bieber's "Baby" on YouTube, and earned U.S.$8-million through the site in 2012 alone ("PSY's 'Gangnam style' hits one billion," 2012; Leong, 2014). Given this almost overnight fame, *The Washington Post* described Psy as a "global pop tsunami from South Korea" (Richards, 2012), and *Newsweek* called him an "Internet anomaly" and declared his song to be "the biggest thing since the Macarena" (Stern, 2012). *Rolling Stone* also commented that "single-handedly shattering a century's worth of Anglo-American pop hegemony is a tough gig" and called *Gangnam Style* "the fastest-spreading Asian viral phenomenon since SARS" (Hiatt, 2012).

Billboard attributes its success to its "accessible electro-dance production, with zippy synths that lead to a breakdown with easy-to-remember lyrics," all of which appeals to both "Western and Eastern listeners" and could instruct other "international acts on how to successfully break the U.S. language barrier" (Blistein, 2012). Psy's connection to the United States as a former student at Boston University and Berklee College of Music in 1996 has also been widely mentioned, especially in Korea, as a factor that enabled Psy to respond to the global fame more immediately and professionally (Stern, 2012). For Psy himself, however, the success was rather the result of painstaking efforts: "me and my choreographers in Korea spent 30 nights doing every animal," he said, referring to his signature horse-riding dance (Stern, 2012).

Nonetheless, YouTube, a product of media digitalization and convergence, cannot be discounted as a contributing factor (Havens and Lotz, 2012). Indeed, Psy's case resembles that of Susan Boyle, of "Britain's Got Talent" fame, who received global attention after her performance on that program subsequently appeared on YouTube ("Korean dramas," 2010). The contribution of the Internet to transnational consumption of cultural products is indeed powerful. The production of over 500 tribute videos by individuals around the globe certainly confirms Psy's contribution to broadening accessibility to Korean cultural products ("The 'Gangnam Style' tribute supercut," 2012).

THE KOREAN WAVE IN NORTH AMERICA AND THE IMPLICATIONS
FOR DIASPORIC MEDIA

The Korean Wave arrived in North America well ahead of Psy's *Gangnam Style*. In the mid-2000s, cable and broadcasting television provided Korean dramas to over 25 million households in the U.S., and, particularly in the Bay Area, they earned higher ratings than ABC's *Extreme Makeover* ("Survey shows most U.S. fans of Korean dramas," 2006; Y. Kim, 2007, pp. 146–147). The popularity of Korean drama cannot be discussed without *Jewel in the Palace* (or *Dae Jang Geum*), which is often considered the key contributor to its success. The *San Francisco Chronicle* reported that more than 100,000 people watched the drama in the Bay Area alone ("U.S. audiences," 2005). Hollywood is also interested in Korean cinema. For example, Chan-wook Park's *Oldboy* and Ki-duk Kim's *3-Iron* were remade and screened in 2005 (Mazurkewich, 2005).

Benefiting from this earlier groundwork, a new type of Korean diasporic media is emerging to initiate what may become the Korean American Wave. One successful case is DramaFever, an online streaming service. This is indeed a case of broadening accessibility not only to Korean cultural products for a broader audience but also to Korean diasporic media for industry stakeholders interested in cross-industry partnerships. Launched in 2009 by two second-generation Korean Americans, Seung Bak and Suk Park, with one Korean drama series, the company has grown to become a leading online streaming service with more than 13,000 episodes of Korean dramas, Latin American telenovelas, and many Asian television shows and movies from 12 countries – a portion of which are syndicated to Hulu, Netflix, Amazon, and iTunes (see DramaFever, n.d.; Longwell, 2016). Such a cross-cultural variety of programs reflects the company's user demographics: 40% white, 30% Latino, 15% African American, and 15% Asian (Edelsburg, 2016). Unlike most Korean media in North America, DramaFever is consumed more by non-Korean than Korean users.

DramaFever's popularity among Latinos is particularly interesting. The *Latin Post* reports that DramaFever's viewership in Latin America increased by 250% from 2014 to 2015, which makes that region the second-largest market after the United States ("DramaFever logs," 2016, paras. 2–3). The *Latin Post* attributes DramaFever's success to the "hiring of professional translators, the start of an affiliate marketing program that established Korean fansites in the region and the launch of local-language mobile apps" (para. 4). Professional translation is considered particularly important as a way to fight effectively against piracy sites and to "differentiate" services by offering titles with quality translation in a timely manner (para. 5).

Like DramaFever's user demographics, the company's corporate trajectory is uncommon for Korean media, which are usually founded and maintained based on local immigrant capital or transnational media from Korea. DramaFever, in contrast, was acquired by a Japanese investment company, SoftBank, in 2014 and was sold a year later to Warner Bros., which is apparently making significant moves into the online streaming market through Turner Broadcasting's purchase of iStreamPlanet and the launch of HBO Now (Frater, 2015; Holloway, 2016). The "corporate synergy" from the purchase of DramaFever is already surfacing (Longwell, 2016, para. 4). Conan O'Brien appeared in the Korea drama *One More Happy Ending* during his visit to Korea in early 2016 for his TBS talk show *Conan,* and the entire show is now available on DramaFever (paras. 1–2). Note that TBS is owned by Time Warner, which also owns Warner Bros. (para. 4). As mentioned earlier, mainstream-diasporic media partnerships are not uncommon: Canada's Star Media Group–*Sing Tao Daily* and the U.S.'s Telemundo-NBC and Black Entertainment Television (BET)–Viacom are a few examples (Jin and Kim, 2011; Rutenberg, 2002; Matsaganis et al., 2011). Nonetheless, DramaFever sets a precedent by being the first of its kind of this scale in the Korean diasporic media sector – and one that is still expanding.

The implications for Korean diasporic media in North America of all these changes brought about by the Korean Wave and the Korean American Wave require continuous research attention. One of the benefits of the Korean Wave is the contribution to improving cultural literacy about Korea, mediated by the consumption of Korean cultural products. The fact that over 90% of Korean drama fans are non-Korean supports this hypothesis, although awareness does not necessarily lead to putting cultural literacy into practice. Nonetheless, from a market perspective, cannibalization within the Korean diasporic media sector can be a concern. Increasing the number of online streaming services is certainly a potential threat to Korean media on traditional platforms, especially those operating largely in the cable and satellite sectors. Based on service fees alone, the old-platform diasporic media have no competitive edge over online services, since their monthly charges are almost equivalent to the annual fee for DramaFever, for example. The rapid transition to online services suggests that it is time for Korean media operating in traditional sectors to respond to the market changes more proactively.

Conclusion

This chapter explored the city-specific and ethnicity-specific factors that offer opportunities and challenges in broadening availability and accessibility of Korean discourse to a wider audience and in facilitating two-way intercultural dialogue. Ball-Rokeach's communication infrastructure theory is useful in looking at the relationships among residents, media, and community organizations. The examination of Korean media in these two cities suggests that it is equally useful to identify key agents in each component.

Although Chapter 6 will discuss policy issues in more detail, one of the most important city-specific factors identified is the immigration history and younger-generation leadership in community affairs. The early peak of Korean immigration to L.A. – owing largely to the Immigration and Nationality Act of 1965 and the demand for immigrant labour from L.A.'s garment industry – has naturally produced a larger younger-generation population than in Vancouver. The leadership of young Koreans in multiethnic organizations based in Koreatown is specific to L.A.'s Korean community and creates positive synergy with first-generation media and CSOs. Another city-specific factor is the strong presence of transnational media branches in L.A.'s Korean media sector. The tension between transnational media and local immigrant media has both positive and negative impacts. On the positive side, the financial capacity of the transnational branches to mobilize intercultural initiatives such as "The Korea Times" English website, the Anabada Flea Market, and the U.S. ad team certainly contributes to broadening access to Korean media for members of the broader society as well as for community, political, and industry interest groups. More in-depth community-wide audience research is needed, however, in order to measure the actual impact of these initiatives.

Commonalities between Korean media in the two cities, on the other hand, suggest that certain traits are ethnicity-specific, bound particularly to Korean media. First, although L.A. offers Korean media by and for younger-generation Korean Americans, producers and consumers of Korean media are predominantly Korean immigrants. Decades of Korean journalism in North America – 30 years in Vancouver and 50 years in L.A. – have produced local Korean journalists who are capable of cultural translation. Nonetheless, the limited sociocultural capital still stands as a barrier, especially for those media or journalists that are newly established, in broadening availability and accessibility for a broader audience. Another commonality between the two cities is the Korean media's relationship with first-generation CSOs.

While there is a mutual understanding of the interests and benefits of cross-institutional collaboration within the community, their role as "collective actors" is still weak. In contrast, the relationship with multiethnic CSOs is emerging as a positive force. The younger-generation leadership in those organizations in L.A. organically builds bridges to the Korean community with many intercultural initiatives. In Vancouver, it is Korean community workers at multiethnic CSOs that strive to bridge the gap between various communities with broader community initiatives. Korean representatives at immigrant service organizations such as SUCCESS actively serve as a liaison between the local Korean community and not-for-profit immigrant services by advocating for the Korean community to the broader society and by providing access to the Korean community for a wide variety of community interest groups.

Finally, the relationship with mainstream media is equally weak in both cities. While L.A.'s Korean media are more engaged with mainstream media through various partnerships, interaction among individual journalists from these two media groups is largely ad hoc, limited to issues related to Korea and Koreans. This raises questions about the cultural literacy of mainstream journalists in their capacity to cover diasporic communities. A hopeful sign is diasporic-mainstream media collaboration, as exemplified between *Sing Tao Daily* and *The New York Times* in revealing the exploitation of labour in the beauty industry. This partnership suggests the possibility of new collaborations in the years to come.

In addition to city-specific and ethnicity-specific factors, new emerging trends add a new dynamic to the Korean diasporic media sector. One notable trend is the spread of the Korean Wave in North America and the growing popularity of Korean cultural products. This external force positively contributes to increasing the value of Korean diasporic media in the broader media system. More and more majority audiences are tuned into local Korean channels to watch Korean dramas, according to media practitioners. What is more, the Korean American Wave is building in the United States through the involvement of the younger generation in media businesses such as DramaFever. This new phase of diasporic media requires continued research attention, especially audience research into the relationship between the consumption of Korean cultural products and cultural literacy about Korea, in order to understand more fully the actual impact of Korean media and the Korean Wave.

All of these factors suggest that both cross-generational collaboration within the diasporic community and cross-cultural institutional collaboration with the broader community, including political and industry interest groups, are critical in increasing the intercultural capacity of young diasporas. The lack of sociocultural capital (i.e., cultural and official language proficiency) often limits Korean media's efforts to play a strong meso storyteller role within and across communities, as Ball-Rokeach's communication infrastructure theory envisions (see Chapter 1), so as to extend their availability and accessibility to the broader community. The findings from this study contribute to communication infrastructure theory by showing that for young diasporic media that lack sociocultural and economic capacity, identifying active agents within each constitutive element of communication infrastructure is important. In the case of Korean media, it is younger-generation community leaders, multiethnic CSOs, and market leaders that play a significant catalyst role in broadening availability and accessibility. Growing possibilities for intercultural outreach seem to be derived through heightened synergy from collaboration among these agents as well as with their counterparts.

That said, the expectation for diasporic media in the years to come is that they will make a conscious effort to identify catalytic agents and establish institutional bonds within and across communities. Certainly, for young diasporas, intercultural outreach is not an immediate priority, since assisting new immigrants in their settlement and integration is already a challenging business. Nonetheless, this examination of Korean media has demonstrated that intercultural outreach is also in the best interest of diasporic media – on sociocultural, economic, and political fronts – in order for them to develop intercultural strategies and reach out to broader society. It is a matter of timing – of identifying at which point in these media organizations' development these strategies will matter. An equally strong conscious effort is required on the part of the dominant structure, whether that be mainstream media or the government. What can be done to establish a support system in the dominant structure? The final chapter will discuss the policy areas in need of attention.

6
The Intercultural Media System and Related Policy Areas

International migration continues to increase around the globe, and Canada and the United States are no exceptions to this trend. Given this flow of migration, the expansion of existing diasporic communication infrastructure, along with the development of new communicative space, is likely. This potential growth grants further importance to the study of diasporic media, especially that of young diasporas, and their implications for the broader media system. The fundamental question is this: Is the media system in a multicultural society *multicultural*, with multicultural options available and accessible *only* for members of individual diasporic communities, or *intercultural*, with these options available and accessible for the rest of society *as well*? Ultimately, is it capable of assisting individuals within a multicultural society in acquiring cultural literacy about communities to which they do or do not belong – and of facilitating functioning democracy amidst cultural and linguistic differences? Given these urgent questions, diasporic media practices are indeed an important public policy concern and priority.

At the turn of the century, the CRTC invited public comments on the need for over-the-air ethnic television in Vancouver (CRTC, 2001b). The responses to this call can be grouped into the following benefits: fulfillment of citizenship, sense of belonging and social cohesion, affordability, and geo-ethnic storytelling. One of the comments illustrates the need for ethnic television as an essential element in the process of integration:

> While we are learning English, it is just as important for us to know what is happening in our new country and in the world, so we can make informed decisions until such time that we are fluent. There are no benefits to keeping over 800,000 of Vancouver's population ignorant about Canada and many benefits to giving them

access to useful information and education. (Wai Sin and family, Comment #372)

The argument is that free ethnocultural options in the broader media system are not only a sign of welcome but also a necessity for immigrants to be adequately informed about here and to make informed decisions. But the same is true for the rest of society: it is equally important that ethnocultural options be available and accessible to members of the broader society so they can be adequately informed about growing ethnocultural communities and make informed decisions. So far, the debates on diasporic media have focused on availability of these options for ethnocultural audiences without paying attention to accessibility of these already available options for a broader audience. Accessibility has been left to individual organizations' discretion rather than understood as a public policy matter. In responding to this gap, this book attempted to open a discussion on possible ways to broaden availability and accessibility to diasporic discourse for all members of society. More importantly, accessibility should not be limited to interest groups but expanded to individual members of society for the vigorous exercise of citizenship based on sufficient cultural literacy. Advancing from a multicultural media system to an intercultural media system, however, requires a collective effort, and policy support is integral to this effort.

The notion of an *intercultural media system* advances theoretical and policy debates concerning multiculturalism and media with respect to cultural diversity. As discussed in Chapter 1, the debates on "multicultural citizenship," "institutional integration," "the multi-ethnic public sphere," "interactive media infrastructure," "the right to communicate" and "the right to be understood," and "the politics of voices and listening," among other topics, all emphasize effective two-way, intercultural communication (see, e.g., Kymlicka, 1995, 2001, 2002; Husband, 1998; Downing and Husband, 2005; Dreher, 2009). In particular, Kymlicka's notion of multicultural citizenship and institutional integration envisions having new options created within rather than outside of the dominant structure (or "anglophone culture") to make it "richer and more diverse" (Kymlicka, 1995, pp. 78–79).

However, a truly functioning institutional integration requires two-way flow of information by having these new ethnocultural options available as well as accessible for *all* members of society for proper cultural integration of *both* minority and majority cultures. The findings from this study suggest that these new options may not be easily integrated into the dominant structure, for sociocultural and economic reasons. Thus, without establishing a proper mechanism that enables accessibility of these new options for members of the broader society, they are unlikely to make the structure richer and more diverse; rather, they are likely to serve only as *media for the Other*, not *media for all*. This distinction currently continues, while the relationship between diasporic and mainstream media remains distant. What is more, those options that are developed outside of the dominant structure – such as the initiatives of the majority of young diasporic media in the print sector – are likely to remain largely unknown outside of ethnic enclaves.

What, then, should be done to make these options available and accessible for all members of the broader society? Many have argued that government intervention is critical (Kymlicka, 2002; Downing and Husband, 2005; Dreher, 2009). But what exactly should the government be expected to do? Based on the comments from media practitioners and civil society organization (CSO) leaders, this chapter provides policy recommendations for government, media sectors, industry associations, and academic institutions to consider in their efforts in building an intercultural media system.

Policy Areas

One of the most notable city-specific factors is the regulatory context of each city, which is certainly influenced by the status of multiculturalism in each country. Canada's official commitment to multiculturalism accepts immigrants as permanent members of society and lays out policy and regulatory frameworks to facilitate their social integration. As discussed in Chapter 2, policy directives such as the "Building on Success: A Policy Framework for Canadian Television" (CRTC, 1999a) and the "Ethnic Broadcasting Policy" (CRTC, 1999b) are in place to ensure fair and accurate representation of ethnic minorities and ethnic programs in Canadian broadcasting, although these policies are not necessarily reflected in practice. Measures such as these are absent in the United States; although the Federal Communications Commission (FCC) does emphasize ownership and viewpoint diversity through its "diversity objective," but again, its effectiveness is another question. Chapter 2 discusses how these measures work at the present time. Indeed, all these measures focus on availability of but not accessibility to diasporic media. What does this focus mean for media practitioners, and what do they really need? What are the policy measures that can be considered to widen both availability and accessibility and that work towards building an intercultural media system?

MULTICULTURAL CONTENT RULES

Canadian content rules contribute to availability of diasporic discourse by encouraging local diasporic media production. This protective measure, which is intended to guard the Canadian media industry from U.S. media expansion by encouraging Canadian creators to produce local content, applies equally to ethnic television: 60% of overall content and 50% during the evening broadcast period should be made in Canada by Canadian creators (CRTC, 1999b). Ethnic specialty services are also subject to similar requirements, but with a proportion of 15% Canadian content compared to 35% for English and French specialty services (CRTC, 2000).

While the Canadian content rules have benefits, the case of Korean media suggests a few areas of possible development. First, Canadian content rules are conditional on the producers' commitment to local production and ability to mobilize financial and sociocultural capital to realize this level of production. All producers interviewed for this study expressed a high commitment to local content. Commitment is high partly owing to a genuine interest in local production and partly as a survival strategy, in anticipation of Korean transnational media potentially expanding into Canada, as they have in the United States. Nevertheless, a high level of commitment does not necessarily mean a high level of production. A lack of resources, owing largely to internal restructuring during the economic recession, makes it difficult even to maintain the current level of Canadian content. Local producers simply do not have the capacity to commit most of their local staff to the production of a half-hour program (e.g., *TV Korea Magazine*). In this sense, the Canadian content rules are often more of a burden than an incentive.

Second, as many media scholars have pointed out, the definition of Canadian content is ambiguous (Armstrong, 2010; Vipond, 2000). What does "Canadian content" mean? What should Canadian content in multicultural Canada entail? Does the Canadian content program reflect the changing ethnocultural profile of Canada? Perhaps it is time to redefine the criteria for Canadian content. If the original intent of the requirement was to strengthen Canadian identity through real Canadian cultural production by Canadian creators, wherein the Canadian identity reflects the "multicultural and multiracial nature of Canadian society" (Broadcasting Act 1991, see Chapter 2) in any sense, a certain requirement for multicultural content needs to be emphasized. Currently, the Canadian content rules focus on Canadian creation of various genres (e.g., drama, documentary, children's programming), but there is no requirement for multicultural content within the Canadian content. The current rule imposed on ethnic television (although adjustable by conditions of licence) and Category 2 ethnic specialty services are the only rules that would allow for specifically multicultural content, assuming that multicultural and third-language producers are likely to produce multicultural and third-language content. This is, in fact, the basic assumption that the FCC's minority ownership objective relies on.

Also worthy of consideration is the revitalization of OMNI's multilingual local daily news or the creation of a similar program. It is unfortunate that Canada's only multilingual daily news on a multicultural television station had to be sacrificed – with Korean News removed first – because of the forces of the political economy of the news industry (see Chapter 3). Although this news program was originally offered in the respective languages of the communities it served, if it had been offered with subtitles, it certainly would have served as a window to everyday multiethnic discourse and possibly contributed to filling the gap in public discourse. How local Chinese, Punjabi, and Korean communities interpret and narrate the same event can diversify viewpoints. Official-language or multilingual subtitle services are critical to serve this function. (See the following section for further details.)

The United States, in contrast, does not have an American content requirement; however, public-interest obligations imposed on broadcasting licensees are in place (see Chapter 2). The use of local talent, the development of children's and educational programs, and the reservation of three hours a week in the broadcasting schedule for these programs are part of licence-renewal requirements (Grant and Wood, 2004). As an extension of these requirements, multicultural programs or multilingual programs with subtitles could be considered in order to reflect the interests of local diasporic communities. This idea is consistent with the diversity of viewpoints as outlined in the FCC's "Statement of Policy on Minority Ownership of Broadcasting Facilities, 1978": "Adequate representation of minority viewpoints in programing serves not only the needs and interests of the minority community but also enriches and educates the non-minority audience," thus enhancing cultural literacy (FCC, 1978, p. 3) Policy support for relaxed airtime fees for the distribution of minority productions could also achieve the same goal. In fact, the relatively weak financial status of minority media owners and the ongoing underrepresentation of minority journalists in the newsroom pose challenges for minority productions to get on the air.

The success of this measure depends on the financial capacity of producers. In L.A., as is the case in Vancouver, Korean media are aware of such requirements (Media Practitioner 23); however, meeting them is dependent on the discretionary decision of individual media outlets, and production is often kept to a minimum level. Despite the presence of transnational capital and a relatively bigger market size, local production is still a challenge, owing in large part to high airtime fees, easy access to imported content, and the changes in local market conditions. The proliferation of digital Korean channels carrying only imported content from Korea only lowers the competitiveness of the market. As a result, local production in L.A., other than daily news, was limited at the time of the study to a few programs such as TVK24's *Story G,* as mentioned in Chapter 4.

INTERCULTURAL JOINT PRODUCTION

Within this policy environment, one of the ways of broadening the availability of local multicultural content is intercultural joint productions between diasporic and mainstream media or among diasporic media from diverse diasporic communities. While Canadian broadcasting policies reinforce the commitment to appropriate and accurate representation of ethnocultural minorities (CRTC, 1999a, 1999b), these policies generally encourage individual commitment rather than joint commitment through cross-cultural and cross-racial collaborative work, reflecting the "multicultural and multiracial nature of Canadian Society" (see Chapter 2). Policy support for intercultural joint production would be timely. As discussed in Chapters 3 and 4, many intercultural projects pursued by Korean media in both cities confirm that the benefit of intercultural collaboration is being recognized by both sides.

The same measure could be extended to the print sector. Generally, the print media sector, in which diasporic media are concentrated, is out of the regulatory loop. By nature of the medium, newspapers are developed largely outside of the broader system (or the dominant structure). Efforts to link Korean media with mainstream media institutions are evident through various types of business partnerships: examples are Vancouver's *Canada Express* and its exclusive licensing with Canwest and L.A.'s *The Korea Times's* (*Hankook Ilbo*) and *The Korea Daily's* (*JoongAng Ilbo*) joint delivery system with the *Los Angeles Times*. Nonetheless, all of these efforts are still predominantly one-way, limited to making broader public discourse available and accessible to the Korean community and not the other way around. A hopeful sign is that mainstream print media are responding, one example being the aforementioned coverage of New York's nail salons in *The New York Times* and the availability of the story in Korean, Chinese, and Spanish (see Chapter 5). Certainly, such collaboration widens accessibility for all audiences.

Multilingual services

If multicultural content rules were to require production of new content, official-language subtitle services for third-language programs and multilingual subtitle services for official-language programs would make existing productions available and accessible for a wider audience and contribute to improving cultural literacy for all. After all, it is this accessibility that increases awareness of issues that matter. In broadcasting, the official-language subtitle services for third-language programs has been suggested by Canadian media scholars Beaty and Sullivan (2006), who argue that official-language subtitles for more third-language programs could help reach a broader audience. Right now, this kind of service is left to an individual media outlet's discretion, which is one of the reasons why Korean media outlets lacking socio-cultural and economic capital cannot reach a broader audience. In the broader intercultural media system, the same logic can also be applied in reverse to multilingual subtitles for official-language programs.

Translation services are equally important for print media. The nail-salon story mentioned above is a perfect example – it's another story that was covered and discussed in the Chinese community in New York for over a decade and is now available to a broader audience through multilingual translation. In addition, the story reached an audience beyond the United States: new readers based in South Korea clicked on *The New York Times* website for the first time. This type of two-way effort for mutual exposure is a cost-effective way to enhance cultural literacy, considering the hefty investment required for production of new content.

Greater role of the public sector

Currently, multicultural and multilingual endeavours are led by diasporic media in the private sector, and Korean media are no exception. In Canada, for example, Rogers's OMNI and Shaw's Multicultural Channel (SMC) serve more than 20 linguistic communities in collaboration with local independent producers from diasporic communities. Particularly, SMC offers free airtime to independent producers as part of its community programming. Such an endeavour lifts the burden of airtime fees – which often hinder local production, as demonstrated by L.A.'s Korean television services – and encourages multilingual programs to get on the air. The absence of similar initiatives by the CBC, other than *Hockey Night in Canada* in Punjabi, calls for a greater role to be played by the public sector.

During the time of study, Korean-language services were available on all television platforms (terrestrial, cable, satellite, and online streaming), with a high concentration in the cable and satellite sectors, such as Shaw's TV Korea and All TV, Time Warner's KBS World, DirecTV's Korean Direct, and Dish Network's Tiger Pack among its "International Packages."[1] These options in the private sector offered only limited accessibility for a broader audience owing to sociocultural and economic barriers. Socioculturally, as discussed above, English subtitles are provided only to selected programs, mainly entertainment programs (e.g., drama, documentaries), and are not at all provided for everyday local evening news, thereby preventing non–Korean-speaking audiences from accessing local daily news from the Korean community. Interestingly, these options are in contrast to the aggressive marketing of online streaming services such as DramaFever, which provides English and Spanish subtitles on all of its programs as they are released. On an economic level, most Korean channels are paid services provided to subscribers. Digital channels certainly multiplied free options; however, only producers with more solid programming could realize these digital channels as real options. During the time of study, much of the airtime on these channels was dedicated to advertising. Given this situation, a greater role for public broadcasting is in demand. What is important to note, however, is that availability of multicultural content, let alone third-language content, should come first, prior to any discussion on sociocultural and economic barriers to the accessibility of this content.

INTERCULTURAL READINESS OF MAINSTREAM INDUSTRY AND ACADEMIC INSTITUTIONS

Availability and accessibility of diasporic discourse can be improved through various institutional collaborations. Aside from the intercultural joint productions discussed above, policy support for mainstream industry and academic institutions to help them improve institutional readiness for multiethnic membership is needed. First, affiliation with media industry associations is particularly important for diasporic media, given the absence of a regulatory framework for the print media sector. The awareness of existing mainstream media associations, such as the B.C. Press Council and the Canadian Association of Journalists, was generally low among the Korean media practitioners interviewed. None of these were mentioned during the interviews and no Korean media practitioners served on any of these boards. Commonly mentioned during the interviews were comments such as "I have never heard of the B.C. Press Council, but I am definitely willing to find out more about it" (Media Practitioner 5) or "there is no practical reward [for membership of this nature]" (Media Practitioner 1).[2] Without knowing what is out there, participation cannot be expected. The low awareness of, and participation in, media associations is partially attributable to voluntary rather than mandatory participation of media outlets in these industry networks.

Nevertheless, the lack of awareness or interest on the part of Korean media is not solely to blame for the lack of institutional affiliation. It is equally important for mainstream media associations to be multiculturally equipped to work with multiethnic members. An interesting case shared by a Korean media publisher in Vancouver suggests that the level of multicultural readiness on the part of mainstream associations is equally important (Media Practitioner 3). This publisher recalled his initial contact with a local industry association in the print sector. Although the publisher is now a standing member of the association, his membership did not come easy. The membership application was initially rejected for the sole reason that the association had no capacity to review a non-English publication. The association instead offered him an associate member position, which grants all but voting rights. When he refused, the association asked him to provide an English translation of the entire publication for review at his own expense. The publisher instead offered to provide a Korean-English interpreter for one day to assist the association in reviewing his publication. The offer was accepted, and he finally received a full membership once the review was completed. Why was the membership so important? The publisher answered, "It is a breakthrough for all non-English publishers" (Media Practitioner 3). This case suggests that multicultural readiness is a concern for both sides. On the part of most Korean media practitioners, the case above being an unusual exception, the existence and significance of mainstream media industry associations are rarely recognized. On the part of mainstream media associations, multiethnic membership is still new and no system is yet in place to accommodate multiethnic members.

Voluntary participation in ethnic media associations, however, is more common. The Canadian Ethnic Media Association (CEMA) and New America Media (NAM), for example, list approximately 1,300 and 3,000 broadcasting, print, and online media organizations, respectively. Policy support for these associations to serve as a venue for diasporic media organizations is important to facilitate these media in identifying themselves and connecting with their industry counterparts. For young diasporic media like Korean media, the gain from collaboration with NAM is tremendous. NAM is front and centre in making ethnic voices from diverse ethnocultural groups available to a broader audience; "NAM produces, aggregates and disseminates multimedia content and services for and from the youth and ethnic media sectors" (see New America Media, n.d.). Efforts such as this one are critical in broadening availability and accessibility of diasporic discourse for a broader audience.

During the time of study, the visibility of L.A.'s Korean media in "ethnic media" circles, such as the Asian American Journalists Association (AAJA) and NAM, was indeed high through membership or participation as board members (e.g., Korean-American journalists serving as board directors). S.L. Yoo of *The Korea Daily Washington D.C.* received the award for Best Immigration Coverage from New America Media at the second Ethnic Media Awards in Washington, D.C., with an article titled "Immigration Status Not a Factor in Receiving WIC Benefits" (S.E. Lee, 2011). *The Korea Daily Washington D.C.* reported that Yoo was the only Asian reporter among the 14 ethnic media reporters awarded (S.E. Lee, 2011). J.H. Cho of *The Korea Daily New York* was also selected as a New York Community Media Alliance 2010 fellow (Ahn, 2010).

Policy support for the community outreach efforts of journalism schools is also important. The CUNY Graduate School of Journalism's Center for Community and Ethnic Media (CCEM), for example, is at the forefront of this initiative. In addition to the ethnic media directory developed in-house, the center offers "Translating NYC," where English translation of stories from various diasporic media appear (see CUNY Graduate School of Journalism, CCEM, n.d.). It is a challenge for any diasporic community to establish a communication infrastructure that attends effectively to both internal and external communication. Cross-institutional collaboration creates synergies in this area and enables the broadening of availability and accessibility of diasporic discourse.

Media-academia collaboration also serves the marketing and professional needs of diasporic media – the two important areas that Korean media practitioners want to see improved. In terms of marketing, while a majority of leading media outlets offer media kits, which consist of basic corporate information as well as target market information, regular tracking data on audience media consumption are rare. Only the leading Chinese media outlets have been able to conduct audience research (e.g., 2005 Vancouver Chinese media habits study, 2007 Canadian Chinese Media Monitor by Fairchild TV, 2005 Chinese newspaper readership study by *Sing Tao Daily*, 2006 study on Chinese American media consumption and purchasing behaviour survey by the *World Journal*).[3] No studies on this scale were conducted by Korean media. *The Korea Daily*'s (or *JoongAng Daily* or *JoongAng Ilbo*) 2010 online survey on readership patterns was the only audience readership study that has been done on Korean audiences in Vancouver in recent years (see Chapter 3). Market research, however, is an increasingly important diasporic media project, especially since the placement of mainstream ads (both government and corporate ads) remains an ambitious goal. This research is particularly important for L.A.'s Korean media outlets that are proactively reaching out to mainstream advertisers through their so-called U.S. ad teams.

In academia, audience research on Korean American viewership in the United States has been conducted by Korean scholars including a study of satellite television viewership of Korean immigrants in L.A. (Moon and Park, 2007) and Texas (C. Lee, 2004) and a study of media consumption patterns of Korean immigrants in Chicago (Moon, 2003). Although social science research and market research have different goals and methods, they are complementary; together, they respond to the growing recognition among marketers of ethnographic research on consumers. Wider circulation of academic research to the diasporic media sector is an important responsibility for communication and journalism schools.

In terms of professional needs, there is an aspiration for professional development within the Korean media sector. Cultural literacy training is one possible area of focus. Some CSO leaders noted that a lack of cultural literacy often leads to reactive rather than proactive approaches to the coverage of diasporic communities and results in the reinforcement of stereotypes

(Community Worker 3 and CSO Leader 2). For example, discussions about diasporic communities at a local government level often circle aimlessly around "what government should do" in response to requests from diasporic communities rather than proactively questioning "what government can do" or "what governments and communities can do together" (Community Worker 3). Cultural literacy training as part of journalistic training is thus important to improving the cultural literacy of journalists, who in turn influence the cultural literacy of audiences (CSO Leader 2). Such training is equally important for Korean diasporic media journalists as a way of "confronting their own stereotypical prejudice, assumptions" (CSO Leader 2). Ad hoc fact checking without an understanding of deeper sociocultural implications only essentializes cultural differences. It takes *both*, not *either*, to be culturally literate enough to have a meaningful conversation.

FINANCIAL SUPPORT

Another type of support needed to help young diasporic media like Korean media make their content more available and accessible is financial support. During the interviews, one of the most commonly mentioned suggestions for additional revenue was the placement of government ads. The prevailing perception among interviewees was that diasporic media outlets are not sufficiently considered in the ad placement selection process. Only one or two of these ads are placed each year (Media Practitioners 1 and 7):

> We get government ads only during election time. However, governments can consider using diasporic media to make major government announcements such as the Harmonized Sales Tax. Also, during major events such as the Olympics, they can consider using diasporic media to invite more participation across communities – for example, volunteer recruiting. (Media Practitioner 6)

The situation is the same for corporate ads. Only about three percent of the newspaper ads are placed by mainstream advertisers, and these are mainly local professional services targeting the Korean community (e.g., Simpson, Thomas, and Associates) rather than multinational corporations (e.g., McDonald's), although ads from the latter are not completely absent.

The situation for Korean media in the United States is similar. The placement of government ads is the source of revenue most desired by media practitioners but is least likely to be satisfied. Mainstream media, according to practitioners, are the major recipients of government ads, and only a few make it to Korean media. Some examples of government ads found during the time of study are ads for Census 2010, Flu Shot L.A., and iWatch. The benefit of government ads, of course, is the higher ad rate, which is incomparable to the going rate for local enclave businesses. "Although we do not get as much as *The L.A. Times*," said one media practitioner, "we do get major ads from the government. The ad rate is much higher, since the government already has the rate set for mainstream media" (Media Practitioner 32). The situation is the same for corporate ads. Although some major transnational corporations appear in Korean media – such as McDonald's, Verizon, State Farm, and Toyota – the actual number is still minimal. This low level of popularity of Korean media among mainstream advertisers may be attributed to skepticism about the size of the audience, among other reasons. One media practitioner commented that the Asian market is growing but is still not considered to form a critical mass:

> Yes, the English-speaking population is growing, but not to the level where we need to change our programming or there is ad support ... When you put all English-speaking Asians, Chinese, Korean, whatever, together, it's a growing population ... but the number only goes up to five percent and the number is the number ... It's not there yet. (Media Practitioner 22)

Another area that affects the financial stability of some media businesses is airtime fees. Korean television services in L.A., whether provided by transnational or immigrant media, provide programs through brokerages who lease airtime from licence holders. Because of the foreign-ownership restrictions, transnational media are not eligible for ownership. Local immigrant media are eligible for ownership but are financially less capable. As discussed in Chapter 4, high airtime fees hinder local production by redirecting resources from content development. Korean media practitioners complained that these fees account for a significant portion of direct expenses and the increase in airtime fees at every renewal has pushed some outlets out of the market. Indeed, most of the advertising revenue generated from the Korean enclave businesses is used to pay airtime fees. The study of Y.R. Hong, Hong, Lee, Kim, and Chae (2009) on overseas Korean-language broadcasting, conducted for the Korea Communications Commission (KCC), confirms that over 70% of the expenses of Korean television companies operating in the United States are attributed to airtime fees. In the current market-driven pricing of airtime fees, the availability and accessibility of minority programs, let alone Korean American productions, is difficult. In compliance with the FCC's emphasis on diversity, financial assistance (e.g., discounted airtime fees) for Korean American services could be considered. The FCC's current financial measures are, however, inadequate for Korean media, since these measures aid minority ownership, such as bidding credits and tax certificates. None of these were mentioned during the interviews (see Chapter 4), reflecting the reality that a majority of Korean media outlets are program providers.

The road ahead for existing Korean television stations is increasing competition with online services. English-subtitled KBS World programs are available on YouTube for free, and online streaming services such as DramaFever charge only U.S.$0.99 to $8.33 per month, when cable and satellite services still charge additional fees for international packages, on top of base subscription fees. Given new changes in the market, Korean content on traditional media platforms is losing its competitiveness.

Conclusion

The presence of an intercultural media system is an important precondition for a functioning democracy in a multicultural society. In this system, mainstream and diasporic media are not only available but also accessible to all members of society. This means that voices from diverse communities are adequately created, circulated, contested, and cultivated in everyday discourse and that all members of society experience a full sense of belonging and have sufficient cultural literacy to make informed democratic choices. This system directs the flow of information from multiple sources to multiple receivers, thereby facilitating two-way mainstream–diasporic communication. The present system, however, enables only one-way communication of mainstream discourse to diasporic communities. The headlines of mainstream news are available to diasporic communities through diasporic media, but those of diasporic communities are less likely available to the broader society, if at all.

Building an intercultural media system requires a collective effort on the part of government, media sectors, industry associations, and academic institutions. This book has examined structural and institutional conditions for diasporic media through a case study of Korean media in Vancouver and Los Angeles. Following the discussion on institutional conditions of diasporic media in the previous chapter, this chapter revisited the discussion in Chapter 2 on structural conditions and their influence on availability and accessibility of diasporic media. How current media policies and practices work in general, and how Korean communities and their media operate in particular, under those structural conditions helps us understand the rapidly transforming media system in a multicultural society. Interviews with Korean media practitioners offered insight into multiculturalism and media theories and policies. Beyond those policy areas previously discussed in Chapter 2, potential policy areas in need of further attention were identified, which help improve availability and accessibility of diasporic discourse for all members of society.

The findings of this study suggest that the status of multiculturalism as a theory or political philosophy does make a difference in policy directives for immigration, citizenship, and media undertakings; however, the impact on actual outcomes is limited. Canada's official constitutional recognition of multiculturalism means that immigrants are accepted as permanent members of society and that social programs are offered that assist them in their settlement and integration. Diasporic media are recognized in the Broadcasting Act, and policy measures are established specifically for ethnic broadcasting. The "Policy Framework for Canadian Television" (CRTC, 1999a) and the "Ethnic Broadcasting Policy" (CRTC, 1999b), for example, set out directives for ethnic broadcasting. Furthermore, measures such as Canadian content rules have been shown to contribute to local diasporic production, as demonstrated in the case of TV Korea. The United States, in contrast, does not officially support group-differentiated measures, and only a few measures, such as minority ownership and viewpoint diversity, are in place as part of the FCC's broader "diversity objective." However, the end result is similar in Vancouver and L.A. regardless of the policy structure, since the current policies do not adequately address the real needs of diasporic media, whose limited financial and sociocultural capital – amidst the constant changes in the global economy, technology, and policies and constitutions in Canada, the United States, and Korea– continually challenge diasporic media's efforts to broaden availability and accessibility.

Clearly, more targeted policy support for capacity building for both diasporic and mainstream media is critical. First, multicultural content rules – in addition to Canadian content rules in Canada and children's and educational program requirements in the United States – are desirable. The existing measures only vaguely reinforce the notions of a "multicultural and multiracial nature" or "viewpoint diversity" (see Chapter 2) with no specific regulatory obligation or consequence if these conditions are unmet. Furthermore, intercultural joint productions and multilingual subtitle services could facilitate both the creation of new multicultural content and the wider distribution of existing content.

Policy support that improves the role of the public service and the multicultural readiness of industry and academic institutions is also desirable. In particular, Korean media's intercultural initiatives reflect an aspiration for institutional connection with mainstream institutions; however, these aspirations often fail to receive reciprocal interest or commitment from mainstream institutions. Finally, a desirable change would be more localized financial support through the placement of government ads and/or subsidies to support marketing efforts such as media monitoring and diasporic media-academia joint research. Current financial support measures focus on business transactions related to ownership; however, ownership is a rather distant concern for many Korean media organizations that are program providers rather than broadcasting owners, particularly in the United States.

In considering these policy supports, group-differentiated support for diasporic communities in varying stages of development of communication infrastructure is critical. In general, the policy discourses in both countries tend not only to group all ethnocultural minorities bluntly as members of the "visible minority" but also to group them together with other minority groups such as women, Aboriginals/Native Americans, people with special needs, and sometimes seniors, without due consideration for the diversity between and within each of these groups. Thus, a more careful engineering of policies with respect to group differentiation would be advantageous. It is important to note, however, that these policy recommendations are largely based on the study of Korean diasporas; thus, generalization to other groups must be done with caution. Nevertheless, these recommendations highlight policy areas to consider in supporting young diasporic media in developing their communication infrastructure and expanding their contribution to building an intercultural media system.

In summary, intercultural communication is a shared responsibility among government, media sectors, industry associations, and academic institutions. An intercultural media system requires institutional commitment and carefully crafted policies that address availability and accessibility of diverse voices for all members of society. Under the current media system, diasporic communities are likely to be better informed about broader society than the broader society is about diasporic communities. Echoing the aforementioned comment from the public hearing on over-the-air ethnic television in Canada: keeping over 800,000 members of Vancouver's population ignorant about their new home has no benefits. Conversely, keeping the rest of the population ignorant about their diasporic neighbours also has no benefits and many drawbacks. To truly accommodate deep diversity in perspectives and enable everyone to exercise their citizenship fully in a multicultural society and functioning democracy, it is important to think carefully about the ways to improve the cultural literacy of members of a multicultural society. Diasporic media is certainly one avenue toward this goal, if they are made widely available and easily accessible to *all*.

Notes

INTRODUCTION

1 These figures show a growth of international migrants in the population since 1990, when the proportions in Canada and the United States were 16% and 9%, respectively (Kobayashi et al., 2011, p. xvii).

2 Such demographic composition has been quite consistent since the early 2000s, when 70% of Canadian immigrants lived in three major cities (Toronto, Vancouver, and Montreal) and 66% of U.S. immigrants lived in five major cities (New York, Los Angeles, Chicago, Houston, and Philadelphia; Citizenship and Immigration Canada, 2001; U.S. Census Bureau, 2000).

3 Wood and Landry (2008, p. 250) define "cultural literacy" as "the ability to read, understand and find the significance of diverse cultures and, as a consequence, to be able to evaluate, compare and decode the varied cultures that are interwoven in a place." See Chapter 1 for a full discussion.

4 Korea's new election law was passed on February 5, 2009, and extended voting rights to overseas Koreans who are 19 years old or older (Ryu, 2009). Overseas Koreans eligible to vote are Korean citizens, mainly permanent residents and temporary visitors in respective regions. S.C. Park of Kyungki University (South Korea) estimated that the eligible voters around the world in 2010 numbered 2,295,937 and that nearly 40% (or 879,083) of those were located in the United States (D.Y. Chung, 2010c).

5 For agreement, the average values for Percentage Agreement and Cohens' Kappa are high – 88.6% and 0.81, respectively – while the optimal score for Cohen's Kappa is 0.8 or greater (Macnamara, 2005). For covariance, Pearson's r for interval variables was 0.938.

CHAPTER 1: CONCEPTUALIZING MEDIA IN A MULTICULTURAL SOCIETY

1 According to Kymlicka (1995, p. 76), societal culture is "a culture which provides its members with meaningful ways of life across the full range of human activities, including social, educational, religious, recreational, and economic life, encompassing both public and private spheres." Kymlicka (1995, pp. 26–33) writes of three categories of "group-differentiated rights," separating national minorities (e.g., Aboriginals) from polyethnic minorities (immigrants): "self-government rights" for the national minority, which guarantee "some form of political autonomy or territorial

jurisdiction"; "polyethnic rights," which guarantee financial support and legal protection for certain cultural and religious practices; and "special representation rights," which guarantee representation of minorities for political leadership.

CHAPTER 2: MULTICULTURAL OR INTERCULTURAL?

1 The points system ended the racist immigration policy by selecting immigrants based on the following criteria: level of education, vocational preparation, knowledge of one or both official languages, and occupational demand in Canada (Abu-Laban and Gabriel, 2002, p. 45). The passing score was 50 out of 100 and was raised to 70 in the early 1990s (p. 45).

2 The Canadian Experience Class was introduced in 2008 to enable "people who meet a minimum language requirement and have at least one year of skilled work experience in Canada to transition to permanent residence" (Citizenship and Immigration Canada, 2013).

3 Canadian production is defined as programs that (1) are "produced in-house by a licensee of the CRTC"; (2) "satisfy the CRTC's own certification system"; (3) are "certified by the Canadian Audio-Visual Certification Office (CAVCO), a division of the Department of Canadian Heritage"; (4) are "produced internally by the National Film Board of Canada (NFB)"; or (5) are "certified pursuant to one of the international co-production treaties negotiated by the Department of Canadian Heritage (and called official co-productions to distinguish them from other kinds of domestic and international co-productions)" (Armstrong, 2010, p. 100). The rules currently require conventional private television licensees to "devote not less than 60% of the broadcast year and not less than 50% of the evening broadcast period (6 p.m. to midnight) to Canadian programs" (CRTC 1999a).

4 A brokerage is "the purchase of blocks of radio and television time by independent ethnic producers who determine the program content and commercial messages and derive revenues from the advertising contained therein" (Roth, 1998).

5 In the discussion of media policies, the term "ethnocultural" is used in place of "diasporic" in order to be more consistent with the names of existing services (e.g., ethnic pay & specialty services) and policies (e.g., Ethnic Broadcasting Policy). Nonetheless, it is essentially "diasporic" as this book advocates "diasporic media" over "ethnic media."

6 As mentioned earlier, the "Category 2 specialty services" was created in 2002 in response to the needs of diverse communities (CRTC, 2002).

7 The Federal Communications Commission (FCC) is a U.S. federal regulatory agency that is equivalent to the CRTC in Canada.

8 According to the Form 395-B, "minority group" is "American Indian or Alaskan Natives; Asian or Pacific Islanders; Black, not of Hispanic origin; Hispanics, Whites, not of Hispanic origin" (FCC, 2000).

9 "Nonvisible minority" here are those who are not a "visible minority." Statistics Canada (2015) uses the term "visible minority" as defined by the Employment Equity Act of Canada: "persons, other than Aboriginal peoples, who are non-Caucasian in race or non-white in colour." This definition further specifies that "The

visible minority population in Canada consists mainly of the following groups: Chinese, South Asian, black, Arab, West Asian, Filipino, Southeast Asian, Latin American, Japanese, and Korean."

10 The Canadian Television Fund (CTF), a nonprofit corporation, was created by the Department of Canadian Heritage, the Cable Production Fund, and Telefilm Canada in 1996 (Armstrong, 2010, p. 134). Later in 2009, the Government of Canada announced the amalgamation of the CTF and the Canada New Media Fund to establish the Canada Media Fund (p. 137).

11 Lincoln et al. were referring to statements 31 and 32 in the Ethnic Broadcasting Policy (CRTC, 1999b).

12 Canadian editorial content is "editorial content (text and photographs, graphics and illustrations) created or translated by a Canadian citizen or a permanent resident of Canada within the meaning of the Immigration and Refugee Protection Act. Translated editorial content by a citizen or a permanent resident of Canada within the meaning of this Act will be considered Canadian editorial content if the editorial content is translated into one of the two official languages. Note: translation does not modify the nature of the editorial content" (Canada, Ministry of Public Works and Government Services, 2015, p. 22).

An ethnocultural periodical is "a periodical that primarily serves or is primarily concerned with a commonly recognized specific cultural or racially distinct community or specific linguistic group using other than Canada's official languages. An eligible ethnocultural periodical may be published in any language" (p. 24).

CHAPTER 3: KOREAN DIASPORIC MEDIA IN VANCOUVER

1 Note that this overview is based on the data collected during the fieldwork conducted from 2009 to 2011. A follow-up mapping of the Korean media sector is required to understand the up-to-date status of these media outlets. Some outlets closed their businesses during or after the time of this study, such as TV Korea in 2011, *The Korean Canadian News* in the early 2010s, and *The Korea Times* in 2015.

2 Some European diasporic media that the Cultural Diversity and Ethnic Media in BC project (Murray et al., 2007) identified date back to the early 1900s: *Swedish Press* (est. 1929), *L'Eco d'Italia* (*Il Marco Polo*; 1956), and *De Hollandse Krant* (1969). The majority of Asian media were founded in the 1970s: Mainstream Broadcasting Corporation, CHBM-AM1320, and *Link* (1973); *World Journal* (1976); and *Vancouver Shinpo* and *Indo-Canadian Times* (1978).

3 This schedule is no longer available on the SMC's website. However, the author is in possession of a copy of the schedule obtained during the time of the study.

4 All of the seven largest diasporic media outlets in British Columbia belong to the Chinese community, with the largest (Talentvision) employing 150 full-time employees, followed by 125 employees for *Sing Tao Daily* and 111 employees for *Ming Pao* (Murray et al., 2007, pp. 152–153).

5 *Hallyu* (or the Korean Wave) has been described as "the flood of Korean pop culture – films, pop music and especially TV dramas – into the rest of East Asia" (Huat and Iwabuchi, 2008, p. 2).

6 Some interviews with Media Practitioners, CSO leaders, and Community Workers in this chapter were conducted in Korean and translated to English. Some headlines and quotes were originally Korean and translated to English.

7 The z-test that compares column proportions determines whether the differences presented in figures are statistically significant. See the note below each table, which says that "each subscript letter denotes a subset of column categories whose column proportions do or do not differ significantly from each other at the .05 level." Different subscript letters indicate statistical significance between the column categories.

8 In Table 3.3, the portion of sports news is significant (30%), owing to the Vancouver 2010 Paralympics Games that took place during the time of data collection.

9 Religion (11%) is sporadic: a nationally renowned Buddhist monk passed away during the time of data collection. Crime/violence (15%) can also be intermittent: there was a sexual assault case widely discussed in the media in Korea (*The Korea Times*, March 12, 2010, B1; OMNI, March 11, 2010).

10 Members of the 1.5 generation (or *Il-chom-o-se*) are "those born in Korea but who arrived in the United States as children or young adults" (Martin, 2005, p. 73).

11 Ken Beck Lee (Liberal) ran in the same riding (New Westminster-Coquitlam) as Yonah Martin (Conservative). He failed to win in the election (with 2,514 votes), losing to Fin Donnelly (NDP, with 12,129 votes; Kwon, 2009b).

12 The Korean business directories that were available during the time of study included Koreatimes Business Directory, Hanin Yellowpages, Telephone Directory of Korean Canadian in British Columbia, and Korean Yellow Pages.

13 During the time of study, All TV (Category 2 Korean specialty TV) was available through Shaw and Telus at an additional $15.95 and $15.00, respectively.

14 These newspapers are *The Province, The National Post, The Saskatoon StarPhoenix, The Calgary Herald, The Montreal Gazette, The Windsor Star, The Vancouver Sun, The Regina Leader-Post, The Edmonton Journal, The Times-Colonist* (Victoria), and *The Ottawa Citizen* (Murray et al., p. 20).

CHAPTER 4: KOREAN DIASPORIC MEDIA IN LOS ANGELES

1 Note that the overview is based on the data collected during the fieldwork conducted from 2009 to 2011. A follow-up mapping of the Korean media sector is required to understand the up-to-date status of these media outlets. Some outlets closed their businesses during or after the time of this study, such as JBC AM1230 in 2011 and *KoreAm Journal* in 2015.

2 KBS and MBC are two public broadcasters that have been active in Korea since 1980, when President Chun turned the media industry into an "oligopoly" of these two broadcasters (D. Shim, 2008, p. 23). SBS was the first commercial television station in Korea and has operated since 1991, when it was granted a licence upon the enactment of the new Broadcasting Law in 1990 (p. 23).

3 *Korea Herald Business* is a daily business newspaper in Korea. However, the L.A. office is operated not as a branch but as a franchise, affiliated only through content sharing. It is the same operational format as is found in Vancouver's *The Korea Daily* and *The Korea Times*.

4 The directories that were available during the time of study included *The Korea Times*'s Korean Business Directory (as well as online: http://yp.koreatimes.com/), *The Korea Daily*'s Korean Business Directory, (http://yp.koreadaily.com/main. asp?bra_code=L.A.), the Radio Korea Business Directory (Radio Korea, n.d.-a), the Rakotel online (Radio Korea, n.d.-b), and Koreatown 114 (formerly California 114.com).

5 The history of the Latino media is much longer, with *La Opinión*, a Spanish-language daily newspaper, founded in 1926, and Univision, a Spanish-language television network, founded in 1962 (http://laopinion.com, http://www.univision. com). The history of Japanese media goes back even further, to 1903, when *Rafu Shimpo*, a Japanese/English-language daily newspaper was launched (http://www. rafu.com). The newspaper struggled throughout the economic recession and hit a low in 2010, when the community held a "Save the Rafu" town hall meeting to seek ways to continue its operation (Watanabe, 2010). The paper was still in operation as of 2015.

6 Along with the main evening news (TVK News Wide), TVK24 also offered a mid-day news program for viewers in the eastern region (TVK News Live). TVK24 offered TVK News Live and TVK News English Edition during the sampling period in March 2010; however, the company discontinued the services shortly thereafter.

7 Some interviews with Media Practitioners, CSO leaders, and Community Workers in this chapter were conducted in Korean and translated to English. Some headlines and quotes were originally Korean and translated to English.

8 The content analysis was based on six Korean-language television evening news programs (KBS America News, MBC News Tonight, SBS Evening News, KTN News, TVK News Wide, and LA18 Prime Time Local News), one English-language television news (TVK News English Edition), three Korean-language radio evening news programs (Radio Korea, Radio Seoul, and JBC), and the front page of each section of the four Korean-language daily newspapers (*The Korea Times, The Korea Daily, Koreatown Daily,* and *Korea Herald Business*).

9 These media outlets can be categorized by source of capital: local immigrant media, transnational media, and multicultural media. Local immigrant media outlets are TVK News Wide (TVK24), TVK News English Edition (TVK24), *Koreatown Daily, Korea Herald Business,* and Radio Korea. Transnational media outlets are KBS America, MBC America, SBS International, KTN-TV (of *The Korea Times*), Radio Seoul (of *The Korea Times*), JBC (of *The Korea Daily Vancouver*), *The Korea Times,* and *The Korea Daily*. Finally, multicultural media outlet refers to LA18's Prime Time Local News.

10 KTN-TV (as well as Radio Seoul) is affiliated with *The Korea Times* and is thus categorized as transnational media.

11 Some of the sections are News to People, Sports, Koreatown, Entertainment, Business, Food, Student Reports, Hot Links, Good News, Education, Health, and Opinion.

12 The word *Anabada* is a Korean blend of "save (a), share (na), exchange (ba), and reuse (da)."

13 The Korean population in each of San Bernardino and Riverside Counties accounts for approximately 10,000 (U.S. Census Bureau, 2010b).

14 Some of the labour-intensive businesses often discussed are "grocery/green grocery retail, fish retail, retail of manufactured goods imported from Asian countries, dry cleaning and manicure services, and garment manufacturing" (Min, 2006b, p. 239). Among these, the "grocery/liquor retail" is "most popular" among Koreans (p. 239).

15 The newspaper ads analyzed were the ads on the front page of each section in *The Korea Times*, *The Korea Daily*, *Koreatown Daily*, and *Korea Herald Business*. The television and radio ads analyzed were the ads shown or mentioned during the evening news on KBS America News, MBC News Tonight, TVK News Wide, TVK News English Edition, KTN News, LA18 Prime Time Local News, Radio Korea Evening News, Radio Seoul Evening News, and JBC Evening News. Out of the 14 outlets tracked in this study, SBS Evening News was excluded since the archived news segments available on its website did not contain ads.

16 MBC News Tonight is a 10-minute local news program inserted in the middle of MBC News Live, which is imported from Korea. Thus, only the ads shown before and after MBC News Tonight are included here.

CHAPTER 5: LOCALITY, ETHNICITY, AND EMERGING TRENDS

1 The traditional role of "middleman minority" – that is, businesses that are located "between low-income minority consumers and large companies, often distributing merchandise made by predominantly White-owned corporations to African American and Latino customers" – systematically positioned Korean entrepreneurs in vulnerable situations (Min, 1996, p. 3).

2 Some interviews with Media Practitioners, CSO leaders, and Community Workers in this chapter were conducted in Korean and translated to English. Some headlines and quotes were originally Korean and translated to English.

3 As quoted in the introductory chapter, "cultural literacy" is "the ability to read, understand and find the significance of diverse cultures and, as a consequence, to be able to evaluate, compare and decode the varied cultures that are interwoven in a place" (Wood and Landry, 2008, p. 250).

4 Note that this article was published in 2008, prior to the amendment of the Korean election law.

5 This figure excludes both the content sales to overseas Korean media and DVD/video sales (Republic of Korea, Ministry of Culture, Sports, and Tourism, 2011).

CHAPTER 6: THE INTERCULTURAL MEDIA SYSTEM AND RELATED POLICY AREAS

1 During the time of study, Dish Network, for example, offered 200 international channels in 28 languages. For more details, see Dish TV U.S.A. (n.d.).

2 Some interviews with Media Practitioners, CSO leaders, and Community Workers in this chapter were conducted in Korean and translated to English. Some headlines and quotes were originally Korean and translated to English.

3 *The World Journal* (est. 1976) is a Chinese-language newspaper distributed in major cities in the United States and Canada. For more details, see *The World Journal* (n.d.).

References

'A-na-ba-da Jang-tuh' Ta-in-jong-do Cham-yuh ... Choe-dae Joo-min-hang-sa-roh [Anabada market, joined by other ethnic communities ... the largest community event]. (2010, March 15). *Korea Daily L.A.* Retrieved from http://www.koreadaily.com/news/read.asp?art_id=1001187.

Abu-Laban, Y., & Gabriel, C. (2002). *Selling diversity.* Peterborough, ON: Broadview Press.

Ahn, J. Y. (2010, March 11). Bon-ji Cho-jin-hwa Ghi-ja, NYCMA Fel-low (fellow) Sun-jung [Our paper's reporter Jinhwa Cho, selected as a NYCMA fellow]. *The Korea Daily New York.* Retrieved from http://www.koreadaily.com/news/read.asp?art_id=999679.

Alasuutari, P. (2004). *Social theory and human reality.* London, UK: Sage.

All T.V. (n.d.). All TV History. Retrieved from http://www.alltv.ca/alltv_history.

Ang, I. (2002). *On not speaking Chinese: Living between Asia and the West.* London, UK: Routledge.

–. (2006). On the politics of empirical audience research. In M. G. Durham & D. M. Kellner (Eds.), *Media and cultural studies: Key works* (pp. 174–194). Malden, MA: Blackwell.

Armstrong, R. (2010). *Broadcasting policy in Canada.* Toronto, ON: University of Toronto Press.

Associated Press. (2014, May 31). Psy's Gangnam style reaches 2 billion views on Youtube. *CBC News.* Retrieved from http://www.cbc.ca/news/entertainment/psy-s-gangnam-style-reaches-2-billion-views-on-youtube-1.2660687.

Bailey, O. G. (2007). Transnational identities and the media. In O. G. Bailey, M. Georgiou, & R. Harindranath (Eds.), *Transnational lives and the media: Re-imagining diaspora* (pp. 212–230). Basingstoke, UK: Palgrave Macmillan. http://dx.doi.org/10.1057/9780230591905_12.

Ball-Rokeach, S. J., Kim, Y. C., & Matei, S. (2001). Storytelling neighborhood: Paths to belonging in diverse urban environments. *Communication Research, 28*(4), 392–428. http://dx.doi.org/10.1177/009365001028004003.

Beaty, B., & Sullivan, R. (2006). *Canadian television today.* Calgary, AB: University of Calgary Press.

Bech, L. (2015, June 10). Can mainstream US media tap into non-English-speaking audiences? *Columbia Journalism Review*. Retrieved from http://www.cjr.org/innovations/can_mainstream_us_media_tap_into_non-english_audiences.php.

Bell Media Inc. (2013). *Corporate cultural diversity report 2012*. Retrieved from http://www.crtc.gc.ca/fra/BCASTING/ann_rep/bmcd.doc.

Benson, R., & Powers, M. (2011). Public media and political independence. Washington, DC: Free Press.

Bissoondath, N. (1994). *Selling illusions: The cult of multiculturalism in Canada*. Toronto, ON: Penguin.

Blistein, J. (2012). Psy Gangnam Style. *Billboard, 124*(34), 29.

Brady, D. (2012, Oct 1). The man behind the moves: Psy of 'gangnam style' fame. *Business Week*.

Brinkerhoff, J. M. (2009). *Digital diasporas: Identity and transnational engagement*. Cambridge, UK: Cambridge University Press. http://dx.doi.org/10.1017/CBO9780511805158.

British Columbia. B.C. Stats. (2001, October 5). Infoline report: Immigrants from South Korea. Retrieved from http://www.bcstats.gov.bc.ca/Publications/Infoline/Infoline Archives/InfolineArchives2001.aspx.

Brodie, J. (2002). Citizenship and solidarity: Reflections on the Canadian way. *Citizenship Studies, 6*(4), 377–394. http://dx.doi.org/10.1080/1362102022000041231.

Browne, D. R. (2005). *Ethnic minorities, electronic media, and the public sphere: A comparative study*. Cresskill, NJ: Hampton Press.

Brubaker, R. (2004). *Ethnicity without groups*. Cambridge, MA.: Harvard University Press. http://dx.doi.org/10.1017/CBO9780511489235.004.

Burnet, J. R., & Palmer, H. (1988). *Coming Canadians: An introduction to a history of Canada's peoples*. Toronto, ON: McClelland and Stewart.

Ca-na-da (Canada) Chong-li Dong-hang Chui-jae [First (Korean) media in Canada to accompany Canadian prime minister]. (2009, November 27). *The Vancouver Korean Press*. Retrieved from http://www.vanchosun.com/news/main/frame.php?main=1&boardId=18&bdId=33051.

Cameron, E. (Ed.). (2004). *Multiculturalism and immigration in Canada: An introductory reader*. Toronto, ON: Canadian Scholars' Press.

Canada, Ministry of Justice. (1997). Direction to the CRTC (ineligibility of non-Canadians) SOR/97–192. Retrieved from http://laws-lois.justice.gc.ca/eng/regulations/SOR-97-192/index.html.

Canada, Ministry of Public Works and Government Services. (2015). Canada Periodical Fund aid to publishers: Applicant's guide 2016–2017. Retrieved from http://www.pch.gc.ca/DAMAssetPub/DAM-mags-mags/STAGING/texte-text/fcp_guide_2016-2017_1443723428248_eng.pdf?WT.contentAuthority=12.1.1.

Canada Media Fund. (2016, March). *Diverse Languages Program guidelines 2016–2017*. Retrieved from http://www.cmf-fmc.ca/getattachment/83ca44a4-cb53-41a4-b07f-82b8b1e039e8/2016-17-Diverse-Languages-Guidelines.aspx.

–. (n.d.). Diverse Languages. Retrieved from http://www.cmf-fmc.ca/programs-deadlines/programs/diverse-languages.

Canadian Association of Broadcasters (CAB). (2004, July). Reflecting Canadian: Best practices for cultural diversity in private television. Task Force for Cultural Diversity on Television. Prepared by Richard Cavanagh of CONNECTUS Consulting Inc. Retrieved from http://www.cab-acr.ca/english/social/diversity/taskforce/report/cdtf_report_jul04.pdf.

Canadian Broadcasting Act (1991). Broadcasting Act (S.C. 1991, c. 11). Government of Canada. Justice Laws. Retrieved from http://www.laws-lois.justice.gc.ca/eng/acts/B-9.01/.

Canadian Ethnic Media Association. (n.d.). Directory. Retrieved from http://cema directory.com.

Canadian Radio-Television and Telecommunications Commission (CRTC). (1985, July 4). A broadcasting policy reflecting Canada's linguistic and cultural diversity. Public notice CRTC 1985–139. Retrieved from http://www.crtc.gc.ca/eng/archive/1985/PB85-139.htm.

–. (1997, April 2). Amendments to the commission's employment equity policy. Public notice CRTC 1997–34. Retrieved from http://www.crtc.gc.ca/eng/archive/1997/PB97-34.HTM.

–. (1999a, June 11). Building on success: A policy framework for Canadian television. Public notice CRTC 1999–97. Retrieved from http://www.crtc.gc.ca/eng/archive/1999/PB99-97.htm#t6.

–. (1999b, July 16). Ethnic broadcasting policy. Public notice CRTC 1999–117. Retrieved from http://www.crtc.gc.ca/eng/archive/1999/PB99-117.HTM.

–. (2000, January 13). Licensing framework policy for new digital pay and specialty services. Public notice CRTC 2000–6. Retrieved from http://www.crtc.gc.ca/eng/archive/2000/PB2000-6.htm.

–. (2001a, August 31). Amendments to All TV Inc.'s conditions of licence pertaining to the nature of the service and the broadcast of advertising material. Decision CRTC 2001–538. Retrieved from http://www.crtc.gc.ca/eng/archive/2001/DB2001-538.htm.

–. (2001b, February 28). Report to the Governor in Council on the earliest possible establishment of over-the-air television services that reflect and meet the needs of the multicultural, multilingual and multiracial population of the Greater Vancouver Area. Public notice CRTC 2001–31. Retrieved from http://www.crtc.gc.ca/eng/archive/2001/PB2001-31.htm.

–. (2002, September 12). New licensing framework for specialty audio programming services. Broadcasting public notice CRTC 2002–53. Retrieved from http://www.crtc.gc.ca/eng/archive/2002/pb2002-53.htm.

–. (2004, December 16). Improving the diversity of third-language television services. Broadcasting public notice CRTC 2004–96. Retrieved from http://www.crtc.gc.ca/eng/archive/2004/pb2004-96.htm.

–. (2007). Broadcasting policy monitoring report 2007. Retrieved from http://publications.gc.ca/collections/collection_2007/crtc/BC9-1-2007E.pdf.

–. (2008a, January 15). Regulatory policy: Diversity of voices. Broadcasting public notice CRTC 2008–4. Retrieved from http://www.crtc.gc.ca/eng/archive/2008/pb2008-4.htm.

–. (2008b, March 17). Regulatory policy: Equitable portrayal code. Broadcasting public notice CRTC 2008–23. Retrieved from http://www.crtc.gc.ca/eng/archive/2008/pb2008-23.htm.

–. (2008c, October 30). Regulatory policy: Regulatory frameworks for broadcasting distribution undertakings and discretionary programming services. Broadcasting public notice CRTC 2008–100. Retrieved from http://www.crtc.gc.ca/eng/archive/2008/pb2008-100.htm.

–. (2011, July). *Communications monitoring report.* Retrieved from http://onscreen manitoba.com/wp-content/uploads/2013/09/CRTC-Communications-Monitoring-Report-July-2011.pdf.

CBC News. (2011, March 3). Kenney fundraising letter breaks rules: NDP. Retrieved from http://www.cbc.ca/news/politics/kenney-fundraising-letter-breaks-rules-ndp-1.1026750.

CBC/Radio-Canada. (2011). *Annual report on the operation of the Canadian Multiculturalism Act 2010–2011.* Retrieved from http://www.cbc.radio-canada.ca/_files/cbcrc/documents/equity/multi-1011-en.pdf.

–. (2014). *2014 CBC/Radio-Canada employment equity annual report to employment and social development Canada (Labour program).* Retrieved from http://www.cbc.radio-canada.ca/_files/cbcrc/documents/equity/employment-equity-2014.pdf.

CBS Los Angeles. (2017, June 22). LA18 to replace local Asian TV programs with English infomercials. Retrieved from http://losangeles.cbslocal.com/2017/06/22la18-cancels-asian-programming/.

Chan, B. (2006). Virtual communities and Chinese national identity. *Journal of Chinese Overseas, 2*(1), 1–32. http://dx.doi.org/10.1163/179325406788639093.

Chang, E. T., & Diaz-Veizades, J. (1999). *Ethnic peace in the American city: Building community in Los Angeles and beyond.* New York: New York University Press.

Chang, E. T. (1988). Korean community politics in Los Angeles: The impact of the Kwangju uprising. *Amerasia Journal, 14*(1), 51–67. http://dx.doi.org/10.17953/amer.14.1.gh65433165261483.

Chang, Y. H. (2009, July 16). 'Dang-sun-dden Han-in Bo-ja-kwan Chae-yong' Gar-de-na (Gardena)-ji-yuk Joo Ha-won Chool-ma-ha-neun B-ra-d-for-d (Bradford) Shi-eui-won [Will hire Korean assistant, if elected, said Bradford, a candidate for State Assembly in Gardena]. *The Korea Daily L.A.* Retrieved from http://www.koreadaily.com/news/read.asp?art_id=878447.

Cheadle, B., & Levitz, S. (2012, November 13). Government paid for media monitoring of immigration minister's image. *The Globe and Mail.* Retrieved from http://www.theglobeandmail.com/news/national/government-paid-for-media-monitoring-of-immigration-ministers-image/article5249773/.

Chen, C., Nguyen, S., Bernick, S., & Chen, J. (2006, August 25). Korean wave fuelled by non-Koreans. *Asianweek.*

Cheng, H. L. (2005). Constructing a transnational, multilocal sense of belonging: An analysis of Ming Pao (West Canadian edition). *Journal of Communication Inquiry, 29*(2), 141–159. http://dx.doi.org/10.1177/0196859904273194.

Cheng, L., & Yang, P. Q. (1996). Asians: The "model minority" deconstructed. In R. Waldinger & M. Bozorgmehr (Eds.), *Ethnic Los Angeles* (pp. 305–344). New York, NY: Russell Sage Foundation.

Cho, H. J. (2011, April 4). [Join in one heart]. *The Korea Daily Vancouver*. Retrieved April, 2012, from http://www.joongang.ca/bbs/board.php?bo_table=g100t200&wr_id=1737.

Choi, I. S. (2010, March 19). In-jong-eui Byuk-eul Huh-moo-neun 'Jang-tuh' [The "market" that breaks down the racial barrier]. *The Korea Daily L.A.* Retrieved from http://www.koreadaily.com/news/read.asp?art_id=1003457.

Choi, S. H. (2010a, May 28). Han-in-hui, Ha-i-ti (Haiti) Doo Bun-jjae On-jung Jun-hae [Korean Society, second fund to Haiti]. *The Vancouver Korean Press*. Retrieved from http://www.vanchosun.com/news/main/frame.php?main=1&boardId=5&bdId =34367.

–. (2010b, October 8). Han-in-hui Shi-min-kwon Shi-hum Joon-bi Gwang-ja Yul-uh [Korean Society hosts a citizenship exam seminar]. *The Vancouver Korean Press*. Retrieved from http://www.vanchosun.com/news/main/frame.php?main=1&board Id=18&bdId=35650.

–. (2010c, December 23). Jul-meun Jung-chi In-jae-yang-sung-ae Him-sseu-get-dah [I will train talented young future politicians]. *The Vancouver Korean Press*. Retrieved from http://www.vanchosun.com/news/main/frame.php?main=1&boardId =5&bdId=36691.

–. (2011, April 1). "Ill-bon Jeh-nan Dop-ghi Wee-hae Gut-ghi Hang-sah Mah-ryun-hat -sseum-ni-dah [Organized a walk-a-thon to help (raise funds) Japan in disaster]. *The Vancouver Korean Press*. Retrieved from http://www.vanchosun.com/news/main/ frame.php?main=1&boardId=5&bdId=37913&cpage1=1&search_keywordtype =&search_type=&search_title=&search_typeId=&search_time1=&search_ time3=&search_view=&search_indexof=&search_start=&search_end=&search_ terms=&search_sort=.

Choi, Y. (2010, August 17). [The 9th Korean Heritage Day Festival: Multicultural day]. *The Korea Daily Vancouver*. Retrieved April, 2012, from http://www.joongang.ca/ bbs/board.php?bo_table=g100t200&wr_id=1292.

–. (2011, February 11). [Korean Canadian indie band leader – Andrew Kim]. *The Korea Daily Vancouver*. Retrieved April, 2012, from http://www.joongang.ca/bbs/board. php?bo_table=g100t200&wr_id=1613.

Chung, A. Y. (2007). *Legacies of struggle: Conflict and cooperation in Korean American politics*. Stanford, CA: Stanford University Press.

Chung, D. Y. (2010a, August 12). Hwak Jool-uh-deun Ko-re-a-to-wn (Koreatown) [Significantly downsized K-town]. *The Korea Times L.A.* Retrieved from http://www. koreatimes.com/article/610223.

–. (2010b, April 14). Juk-geuk Dae-eung Ol-ym-pic (Olympic) Nam-jok Go-soo-hae-yah [Proactive response to secure the south of Olympic]. *The Korea Times L.A.* Retrieved from http://www.koreatimes.com/article/588109.

–. (2010c, May 18). Han-in Jae-whae-kook-min Yoo-kwon-jah 88-man-myung [Overseas Korean voters account for 880,000]. *The Korea Times L.A.* Retrieved from http:// www.koreatimes.com/article/594486.

–. (2011, June 10). Han-in-to-wn (town)-eh Tah-in-jong Kwan-gwang-gek Yoo-chi [Attracting non-Korean tourists to K-town]. *The Korea Times L.A.* Retrieved from http://www.koreatimes.com/article/666754.

Chung, K. H. (2010, April 4). "Sung-gong-gah-doh Jil-joo For-e-ver (Forever) 21 Bee-mil-byung-ghi-neun Jang Hui-jang-eui Doo Dhal", "LA-Ti-me-s (Times), Lin-da E-s-ther (Linda Esther) Jang-sshi Sim-cheung-bo-doh ["Race to success Forever 21, a secret weapon is CEO Jang's two daughters," *LA Times* Linda Esther reports Jang in-depth]. *The Korea Daily L.A.* Retrieved from http://www.koreadaily.com/news/read.asp?art_id=1011222.

Citizenship and Immigration Canada. (2001). Recent immigrants in metropolitan areas: Vancouver – A comparative profile based on the 2001 census. http://www.cic.gc.ca/english/resources/research/census2001/vancouver/intro.asp.

–. (2013). Backgrounder – Canadian Experience Class: Reaching for new heights in 2014. Retrieved from http://www.cic.gc.ca/english/department/media/backgrounders/2013/2013-10-28.asp.

–. (2017). #WelcomingRefugees: Key figures. Retrieved from http://www.cic.gc.ca/english/refugees/welcome/milestones.asp.

Comcast. (2011, May 9). TV One announces expanded carriage on Comcast's Xfinity TV lineup in Chicago and Miami markets. Retrieved from http://corporate.comcast.com/news-information/news-feed/tv-one-announces-expanded-carriage-on-comcasts-xfinity-tvlineup-in-chicago-and-miami-markets.

Conrat, M., Conrat, R., Lange, D., & California Historical Society. (1972). *Executive order 9066: The internment of 110,000 Japanese Americans.* Los Angeles: California Historical Society.

Couldry, N., & Dreher, T. (2007). Globalization and the public sphere: Exploring the space of community media in Sydney. *Global Media and Communication, 3*(1), 79–100. http://dx.doi.org/10.1177/1742766507074360.

County of Los Angeles. (2011). Ethnic newspapers: Los Angeles County. Los Angeles, CA: Public Affairs, Chief Executive Office, County of Los Angeles. Retrieved from http://ceo.lacounty.gov/Forms/Media/Ethnic.pdf.

Creech, K. (2007). *Electronic media law and regulation.* Boston, MA: Focal Press.

Cultural Diversity and Ethnic Media in BC. 2006–07. Media directory. Retrieved from http://www.bcethnicmedia.ca/md_directory.html.

CUNY Graduate School of Journalism, Center for Community and Ethnic Media (CCEM) (n.d.). Translating NYC. Retrieved from https://voicesofny.org/category/translating-nyc/.

Curran, J. (2000). Rethinking media and democracy. In J. Curran & M. Gurevitch (Eds.), *Mass media and society* (3rd ed., pp. 120–154). New York, NY: Oxford University Press.

Dahlgren, P. (1995). *Television and the public sphere: Citizenship, democracy and the media.* Thousand Oaks, CA: Sage.

De Leeuw, S., & Rydin, I. (2007). Diasporic mediated spaces. In O. G. Bailey, M. Georgiou, & R. Harindranth (Eds.), *Transnational lives and the media: Re-imagining diaspora* (pp. 175–194). Basingstoke, UK: Palgrave Macmillan. http://dx.doi.org/10.1057/9780230591905_10.

Deacon, D., Pickering, M., Golding, P., & Murdock, G. (2007). *Researching Communication: A practical guide to methods in media and cultural analysis* (2nd ed.). London, UK: Arnold.

Dish Network. (n.d.). Dish TV packages. Retrieved from https://www.dish.com/packages/.

Dish TV U.S.A. (n.d.). International packages – Korean Tiger Pack. Retrieved from https://www.dishtv.us/tag/korean-tiger-pack.

Do, Anh. (2017, July 1). It's the end of an era: Channel 18 cancels international format that served generations of L.A. immigrants, Los Angeles Times. Retrieved from http://www.latimes.com/local/lanow/la-me-ln-channel-18-closure-20170701-story.html.

Downing, J., & Husband, C. (2005). *Representing 'race': Racisms, ethnicities and media.* Thousand Oaks, CA: Sage.

Downing, J. D. H. (1992). Spanish-language media in the greater New York region during the 1980s. In S. H. Riggins (Ed.), *Ethnic minority media: An international perspective* (pp. 256–275). Newbury Park, CA: Sage. http://dx.doi.org/10.4135/9781483325309.n13.

DramaFever. (n.d.). About us. Retrieved from https://www.dramafever.com/company/about.html.

DramaFever logs 250 percent jump in Latino viewership. (2016, January 29). *Latin Post.* Retrieved from http://www.latinpost.com/articles/112337/20160129/dramafever-logs-250-percent-jump-latino-viewership.htm.

Dreher, T. (2009). Listening across difference: Media and multiculturalism beyond the politics of voice. *Continuum, 23*(4), 445–458. http://dx.doi.org/10.1080/10304310903015712.

Edelsburg, N. (2016, August 1). How DramaFever is bringing international TV to American audiences. *The Drum.* Retrieved from http://www.thedrum.com/news/2015/08/12/how-dramafever-bringing-international-tv-american-audiences.

Einstein, M. (2004). *Media diversity: Economics, ownership and the FCC.* Mahwah, NJ: Erlbaum.

Federal Communications Commission (FCC). (1978, May 25). Statement of policy on minority ownership of broadcasting facilities. FCC78-322. Retrieved from https://apps.fcc.gov/edocs_public/attachmatch/FCC-78-322A1.pdf.

–. (2000, April). Broadcasting station annual employment report (Form FCC 395-B). Retrieved from https://transition.fcc.gov/Forms/Form395B/395b.pdf.

–. (2016). EEO rules and policies for radio and broadcast and non-broadcast TV. Retrieved from https://www.fcc.gov/consumers/guides/eeo-rules-and-policies-radio-and-broadcast-and-non-broadcast-tv.

Fleras, A. (2009). Report theorizing multicultural media as social capital: Crossing borders, constructing buffers, creating bonds, building bridges. *Canadian Journal of Communication, 34,* 725–729.

–. (2011). *The media gaze: Representations of diversities in Canada.* Vancouver: UBC Press.

Folkerts, J., Teeter, D. L., & Caudill, E. (2009). *Voices of a nation: A history of mass media in the United States* (5th ed.). Boston, MA: Allyn and Bacon.

Frater, P. (2015, July 19). SoftBank puts video site DramaFever up for sale again, say reports. *Variety*. Retrieved from http://variety.com/2015/biz/asia/softbank-dramafever -up-for-sale-reports-1201543817/.

Gamson, W. A. (2001). Promoting political engagement. In W. L. Bennett & R. M. Entman (Eds.), *Mediated politics: Communication in the future of democracy* (pp. 56–74). New York, NY: Cambridge University Press.

Gandy, O. (2000). Race, ethnicity and the segmentation of media markets. In J. Curran & M. Gurevitch (Eds.), *Mass media and society* (pp. 44–69). London, UK: Arnold.

The 'gangnam style' tribute supercut (video). (2012, October 24). *The Huffington Post*. Retrieved from http://www.huffingtonpost.com/2012/10/24/gangnam-style-tribute -supercut-video_n_2002643.html.

Georgiou, M. (2002). *Mapping minorities and their media: The national context – The UK*. London, UK: London School of Economics. Retrieved from http://www.lse.ac.uk/ media@lse/research/EMTEL/Minorities/papers/ukreport.pdf.

–. (2005). Diasporic media across Europe: Multicultural societies and the universalism-particularism continuum. *Journal of Ethnic and Migration Studies, 31*(3), 481–498. http://dx.doi.org/10.1080/13691830500058794.

Gitlin, T. (1998). Public sphere or public sphericules? In T. Liebes, J. Curran, & E. Katz (Eds.), *Media, ritual, and identity* (pp. 168–174). New York; London: Routledge. http://dx.doi.org/10.4324/9780203019122.

Glazer, N. (1983). *Ethnic dilemmas, 1964-1982*. Cambridge, MA: Harvard University Press.

–. (2005). American diversity and the 2000 census. In G. C. Loury, T. Modood, & S. M. Teles (Eds.), *Ethnicity, social mobility and public policy: Comparing the USA and UK* (pp. 50–66). NY: Cambridge University Press.

Government of Canada. (1988). Canadian Multiculturalism Act. Retrieved from http:// laws-lois.justice.gc.ca/eng/acts/C-18.7/page-1.html.

Grant, P., & Wood, C. (2004). *Blockbusters and trade wars: Popular culture in a globalized world*. Vancouver, BC: Douglas & McIntyre.

Ha, E. S. (2009, February 23). "Ko-re-a-to-wn (Koreatown) Moon-hwa Boh-jon" Han-in-hui, 5-man dol-lar (dollar) Bat-ah [Preserve Koreatown heritage, Korean Federation receives $50,000]. *The Korea Times L.A.* Retrieved from http://www.koreatimes. com/article/506387.

Hafez, K. (2007). *Media and immigration: Ethnicity and transculturalism in the media age*. Cambridge, UK: Polity Press.

Han, H. S. (2009a, October 23). Oh-hey-shim-sshi Sah-gun 'Moo-jae' [Oh Hyeshim case 'Not guilty']. *The Vancouver Korean Press*. Retrieved from http://www.vanchosun. com/news/main/frame.php?main=1&boardId=17&bdId=32757.

–. (2009b, December 4). Oh-hye-shim-sshi Sah-gun Gah-hae-jah Moo-jae-roh Pool-ryuh-nan-dah [Oh Hyeshim case assailant set free]. *The Vancouver Korean Press*. Retrieved from http://www.vanchosun.com/news/main/frame.php?main=1&board Id=17&bdId=33093.

–. (2010a, July 23). Ma-jor (major) Lea-gue-ro (league) Chut-gir-eum Nae-din Han-in [A Korean player steps into the major league]. *The Vancouver Korean Press*. Retrieved from http://www.vanchosun.com/news/main/frame.php?main=1&boardId=17&bd Id=34960.

–. (2010b, April 30). Van-cou-ver (Vancouver) Shi-jang, Soh-soo-min-jok Mok-soh-ri Deut-dah [Mayor of Vancouver listens to the voices of ethnic minorities]. *The Vancouver Korean Press.* Retrieved from http://www.vanchosun.com/news/main/ frame.php?main=1&boardId=17&bdId=34109.

Havens, T., & Lotz, A. D. (2012). *Understanding media industries.* New York, NY: Oxford University Press.

Hayes, A. (2003). Ethnic and foreign-language press. In D. H. Johnston (Ed.), *Encyclopedia of international media and communications* (pp. 571–585). Amsterdam, Netherlands: Elsevier. http://dx.doi.org/10.1016/B0-12-387670-2/00086-8.

Hermida, A. (2008, July 25). CBC seeks to draw in ethnic audiences. *Reportr.net.* Retrieved from http://www.reportr.net/2008/07/25/cbc-seeks-to-draw-in-ethnic-audiences/.

Hiatt, B. (2012, December 06). Can Psy move past 'gangnam style'? *Rolling Stone, 22.*

Hiller, H. H., & Franz, T. M. (2004). New ties, old ties and lost ties: The use of the Internet in diaspora. *New Media & Society, 6*(6), 731–752. http://dx.doi.org/10.1177/ 146144804044327.

Holcomb, J., Gottfried, J., & Mitchell, A. (2013, November 14). *News use across social media platforms.* Retrieved from http://www.journalism.org/2013/11/14/news-use-across -social-media-platforms/.

Hollifield, C. A., & Kimbro, C. W. (2010). Understanding media diversity: Structural and organizational factors influencing minority employment in local commercial television. *Journal of Broadcasting & Electronic Media, 54*(2), 228–247. http://dx.doi. org/10.1080/08838151003737980.

Hollinger, D. (1995). *Postethnic America: Beyond multiculturalism.* New York, NY: Basic Books.

Holloway, D. (2016, February 23). Warner Bros to buy streaming company DramaFever from SoftBank. *The Wrap.* Retrieved from http://www.thewrap.com/warner-bros -to-buy-streaming-company-dramafever-from-softbank/.

Hong, Y. R., Hong, S. Y., Lee, M. S., Kim, E. J., & Chae, H. S. (2009). Joong-jang-ghi Hae-whae Han-kook-uh-bang-song Hwal-sung-hwa Bang-ahn Yun-goo [Midterm and long-term plans for the revitalization of overseas Korean-language broadcasting]. Korea Communications Commission. Retrieved from http://www.kcc.go.kr/down load.do?fileSeq=27962.

Houpt, S. (2015, May 7). Rogers cuts 110 jobs, ends all OMNI newscasts. *The Globe and Mail.* Retrieved from http://www.theglobeandmail.com/report-on-business-to-cut -jobs-kill-all-omni-newscasts/article24306838.

Huat, C. B., & Iwabuchi, K. (2008). Introduction. In C. B. Huat & K. Iwabuchi (Eds.), *East Asian pop culture: Analysing the Korean wave* (pp. 1–12). Hong Kong: Hong Kong University Press. http://dx.doi.org/10.5790/hongkong/9789622098923.003. 0001.

Husband, C. (1996). The right to be understood: Conceiving the multi-ethnic public sphere. *Innovation: The European Journal of Social Sciences, 9*(2), 205–215.

–. (1998). Differentiated citizenship and the multi-ethnic public sphere. *Journal of International Communication, 5*(1–2), 134–148. http://dx.doi.org/10.1080/13216597.1998.9751869.

Hwang, J. M., Moon, J. H., & Chang, Y. (2010, April 25). 2-man-yuh-myung In-san-in-hae Joo-mal 'Hwa-hap Han-mah-dang' ["Harmony festival," attended by a big crowd of approximately 20,000 this weekend]. *The Korea Daily L.A.* Retrieved from http://www.koreadaily.com/news/read.asp?art_id=1021987.

James, A. (2000). Demographic shifts and the challenge for planners: Insights from a practitioner. In M. Burayidi (Ed.), *Urban planning in a multicultural society* (pp. 15–35). Westport, CT: Praeger.

Jang-ghi-jun-ryak Pil-yo-han To-wn (town) Sun-guh-goo Tong-hap [Long-term strategy is needed to integrate (K)-town electoral district]. (2015, May 29). *The Korea Times L.A.* Retrieved from http://www.koreatimes.com/article/921175.

JBC ra-di-o (radio) Bang-song Joong-dan ... TV Bang-song-sah-up Joon-bee [JBC radio discontinues service to prepare for television business]. (2011, February 28). *The Korea Daily L.A.* Retrieved from http://www.koreadaily.com/news/read.asp?art_id =1162122.

Jin, D. Y., & Kim, S. (2011). Sociocultural analysis of the commodification of ethnic media and Asian consumers in Canada. *International Journal of Communication, 5,* 552–569.

Joppke, C. (2005). *Selecting by origin: Ethnic migration in the liberal state.* Cambridge, MA: Harvard University Press.

Karim, K. H. (2002). Public sphere and public sphericules: Civic discourse in ethnic media. In S. D. Ferguson & L. R. Shade (Eds.), *Civic discourse and cultural politics in Canada: A cacophony of voices* (pp. 230–242). Westport, CT: Albex.

–. (2009). The national-global nexus of ethnic and diasporic media. In L. R. Shade (Ed.), *Mediascapes* (3rd ed., pp. 259–270). Toronto, ON: Thomson Nelson.

Katz, Y. (2005). *Media policy for the 21st century in the United States and Western Europe.* Cresskill, NJ: Hampton Press.

KBS Bang-song S-pa-ni-sh (Spanish)-ro Chung-chee [KBS offers Spanish dubbing and subtitle]. (2008, January 15). *The Korea Times L.A.* Retrieved from http://www.koreatimes.com/article/427188.

Kim, A. H. (2010). *Surveying Korean transnationalism: Pilot test findings from the study on Toronto Korean families.* Toronto, ON: York Centre for Asian Research, York University.

Kim, C. J., & Lee, T. (2007). Interracial politics: Asian Americans and other communities of color. In M. Zhou & J. V. Gatewood (Eds.), *Contemporary Asian America: A multidisciplinary reader* (2nd ed., pp. 526–541). New York: New York University Press.

Kim, C. S. (2011, May 12). Un-ron-sah Sun-guh-gwang-go Huh-yong [Election advertising through media allowed]. *The Korea Times L.A.* Retrieved from http://www.koreatimes.com/article/661195.

Kim, D. S. (2011, June 3). Han-in Jung-chi-in Con-fe-ren-ce (conference) eui-eui [The significance of the Korean-American politician conference]. *The Korea Times L.A.* Retrieved from http://www.koreatimes.com/article/665536.

Kim, I. (1981). *New urban immigrants: The Korean community in New York.* Princeton, NJ: Princeton University Press. http://dx.doi.org/10.1515/9781400855674.

Kim, J. H. (2010, September 29). "Han-in Hwa-hap Keun-jan-chi" Nae-il Haw-ryuh-han Gae-mak [Grand opening of Korean harmony festival tomorrow]. *The Korea Times L.A.* Retrieved from http://www.koreatimes.com/article/618811.

Kim, J. O. (2009, May 13). [Richmond Summer Night Market opens on the 15th]. *The Korea Daily Vancouver.* Retrieved April, 2012, from http://www.joongang.ca/bbs/board.php?bo_table=g100t400&wr_id=579.

–. (2010, August 20). [(The ninth anniversary) Survey on Korean media]. *The Korea Daily Vancouver.* Retrieved April, 2012, from http://www.joongang.ca/bbs/board.php?bo_table=g100t200&wr_id=1298.

Kim, N. Y. (2009, January 30). Jae-whae-kook-min 2012-nyun-boo-tuh Too-pyo [Overseas Koreans vote from 2012]. *The Korea Times L.A.* Retrieved from http://www.koreatimes.com/article/501607.

–. (2011a, June 4). Han-in Choi-cho Joo-han-mi-dae-sah Tan-sang [First Korean American ambassador to South Korea appointed]. *The Korea Times L.A.* Retrieved from http://www.koreatimes.com/article/665671.

–. (2011b, May 4). Han-in Sun-chool Im-myung-jik Jung-chi-in 49-myung [Elected or appointed, Korean American politicians totaled 49]. *The Korea Times L.A.* Retrieved from http://www.koreatimes.com/article/659516.

Kim, S. K. (2012, January 13). In-ter-net (Internet) Sun-guh-woon-dong Kwan-ryun Kwan-gye-bub-jo-moon [Legal provisions related to election campaigns through the Internet]. *E-Daily.* Retrieved from http://news.naver.com/main/read.nhn?mode=LSD&mid=sec&sid1=100&oid=018&aid=0002545723.

Kim, S. M. (2011, June 7). "Cha-she-dae Jung-chi-in Yang-sung Woo-sun" Pa-ra-di-gm (paradigm) Jun-hwan [Paradigm change, training next-generation politicians is a priority]. *The Korea Times L.A.* Retrieved from http://www.koreatimes.com/article/666033.

Kim, V. (2015, December 7). Archivist of the Korean American experience says goodbye to print. *Los Angeles Times.* Retrieved from http://www.latimes.com/local/california/la-me-korean-magazine-20151227-story.html.

Kim, Y. (2007). The rising East Asian "wave." In D. K. Thussu (Ed.), *Media on the move: Global flow and contra-flow* (pp. 135–152). London, UK: Routledge.

Kim, Y. C., & Ball-Rokeach, S. J. (2006). Community storytelling network, neighborhood context, and civic engagement: A multilevel approach. *Human Communication Research 32*(4), 411–439. http://dx.doi.org/10.1111/j.1468-2958.2006.00282.x.

Kim, Y. S. (2011a, January 19). 'To-wn (town) Dan-il-sun-guh-goo' Yoon-kwak Nah-what-dah [Single riding boundary for (K)-town is drafted]. *The Korea Times L.A.* Retrieved from http://www.koreatimes.com/article/639158.

–. (2011b, May 25). Tah-in-jong Goh-gaek Gong-ryak Know-how (know-how) Jae-gong [Provide marketing strategies for non-Korean customers]. *The Korea Times L.A.* Retrieved from http://www.koreatimes.com/article/663808.

Kim, Y. Y. (2001). *Becoming intercultural: An integrative theory of communication and cross-cultural adaptation.* Thousand Oaks, CA: Sage.

Kobayashi, A., Li, W., & Teixeira, C. (2011). Introduction. In C. Teixeira, W. Li, & A. Kobayashi (Eds.), *Immigrant geographies of North American cities* (pp. xv–xxxviii). Don Mills, ON: Oxford University Press Canada.

Kore Asian Media. (n.d.). About Kore. Retrieved from http://kore.am/about/.

–. What is Kore? Retrieved from http://www.kore.am/about/what-is-koream/.

Korea Daily L.A. (2016, January 4). [Al-rim] Young-moon Con-ten-t (content) Ser-vi-ce (service) Shi-jak-hap-ni-dah [(Announcement) Starting English content service]. Retrieved from http://www.koreadaily.com/news/read.asp?art_id=3932727.

–. (n.d.-a). ASK U.S.A. (or *Ask Mikook*) Retrieved from http://www.koreadaily.com/qna/ask/ask_list.asp.

–. (n.d.-b). Our network. Retrieved from http://corp.koreadaily.com/eng/about/network.html.

[*The Korea Daily Vancouver*, first among the Korean media to accompany Prime Minister Harper to Korea]. (2009, November 27). *The Korea Daily Vancouver.* Retrieved April, 2012, from http://www.joongang.ca/bbs/board.php?bo_table=g100t200&wr_id=769.

Korea Times L.A. (2013, January 3). Cha-nnel 44.3 KTN-TV Bang-song Jam-jung Joong-dan [Channel 44.3 KTN-TV ceased service temporarily]. Retrieved from http://www.koreatimes.com/article/20130103/77089.

–. (n.d.-a). Han-kook-il-bo-sa Soh-gae [About us]. Retrieved from http://www.koreatimes.com/info/hkib/hankookilbo/.

–. (n.d.-b). Han-in-up-soh-jun-hwa-boo [Korean business directory] 2008–2009. Vol. 34.

–. (n.d.-c). Yulinmadang. Retrieved from http://community.koreatimes.com/board/index.php?board_no=1.

–. (n.d.-d). *New York Times.* Retrieved from www.koreatimes.com/section/114.

–. (n.d.-e). History. Retrieved from http://www.service.koreatimes.com/info/history.html.

Korean Community Workers Network. (2016). Retrieved from http://www.vanchosun.com/news/files/new_kcwn2016.pdf.

Korean dramas riding a new wave: DramaFever web site delivers shows via Hulu. (2010, May 17). *Chicago Tribune.*

KoreanDirect. (n.d.). *DirectTV.* Retrieved from https://www.att.com/directv/international/korea.html.

Koreatown Youth and Community Center. (2008). KYCC annual report 2007–2008. Los Angeles: Author.

Kosnick, K. (2007). Ethnic media, transnational politics: Turkish migrant media in Germany. In O. G. Bailey, M. Georgiou, & R. Harindranath (Eds.), *Transnational lives and the media: Re-imagining diaspora* (pp. 149–172). Basingstoke, UK: Palgrave Macmillan. http://dx.doi.org/10.1057/9780230591905_9.

Kwak, J. M. (2010, April 30). 'Ghan-pan' Young-uh-roh 'Ul-gool' Bah-ggoon Han-in-up-soh Boo-jjuk Neul-ut-dah [Changing to English signs, a significant increase among Korean businesses]. *The Korea Daily L.A.* Retrieved from http://www.koreadaily.com/news/read.asp?art_id=1024975.

Kwak, M. (2004). *An exploration of the Korean-Canadian community in Vancouver*. Research on Immigration and Integration in the Metropolis. Working Paper Series No. 04–14. Retrieved from http://mbc.metropolis.net/assets/uploads/files/wp/2004/WP04-14.pdf.

Kwon, M. S. (2009a, October 16). Jung-chi-eh Kwan-shim Up-uh-yo [No interest in politics]. *The Vancouver Korean Press*. Retrieved from http://www.vanchosun.com/news/main/frame.php?main=1&boardId=18&bdId=32679.

–. (2009b, November 9). Co-qui-tl-am (Coquitlam) Bo-kwol-sun-guh-suh Han-in Hooboh Nak-sun [Korean candidate failed in Coquitlam by-election]. *The Vancouver Korean Press*. Retrieved from http://www.vanchosun.com/news/main/frame.php?main=1&boardId=17&bdId=32904.

–. (2010a, February 12). Ha-i-ti (Haiti) Jae-gun-ae Han-in-ghi-boo 10-man Dol-lar (dollar) Sseu-in-dah [Korean fund $100,000 contributed to Haiti rebuilding]. *The Vancouver Korean Press*. Retrieved from http://www.vanchosun.com/news/main/frame.php?main=1&boardId=18&bdId=33535.

–. (2010b, April 22). Han-in 2-she Miss-uni-ver-se (Miss Universe) Ca-na-da (Canada)-eh Doh-jun [A second-generation Korean challenges Miss Universe Canada]. *The Vancouver Korean Press*. Retrieved from http://www.vanchosun.com/news/main/frame.php?main=1&boardId=5&bdId=34051.

–. (2010c, May 12). Van-cou-ver (Vancouver) Han-in-choi-cho Sah-jeh Suh-poom Yeh-jung [Ordination of the first Korean priest in Vancouver scheduled]. *The Vancouver Korean Press*. Retrieved from http://www.vanchosun.com/news/main/frame.php?main=1&boardId=18&bdId=34284.

–. (2010d, July 28). Han-in-ee BC-joo Te-nni-s (tennis) Dae-pyo-roh Ddeun-dah [Korean player represents B.C. tennis team]. *The Vancouver Korean Press*. Retrieved from http://www.vanchosun.com/news/main/frame.php?main=1&boardId=5&bdId=34988.

–. (2010e, August 20). Van-cou-ver (Vancouver)-eh-suh Han-kook Chong-sun Yon-seup [Practicing Korea's national election in Vancouver]. *The Vancouver Korean Press*. Retrieved from http://www.vanchosun.com/news/main/frame.php?main=1&boardId=5&bdId=35176.

Kwon, S., & Kim, J. (2013). From censorship to active support: The Korean state and Korea's cultural industries. *Economic and Labour Relations Review, 24*(4), 517–532. http://dx.doi.org/10.1177/1035304613508873.

Kymlicka, W. (1995). *Multicultural citizenship: A liberal theory of minority rights*. Oxford, UK: Clarendon Press.

–. (2001). The new debate over minority rights. In R. Beiner & W. Norman (Eds.), *Canadian political philosophy: Contemporary reflections* (pp. 159–176). Oxford, UK: Oxford University Press.

–. (2002). *Contemporary political philosophy: An introduction*. New York, NY: Oxford University Press.

–. (2007). Ethnocultural diversity in a liberal state: Making sense of the Canadian model(s). In K. Banting, T. J. Courchene, & F. L. Seidle (Eds.), *Belonging? Diversity, recognition and shared citizenship in Canada* (pp. 1–48). Montreal, QC: Institute for Research on Public Policy.

Lee, C. (2004). Korean immigrants' viewing patterns of Korean satellite television and its role in their lives. *Asian Journal of Communication, 14*(1), 68–80. http://dx.doi.org/10.1080/0129298042000195161.

Lee, D. I. (2007, Spring). Thanks anyways Vancouver Sun. Cough cough: Van-cou-ver Sun (Vancover Sun)-eul Han-geul-roh Ick-neun-dah [Reading The Vancouver Sun in Korean]. *Korean, 14*(14), 70.

Lee, E. H. (2008, October 23). Bon-bo Cam-pa-in (campaign) "Han-in-up-chae-reul Eh-yong-hap-shi-dah" [Our paper's "Use Korean businesses" campaign]. *The Korea Times L.A.* Retrieved from http://www.koreatimes.com/article/481728.

–. (2010, August 24). Han-in-up-so 20,261-geh ... Jun-moon-jik Jul-ban-ee-sang [Korean businesses totalled 20,261 ... Over half are professional businesses]. *The Korea Times L.A.* Retrieved from http://www.koreatimes.com/article/612578.

Lee, H. K. (2011, March 22). 'For-e-ver (Forever) 21'1-wee Ol-rat-dah [Forever 21 ranked the first]. *The Korea Times L.A.* Retrieved from http://www.koreatimes.com/article/651086.

Lee, J. H. (2010a, October 26). Ja-dam-hui Ko-re-a-to-wn (Koreatown)-eui Nah-ah-ghal Bang-hyang, To-wn (town) Bal-jun-hat-ji-man Han-in-sah-hui Jo-jik-juk-in Mok-soh-ri Boo-jok ... LA do-wn-to-wn (downtown) Chu-rum Co-mmu-ni-ty (community) Jang-ghi-juk pl-an (plan) She-wo-yah [Roundtable on the future of Koreatown, Koreatown improved but lacks collective voice ... need to develop long-term plans like LA downtown]. *The Korea Daily L.A.* Retrieved from http://www.koreadaily.com/news/read.asp?art_id=1106021.

–. (2010b, March 29). 'We Speak English' 2-cha 'Han-in-to-wn (town) Kyung-jae Sal-ri-ghi Woo-dong' Dol-ip ["We Speak English," the second campaign for the revitaliza-tion of Koreatown, Koreatown economy started]. *The Korea Daily L.A.* Retrieved from http://www.koreadaily.com/news/read.asp?art_id=1008294.

Lee, J. W. (2010, December 2). In-land (inland) Han-in-chook-jae Ham-ggeh Jeul-gyu-yo [Enjoy the Inland Korean Festival together]. *The Korea Times L.A.* Retrieved from http://www.koreatimes.com/article/630845.

Lee, K. (2000). *Overseas Koreans.* Seoul, Korea: Jimoondang.

Lee, K. H. (2010a, January 25). [*Korea Daily* co-organizes Summer Night Market]. *The Korea Daily Vancouver.* Retrieved April, 2012, from http://www.joongang.ca/bbs/board.php?bo_table=g100t200&wr_id=861.

–. (2010b, July 2). ["Korean Festival" in Summer Night Market]. *The Korea Daily Van-couver.* Retrieved April, 2012, from http://www.joongang.ca/bbs/board.php?bo_table=g400t100&wr_id=475&page=9.

–. (2010c, November 14). [Feeling good to exercise voting rights]. *The Korea Daily Van-couver.* Retrieved April, 2012, from http://www.joongang.ca/bbs/board.php?bo_table=g100t200&wr_id=1447.

Lee, M. W. (2006, May 19). [Night Market this weekend?]. *The Korea Daily Vancouver.* Re-trieved April, 2012, from http://www.joongang.ca/bbs/board.php?bo_table=T1003&wr_id=7717 http://www.joongang.ca/bbs/board.php?bo_table=g100t200&wr_id=1447.

Lee, S. E. (2011, February 17). Bon-bo Yoo-seung-rim Ghi-ja NAM (New-A-me-ri-ca-me-di-a) (New America Media) Bo-doh-sang [Our paper's reporter Seung-Rim Yoo receives the New America Media reporting award]. *The Korea Daily Washington D.C.* Retrieved from http://www.koreadaily.com/news/read.asp?art_id=1157239.

Lee, S. J. (2011, June 14). Ko-re-a-to-wn (Koreatown)-en Han-shik-dang-man It-nah-yo? [Are there only Korean restaurants in Koreatown?]. *The Korea Daily L.A.* Retrieved from http://www.koreadaily.com/news/read.asp?art_id=1212160.

Lee, Y. W. (2007, February 2). Nae Mom-en Kang-in-han Han-kook-yuh-sung-eui Pee-gah... [Strong Korean woman's blood is running in my body ...]. *The Vancouver Korean Press.* Retrieved from http://www.vanchosun.com/news/main/frame.php?main=1&boardId=18&bdId=22711.

Leong, M. (2014, August 2). How Korea became the world's coolest brand. *The Financial Post.* Retrieved from http://business.financialpost.com/news/retail-marketing/how-korea-became-the-worlds-coolest-brand.

Leung, L. (2008). Mediating nationalism and modernity: The transnationalization of Korean dramas on Chinese (satellite) TV. In K. Iwabuchi, K. and B. H. Chua (Eds.), *East Asian pop culture: Analysing the Korean wave* (pp. 53–70). Hong Kong; London: Hong Kong University Press.

Li, W. (2007). Chinese Americans: Community formation in time and space. In I.M. Miyares & C. A. Airriess (Eds.), *Contemporary ethnic geographies in America* (pp. 213–232). Lanham, MD: Rowman & Littlefield.

Li, W., & Skop, E. (2007). Enclaves, ethnoburbs, and new patterns of settlement among Asian immigrants. In M. Zhou & J. V. Gatewood (Eds.), *Contemporary Asian America: A multidisciplinary reader* (2nd ed., pp. 222–236). New York: New York University Press.

Light, I., & Bonacich, E. (1988). *Immigrant entrepreneurs: Koreans in Los Angeles, 1965–1982.* Berkeley: University of California Press.

Lim, S. H. (2010, November 12). Joong-ang-il-bo OC-jee-gook Ee-jun Ghi-nyum Jah-dam-hui "Him-bat-eun Han-in Jung-chi-ryuk ... Ne-t-wor-k (network) Geup-hae" [Celebrating *Korea Daily*'s new office in OC, a roundtable on "Urgent need for network for Korean-American political power in momentum"]. *The Korea Daily L.A.* Retrieved from http://www.koreadaily.com/news/read.asp?art_id=1113998.

Lin, W.-Y., & Song, H. (2006). Geo-ethnic storytelling: An examination of ethnic media content in contemporary immigrant communities. *Journalism, 7*(3), 362–388. http://dx.doi.org/10.1177/1464884906065518.

Lincoln, C., Tassé, R., & Cianciotta, A. (2004). *Integration and cultural diversity report of the Panel on Access to Third-Language Public Television Services.* Ottawa, ON: Canadian Heritage. Retrieved from http://publications.gc.ca/collections/Collection/CH44-84-2004E.pdf.

Lindgren, A. (2011, September). Interpreting the city: Portrayals of place in a Toronto-area ethnic newspaper. *Aether: The Journal of Media Geography, 8*(A), 66–88.

Lo, L. (2006). Changing geography of Toronto's Chinese ethnic economy. In D. H. Kaplan & W. Li (Eds.), *Landscapes of the ethnic economy* (pp. 83–96). Lanham, MD: Rowman & Littlefield.

Lögberg-Heimskringla. (n.d.). What is Lögberg-Heimskringla? Retrieved from http:// www.lh-inc.ca/what-is-loegberg-heimskringla/.

Longwell, T. (2016, April 12). Conan O'Brien gets his K-drama on in DramaFever's 'One more happy ending.' *VideoInk*. Retrieved from http://thevideoink.com/news/ conan-obrien-gets-k-drama-dramafevers-one-happy-ending/.

Macnamara, J. (2005). Media content analysis: Its uses, benefits and best practice methodology. *Asia Pacific Public Relations Journal, 6*(1), 1–34.

Mall, R. (1997). Indo-Canadians. In C. Davis (Ed.), *The Greater Vancouver book: An urban encyclopedia*. Surrey, BC: Linkman Press.

Martin, J. C. (2005). *The Korean Americans*. San Diego, CA: Lucent Books.

Martin Spigelman Research Associates (2000, July). *Building community: A framework for services for the Korean community in the Lower Mainland Region of British Columbia*. Prepared for the City of Vancouver, Canadian Heritage, and MOSAIC. Retrieved from https://www.mosaicbc.org/wp-content/uploads/2017/01/Korean-Community-Profile-GVRD.pdf

Matsaganis, M., Katz, V., & Ball-Rokeach, S. (2011). *Understanding ethnic media: Producers, consumers, and societies*. Los Angeles, CA: Sage.

Mazurkewich, K. (2005, May 13). Personal journal: South Korea on stage at Cannes; its filmmakers hit stride, as one movie is contender and others are screened. *The Wall Street Journal*.

McEwen, M. (2007, July). *A report to the CRTC: Media ownership – Rules, regulations, and practices in selected countries and their potential relevance to Canada*. Prepared by Media Strategy Policy Limited. Retrieved April, 2012, from http://www.crtc.gc. ca/eng/publications/reports/mcewen07.htm.

Min, P. G. (1996). *Caught in the middle: Korean merchants in America's multiethnic cities*. Berkeley: University of California Press.

–. (2001). Koreans: An "institutionally complete community" in New York. In N. Foner (Ed.), *New immigrants in New York* (pp. 173–199). New York, NY: Columbia University Press.

–. (2006a). Asian immigration: History and contemporary trends. In P. G. Min (Ed.), *Asian Americans: Contemporary trends and issues* (2nd ed., pp. 7–31). Thousand Oaks, CA: Pine Forge Press. http://dx.doi.org/10.4135/9781452233802.n2.

–. (2006b). Korean Americans. In P. G. Min (Ed.), *Asian Americans: Contemporary trends and issues* (2nd ed., pp. 230–261). Thousand Oaks, CA: Pine Forge Press. http://dx. doi.org/10.4135/9781452233802.n10.

Mitchell, K. (2001). Transnationalism, neo-liberalism, and the rise of the shadow state. *Economy and Society, 30*(2), 165–189. http://dx.doi.org/10.1080/030851401200 42262.

Moon, S. (2003, June). Media consumption patterns of Korean immigrants in the U.S.: A study of Korean immigrants' media uses and gratifications in Chicago's Koreatown. Paper submitted to the Hawaii International Conference on Social Science, Honolulu, Hawaii, June 12–15.

Moon, S., & Park, C. Y. (2007). Media effects on acculturation and biculturalism: A case study of Korean immigrants in Los Angeles' Koreatown. *Mass Communication & Society, 10*(3), 319–343. http://dx.doi.org/10.1080/15205430701407330.

Moon, T.K. (2009, December 25). 'Ir-vi-ne (Irvine) Han-in-eui-nal Chook-jae' Yul-rin-dah [The Irvine Korean Festival is coming]. *The Korea Times L.A.* Retrieved from http://www.koreatimes.com/article/567775.

–. (2010, December 7). Ir-vi-ne (Irvine) Han-in-eui-nal Chook-jae Yul-lin-da [The Irvine Korean Festival is coming]. *The Korea Times L.A.* Retrieved from http://www.koreatimes.com/article/631626.

Moon, T.K., & Lee, J. H. (2010, October 12). Ddeu-guh-wot-dun OC Han-in Chook-jae [Well-received OC Korean Festival]. *The Korea Times L.A.* Retrieved from http://www.koreatimes.com/article/621292.

MP files complaint over Allen's immigrant rant. (2007, September 25). *CTV News.* Retrieved from http://www.ctvnews.ca/mp-files-complaint-over-allen-s-immigrant-rant-1.257677.

Murdie, R. A., & Skop, E. (2011). Immigration and urban and suburban settlements. In C. Teixeira, W. Li, & A. Kobayashi (Eds.), *Immigrant geographies of North American cities* (pp. 48–68). Don Mills, ON: Oxford University Press Canada.

Murray, C.A., Yu, S., & Ahadi, D. (2007). *Cultural diversity and ethnic media in BC: A report to Canadian Heritage Western Regional Office (Study No. 45193670).* Vancouver, BC: Centre for Policy Studies on Culture and Communities, School of Communication, Simon Fraser University. Retrieved from http://www.bcethnicmedia.ca/Research/cultural-diversity-report-oct-07.pdf.

Naficy, H. (2003). Narrowcasting in diaspora: Middle Eastern television in Los Angeles. In K. H. Karim (Ed.), *The media of diaspora* (pp. 51–62). London, UK: Routledge.

National Ethnic Press and Media Council of Canada (NEPMCC). (n.d.). Working to make Canada a true community of communities. Retrieved from http://www.nepmcc.ca/basic/ethnicpress1.htm.

Nawaz, A. (2015, February 13). Young, female, and hooked: Why binge watchers flock to DramaFever. *NBC News.* Retrieved from http://www.nbcnews.com/news/asian-america/young-female-hooked-why-binge-watchers-flock-dramafever-n300246.

New America Media. (n.d.). About New America Media. Retrieved from http://newamericamedia.org/about/.

Nir, S. M. (2015, May 5). The price of nice nails. *The New York Times.* Retrieved from https://www.nytimes.com/2015/05/10/nyregion/at-nail-salons-in-nyc-manicurists-are-underpaid-and-unprotected.html?_r=0.

Ojo, T. (2006). Ethnic print media in the multicultural nation of Canada. *Journalism, 7*(3), 343–361. http://dx.doi.org/10.1177/1464884906065517.

Oliver, M. L. and D. M. Grant. (1995). Making space for multiethnic coalitions: The prospects for coalition politics in Los Angeles. In E.-Y. Yu & E.T. Chang (Eds.), *Multiethnic Coalition Building in Los Angeles: A Two-Day Symposium* (pp. 81–116). Los Angeles, CA: Institute for Asian American and Pacific American Studies.

Ong, A. (1999). *Flexible citizenship: The cultural logics of transnationality.* Durham, NC: Duke University Press.

–. (2003). *Buddha is hiding: Refugees, citizenship, the new America.* Berkeley: University of California Press.

Organisation for Economic Co-operation and Development (OECD). (n.d.). International migration database. Retrieved from https://stats.oecd.org/index.aspx?DataSetCode =MIG.

Park, E. J. W. (2001). Community divided: Korean American politics in post-civil unrest Los Angeles. In M. López-Garza & D. R. Diaz (Eds.), *Asian and Latino immigrants in a restructuring economy: The metamorphosis of Southern California* (pp. 273–288). Stanford, CA: Stanford University Press.

Park, S. J. (2010, April 6). Woo-ri Ham-geh Man-nah-yo 'Anabada' ... 'Bum-co-mmu-ni-ty (community) E-ven-t (event)' Joo-min-deul Ddeu-guh-woon Kwan-shim [Let us meet at the Anabada ... High interest in pan-community event]. *The Korea Daily L.A.* Retrieved from http://www.koreadaily.com/news/read.asp?art_id=1012395.

Park, W. (1994). Political mobilization of the Korean American community. In G. O. Totten (Ed). *Community in crisis: New directions for the Korean American community after the civil unrest of April 1992* (pp. 199–220). Los Angeles: Center for Multi-ethnic and Transnational Studies.

Perlman, A., & Amaya, H. (2013). Owning a voice: Broadcasting policy, Spanish language media, and Latina/o speech rights. *Communication, Culture & Critique, 6*(1), 142–160. http://dx.doi.org/10.1111/cccr.12001.

Pew Research Center. (2006, August 21). *What's next for the ethnic media?* Retrieved from http://www.journalism.org/2006/08/21/whats-next-for-the-ethnic-media/.

–. (2009). *Black-white conflict isn't society's largest.* Retrieved from http://www.pewsocial trends.org/2009/09/24/black-white-conflict-isnt-societys-largest/.

Psy's 'Gangnam Style' hits one billion views on YouTube. (2012, Dec 22). *Asian News International.* Retrieved from http://www.dnaindia.com/entertainment/report-psy -s-gangnam-style-hits-one-billion-views-on-youtube-1780479.

Punathambekar, A. (2014). After Bollywood: Diasporic media in an age of global media capitals. In K. G. Wilkins, J. D. Straubhaar, & S. Kumar (Eds.), *Global communication: New agendas in communication* (pp. 66–82). New York, NY: Routledge.

Raboy, M. (2010). Media. In M. Raboy & J. Shtern (Eds.), *Media divides: Communication rights and the right to communicate in Canada* (pp. 91–119). Vancouver: UBC Press.

Radio Korea. (n.d.-a). Ra-di-o (radio) Ko-re-a (Korea) Up-so-rok [Radio Korea Business Directory] 2008–2009.

–. (n.d.-b). Rakotel. Retrieved from http://www.radiokorea.com/rakotel/.

Ramirez, R. (2011, October). Can mainstream and ethnic media collaborate? *Mediashift.* Retrieved from http://mediashift.org/2011/10/can-mainstream-and-ethnic-media -collaborate285/.

Rant clarified. (2007, September 27). *The Vancouver Sun.* Retrieved April, 2012, from http://www.canada.com/vancouversun/news/story.html?id=19571889-2015-47a3 -b1ae-4c34173ee403&k=68098.

Rennhoff, A. D., & Wilbur, K. C. (2011, June). Local media ownership and viewpoint diversity in local television news. Federal Communications Commission. Retrieved from http://apps.fcc.gov/edocs_public/attachmatch/DOC-308596A1.pdf http://dx. doi.org/10.2139/ssrn.1803256.

Republic of Korea, Ministry of Culture, Sports, and Tourism. (2011). '10-nyun Bang-song P-ro-g-ram (program) Soo-chool Gyoo-mo-neun 1-uk 8700-yuh Man Dol-lar (dollar) [*2010 program export totalled $187,000,000*]. Retrieved from http://www. mcst.go.kr/web/s_notice/press/pressView.jsp?pSeq=11273.

Republic of Korea, Ministry of Foreign Affairs and Trade. (2007). Information on the region: The ROK-US relations. Retrieved from http://www.mofa.go.kr/ENG/countries/northamerica/local/index.jsp?menu=m_30_20_20?.

–. (2009). Jae-whae-dong-po-hyun-hwang [Overseas Koreans] (2009). Retrieved from http://www.mofat.go.kr/webmodule/htsboard/template/read/korboardread.jsp? typeID=6&boardid=232&seqno=323304.

–. (2010). Statistics on Korean migrants. Retrieved April, 2012, from http://www.mofat.go. kr/travel/overseascitizen/index.jsp?mofat=001&menu=m_10_40&sp=/webmodule/ htsboard/template/read/korboardread.jsp%3FtypeID=6%26boarddid=232%26 tableName=TYPE_DATABOARD%26seqno=354018.

Richards, C. (2012, Dec 10). Psy: Regrets, gangnam style. *The Washington Post.*

Riffe, D., Aust, C. F., & Lacy, S. R. (1993). The effectiveness of random, consecutive day and constructed week sampling in newspaper content analysis. *Journalism Quarterly, 70*(1), 133–139. http://dx.doi.org/10.1177/107769909307000115.

Riggins, R. H. (1992). *Ethnic minority media: An international perspective.* London, UK: Sage. http://dx.doi.org/10.4135/9781483325309.

Rong, X. (2015, September 22). The benefits of collaborating with ethnic media. *Poynter.* Retrieved from https://www.poynter.org/news/benefits-collaborating-ethnic-media.

Roth, L. (1998). The delicate acts of "colour balancing": Multiculturalism and Canadian television broadcasting policies and practices. *Canadian Journal of Communication, 23*(4). Retrieved from http://www.cjc-online.ca/index.php/journal/article/view Article/1061/967.

Royal Commission on Bilingualism and Biculturalism. (1967, October 8). General introduction, Book 1: The official languages. Catalogue No. Z1-1963/1-5/1. Retrieved from http://publications.gc.ca/collections/collection_2014/bcp-pco/Z1-1963-1-5-1-1 -eng.pdf.

Rutenberg, J. (2002, April 11). U.S. approves NBC purchase of Telemundo. *The New York Times.* Retrieved from http://www.nytimes.com/2002/04/11/business/us-approves -nbc-purchase-of-telemundo.html.

Ryoo, W. (2009). Globalization or the logic of cultural hybridization: The case of the Korean Wave. *Asian Journal of Communication, 19*(2), 137–151. http://dx.doi.org/ 10.1080/01292980902826427.

Ryu, J. B. (2009, February 7). Il-moon-il-dap-eu-roh Pool-uh-bon Jae-whae-gook-min-too-pyo [Q&A on overseas voting]. *The Korea Times L.A.* Retrieved from http:// www.koreatimes.com/article/503509.

Seo, K. W. (2009a, March 29). Han-in-to-wn (town) Dan-chae-jang Ja-dam-hui 'Ship-gae-ddeui-neun 'To-wn (town) Sang-jing-mool' Shi-geup' [Roundtable for CSO leaders, need for an eye-catching (K)-town typifier]. *The Korea Daily L.A.* Retrieved from http://www.koreadaily.com/news/read.asp?art_id=815381.

–. (2009b, May 28). Han-in-to-wn (town) 'Yeon-bang Sah-juk-ji' Hwak-jung [Koreatown, designated as a Preserve America Community]. *The Korea Daily L.A.* Retrieved from http://www.koreadaily.com/news/read.asp?art_id=853361.

–. (2009c, August 6). LA-han-in-to-wn (town) Sah-juk-ji Seung-in ... Mi-chelle (Michelle) O-ba-ma (Obama) Gong-shik Chook-ha Suh-han [L.A. Koreatown designated as a Preserve America Community ... An official congratulatory letter from Michelle Obama]. *The Korea Daily L.A.* Retrieved from http://www.koreadaily.com/news/read.asp?art_id=888176.

Shim, D. (2006). Hybridity and the rise of Korean popular culture in Asia. *Media, Culture & Society, 28*(1), 25–44. http://dx.doi.org/10.1177/0163443706059278.

–. (2008). The growth of Korean cultural industries and the Korean Wave. In C. B. Huat & K. Iwabuchi (Eds.), *East Asian pop culture: Analysing the Korean Wave* (pp. 14–31). Hong Kong: Hong Kong University Press. http://dx.doi.org/10.5790/hongkong/9789622098923.003.0002.

Shim, M. K. (2010, March 30). We Speak English. *The Korea Times L.A.* Retrieved from http://www.koreatimes.com/article/585222.

Siapera, E. (2010). *Cultural diversity and global media: The mediation of difference.* Chichester, UK: Wiley-Blackwell. http://dx.doi.org/10.1002/9781444319132.

Siegel, A. (1996). *Politics and the media in Canada.* Toronto, ON: McGraw-Hill Ryerson.

Sinclair, J., Yue, A., Hawkins, G., Pookong, K., & Fox, J. (2001). Chinese cosmopolitanism and media use. In S. Cunningham & J. Sinclair (Eds.), *Floating lives: The media and Asian diaspora* (pp. 35–90). Lanham, MD: Rowman & Littlefield.

Spencer, J. (2001). Ethnography after postmodernism. In P. Atkinson, A. Coffey, S. Delamont, J. Lofland, & L. Lofland. (Eds.), *Handbook of Ethnography* (pp. 443–452). SAGE Publications Ltd. http://dx.doi.org/10.4135/9781848608337.n30.

Sreberny, A. (2000). Media and diasporic consciousness: An exploration among Iranians in London. In S. Cottle (Ed.), *Ethnic minorities and the media* (pp. 149–163). Buckingham, UK: Open University Press.

–. (2005). "Not only, but also": Mixedness and media. *Journal of Ethnic and Migration Studies, 31*(3), 443–459. http://dx.doi.org/10.1080/13691830500058828.

Statistics Canada. (2011a). 2011 National Household Survey: Data tables. Catalogue no. 99-010-X2011030. Retrieved from http://www12.statcan.ca/nhs-enm/2011/dp-pd/dt-td/Rp-eng.cfm?LANG=E&APATH=3&DETAIL=0&DIM=0&FL=A&FREE=0&GC=0&GID=1118296&GK=0&GRP=1&PID=105392&PRID=0&PTYPE=105277&S=0&SHOWALL=0&SUB=0&Temporal=2013&THEME=95&VID=0&VNAMEE=&VNAMEF=.

–. (2011b). Linguistic characteristics of Canadians: Language, 2011 census of population. Catalogue no. 98–314–X2011001. Retrieved from http://www12.statcan.gc.ca/census-recensement/2011/as-sa/98-314-x/98-314-x2011001-eng.pdf.

–. (2011c). 2011 National Household Survey: Data tables. Catalogue no. 99-010-X2011029. Retrieved from http://www12.statcan.gc.ca/nhs-enm/2011/dp-pd/dt-td/Rp-eng.cfm?LANG=E&APATH=3&DETAIL=0&DIM=0&FL=A&FREE=0&GC=0&GID=0&GK=0&GRP=0&PID=105395&PRID=0&PTYPE=105277&S=0&SHOWALL=0&SUB=0&Temporal=2013&THEME=95&VID=0&VNAMEE=&VNAMEF.

–. (2015). Visible minority of person. Retrieved from www23.statcan.gc.ca/imdb/p3Var. pl?Function=DECI&Id=257515.

Steele, A. (2009a, October 16). Reduced charges from Maple Ridge sushi restaurant fatal crash anger mother. *Canwest News Service*. Retrieved April, 2012, from http://www.vancouversun.com/news/Reduced+charges+from+Maple+Ridge+sushi+restaurant+fatal+crash+anger+mother/2111354/story.html.

–. (2009b, October 22). Man found not criminally responsible for fatal sushi restaurant crash. *Maple Ridge Times*. Retrieved April, 2012, from http://www.vancouversun.com/news/found+criminally+responsible+fatal+sushi+restaurant+crash/2133362/story.html.

–. (2009c, December 3). Driver in deadly crash into Maple Ridge restaurant wins release. *Maple Ridge-Pitt Meadows Times*. Retrieved April, 2012, from http://www.vancouversun.com/news/Driver+deadly+crash+into+Maple+Ridge+restaurant+wins+release/2299571/story.html.

–. (2010, January 15). Driver in deadly Maple Ridge restaurant crash to get released today. *Maple Ridge Times*. Retrieved April, 2012, from http://www.vancouversun.com/news/Driver+deadly+Maple+Ridge+restaurant+crash+released+today/2446975/story.html.

Stern, M. (2012, November 5). Doin' it "gangnam style." *Newsweek*, p. 49.

Sun, W. (2006). Transnationalism and a global diasporic Chinese mediasphere. In W. Sun (Ed.), *Media and the Chinese diaspora* (pp. 1–25). London, UK: Routledge.

Survey shows most U.S. fans of Korean dramas are non-Koreans. (2006, August 29). *Asian Reporter, 16*(35), 1, 6.

Time Warner. (n.d.) Channel line-ups for "City of L.A." Retrieved April, 2012, from http://www.timewarnercable.com/SoCal/support/clu/clu.ashx?ChannelFilter=All&CLUID=942&Zip=&SortByPackage=true.

Tinsley, H., & Weiss, D. (1975). Interrater reliability and agreement of subjective judgements. *Journal of Counseling Psychology. 22*(4), 358–376. doi: http://dx.doi.org/10.1037/h0076640.

Trevelyan, E., Gambino, C., Gryn, T., Larsen, L., Acosta, Y., Grieco, E., Harris, D., & Walters, N. (2016, November). Characteristics of the U.S. Population by Generational Status: 2013. Report for U.S. Census Bureau. P23-214. Retrieved from https://www.census.gov/content/dam/Census/library/publications/2016/demo/P23-214.pdf.

TVK24. (n.d.). MediaKit. Retrieved from http://www.tvk24.com/sub06_02.php?menu_id=6.

United Nations. (2015). Trends in international migration stock: Migration by destination and origin. Retrieved from http://www.un.org/en/development/desa/population/migration/data/estimates2/data/UN_MigrantStockByOriginAndDestination_2015.xlsx.

U.S. audiences devour South Korean soap opera. (2005, September 3). *China Daily*, p. 10.

U.S. Census Bureau. (2000). The foreign-born population: 2000. Retrieved from http://www.census.gov/prod/2003pubs/c2kbr-34.pdf.

–. (2010a). Selected population profile in the United States: 2010 American Community Survey 1-year estimate. Retrieved from http://factfinder2.census.gov/faces/table services/jsf/pages/productview.xhtml?pid=ACS_10_1YR_S0201&prodType=table.

–. (2010b). Total Asian categories tallied for people with one Asian category only and people with no specific Asian category reported, 2010 Census Summary File 1. Retrieved from https://factfinder.census.gov/faces/tableservices/jsf/pages/product view.xhtml?pid=DEC_10_SF1_PCT5&prodType=table.

–. (2011).Selected population profile in the United States: 2010 American Community Survey 1-year estimate – Korean alone. Retrieved from https://factfinder.census. gov/faces/tableservices/jsf/pages/productview.xhtml?pid=ACS_11_1YR_S0201 &prodType=table.

U.S. Department of State. (2017). Refugee Processing Center, Bureau of Population, Refugees, and Migration. Interactive reporting: Admissions and Arrivals. ireports. wrapsnet.org.

Vertovec, S. (1997). Three meanings of "diaspora," exemplified among South Asian religions. *Diaspora, 6*(3), 277–299.

Vipond, M. (2000). *The mass media in Canada.* Toronto, ON: J. Lorimer.

Võ, L. T. (2004). *Mobilizing an Asian American community.* Philadelphia, PA: Temple University Press.

Waldman, S. (2011, July). With the Working Group on Information Needs of Communities, Federal Communications Commission. Information needs of communities: The changing media landscape in a broadband age. Retrieved from https:// transition.fcc.gov/osp/inc-report/The_Information_Needs_of_Communities.pdf.

Wang, S., & Wang, Q. (2011). Contemporary Asian immigrants in the United States and Canada. In C. Teixeira, W. Li., & A. Kobayashi (Eds.), *Immigrant geographies of North American cities* (pp. 208–230). Don Mills, ON: Oxford University Press Canada.

Watanabe, T. (2010, March 1). L.A.'s Little Tokyo looks to save struggling newspaper. *Los Angeles Times.* Retrieved from http://articles.latimes.com/2010/mar/01/local/la-me -raful-2010mar01.

Winseck, D. (2012). Critical media research methods: Media ownership and concentration. In I. Wagman and P. Urquhart (Eds.), *Cultural industries.ca: Making sense of Canadian media in the digital era* (pp. 147–165). Toronto, ON: James Lorimer.

Wood, P., & Landry, C. (2008). *The intercultural city: Planning for diversity advantage.* Sterling, VA: Earthscan.

World Journal. (n.d.). About us. Retrieved from http://www.worldjournal.com/page-about _us-e/.

Yang, J. (2012). The Korean Wave (*hallyu*) in East Asia: A comparison of Chinese, Japanese, and Taiwanese audiences who watch Korean TV dramas. *Development and Society, 41*(1), 103–147. http://dx.doi.org/10.21588/dns.2012.41.1.005.

Yang, S. J. (2011, May 25). To-wn (town) Sun-guh-goo Dan-il-hwa [(K)-town as a single electoral district]. *The Korea Times L.A.* Retrieved from http://www.koreatimes. com/article/663806.

Yeo, J. Y. (2008, February 6). Mi-gook-sun-guh, Woo-rin Whae Joh-yong-han-gah [The U.S. election, why are we silent]. *The Korea Times L.A.* Retrieved from http://www.koreatimes.com/article/431490.

Yoo, N. (2010, February 19). [Any opposition to the Koreatown boundary?]. *Koreatown Daily.* Retrieved April, 2012, from http://www.koreatowndaily.com/read.php?id=20100219193623&section=local&ss=1&type=fdb.

Yu, S. S. (2015). The inevitably dialectic nature of ethnic media: A review article. *Global Media Journal: Canadian Edition, 8*(2), 133–140.

–. (2016a). Ethnic media as communities of practice: The cultural and institutional identities. *Journalism: Theory, Practice & Criticism.* http://dx.doi.org/10.1177/14648 8491666713.

–. (2016b). Instrumentalization of ethnic media. *Canadian Journal of Communication. 41*(2), 341–349.

–. (2017a). Ethnic media: Moving beyond boundaries. In C. Campbell (Ed.), *The Routledge companion to media and race* (pp. 160–172). London, UK: Routledge.

–. (2017b). Commercialization of journalism: Ethnic media, news production, and business strategies in the digital era. *Journalism Studies.* Retrieved from http://dx.doi.org/10.1080/1461670X.2017.1350116.

Yu, S. S., & Ahadi, D. (2010). Promoting civic engagement through ethnic media. *Platform: Journal of Media and Communication, 2*(2), 54–71.

Yu, S. S., & Murray, C. A. (2007). Ethnic media under a multicultural policy: The case of Korean media in B.C. *Canadian Ethnic Studies, 39*(3), 99–124.

Zandberg, B. (2007, June 27). CanWest targets ethnic readers, produces gibberish. *The Tyee.* Retrieved from https://thetyee.ca/Mediacheck/2007/06/27/Gibberish/.

Zhou, M., Chen, W., & Cai, G. (2006). Chinese-language media and immigrant life in the United States and Canada. In W. Sun (Ed.), *Media and the Chinese diaspora* (pp. 42–74). London, UK: Routledge.

Zolf, D. (1988). The regulation of broadcasting in Canada and the United States: Straws in the wind. *Canadian Journal of Communication, 13*(2), 30–44.

Index

Note: "(i)" after a page number indicates an illustration; "(t)" after a page number indicates a table; "CSO" stands for civil society organization